Spinoza's Political Philosophy

Spinoza Studies
Series editor: Filippo Del Lucchese, Brunel University London

Seminal works devoted to Spinoza that challenge mainstream scholarship
This series aims to broaden the understanding of Spinoza in the Anglophone world by making some of the most important work by continental scholars available in English translation for the first time. Some of Spinoza's most important themes – that right is coextensive with power, that every political order is based on the power of the multitude, the critique of superstition and the rejection of the idea of providence – are explored by these philosophers in detail and in ways that will open up new possibilities for reading and interpreting Spinoza.

Editorial Advisory board
Saverio Ansaldi, Etienne Balibar, Chiara Bottici, Laurent Bove, Mariana de Gainza, Moira Gatens, Thomas Hippler, Susan James, Chantal Jaquet, Mogens Laerke, Beth Lord, Pierre Macherey, Nicola Marcucci, Alexandre Matheron† (cross symbol), Dave Mesing, Warren Montag, Pierre-François Moreau, Vittorio Morfino, Antonio Negri, Susan Ruddick, Martin Saar, Pascal Sévérac, Hasana Sharp, Diego Tatián, Dimitris Vardoulakis, Lorenzo Vinciguerra, Stefano Visentin, Manfred Walther, Caroline Williams.

Books available
Affects, Actions and Passions in Spinoza: The Unity of Body and Mind, Chantal Jaquet, translated by Tatiana Reznichenko
The Spinoza-Machiavelli Encounter: Time and Occasion, Vittorio Morfino, translated by Dave Mesing
Politics, Ontology and Knowledge in Spinoza, Alexandre Matheron, translated and edited by Filippo Del Lucchese, David Maruzzella and Gil Morejón
Spinoza, the Epicurean: Authority and Utility in Materialism, Dimitris Vardoulakis
Experience and Eternity in Spinoza, Pierre-François Moreau, edited and translated by Robert Boncardo
Spinoza and the Politics of Freedom, Dan Taylor
Spinoza's Political Philosophy: The Factory of Imperium, Riccardo Caporali, translated by Fabio Gironi

Forthcoming
Affirmation and Resistance in Spinoza: Strategy of the Conatus, Laurent Bove, translated and edited by Émilie Filion-Donato and Hasana Sharp
Spinoza and Contemporary Biology: Lectures on the Philosophy of Biology and Cognitivism, Henri Atlan, translated by Inja Stracenski
Spinoza's Paradoxical Conservatism, François Zourabichvili, translated by Gil Morejón
Spinoza's Critique of Hobbes: Law, Power and Freedom, Christian Lazzeri, translated by Nils F. Schott

Visit our website at www.edinburghuniversitypress.com/series/SPIN

Spinoza's Political Philosophy
The Factory of Imperium

Riccardo Caporali

Translated by Fabio Gironi

EDINBURGH
University Press

Edinburgh University Press is one of the leading university presses in the UK. We publish academic books and journals in our selected subject areas across the humanities and social sciences, combining cutting-edge scholarship with high editorial and production values to produce academic works of lasting importance. For more information visit our website: edinburghuniversitypress.com

La fabbrica dell'imperium: Saggio su Spinoza by Riccardo Caporali
© Liguori Editore, 2000, 2023
English translation © Fabio Gironi, 2022

Edinburgh University Press Ltd
The Tun – Holyrood Road, 12(2f) Jackson's Entry, Edinburgh EH8 8PJ

First published in hardback by Edinburgh University Press 2000

Typeset in 10/12 Goudy Old Style
by Cheshire Typesetting Ltd, Cuddington, Cheshire

A CIP record for this book is available from the British Library

ISBN 978 1 4744 6759 9 (hardback)
ISBN 978 1 4744 6760 5 (paperback)
ISBN 978 1 4744 6761 2 (webready PDF)
ISBN 978 1 4744 6762 9 (epub)

The right of Riccardo Caporali to be identified as the author of this work has been asserted in accordance with the Copyright, Designs and Patents Act 1988, and the Copyright and Related Rights Regulations 2003 (SI No. 2498).

The Department of Philosophy and Communication (FILCOM) of the University of Bologna has contributed to the funding for the translation of this book.

Contents

Introduction: 'I Am a Good Republican'		1
1.	**Metaphysics and Politics**	20
	Non nimis improprie (Descartes)	23
	'Therefore it will be the cause of itself' (Spinoza)	29
	Causa rerum	35
	Eo sensu	39
	From Metaphysics to Politics	42
2.	**Towards a Political Order**	49
	The Imagination of Order (Premise)	49
	The *Conatus*	54
	Nothing Is More Useful to Man	64
	Natural Law	77
	The Artifice of Nature	87
3.	**A Militant Design: The Theological-Political Treatise**	95
	Philosophy and Theology	99
	Obedience	100
	Universal Faith	113
	The Absolute of the *Respublica*	121
	The Free Republic	128
	The *Pactum*	135
4.	**Between Realism and Project: The Political Treatise**	142
	Realism	145
	Multitudo	152
	The Kinds of State	164
	On Monarchy	168

The Aristocracy	180
Absolutum, sive democratia	195
The Patience of the Excluded	198
Bibliography	206
Works by Spinoza	206
Other Abbreviations	207
Secondary Literature	209
Index	226

Introduction:
'I Am a Good Republican'

I

In the opening lines of the *Tractatus de Intellectus Emendatione* – one of Spinoza's unfinished works, composed on the way towards the *Ethics* – Spinoza appears to outline the relationship between metaphysics, ethics, and politics on the basis of some very precise deductive logic. Having argued that human perfection amounts to the knowledge of the mind's union with 'the whole of Nature', he then adds:

> [t]his, then, is the end I aim at: to acquire such a nature, and to strive that many acquire it with me. That is, it is part of my happiness [*felicitate*] to take pains that many others may understand [*intelligant*] as I understand, so that their intellect and desire agree entirely with my intellect and desire. To do this it is necessary, *first* to understand as much of Nature as suffices for acquiring such a nature; next, to form a society [*societatem*] of the kind that is desirable, so that as many as possible may attain it as easily and surely as possible.[1]

At first sight, *intellectus* would seem to produce happiness which, due to its own impulse towards growth and accumulation, looks towards a *societas*. Metaphysics seems to dovetail into ethics and politics: from metaphysics to politics, passing through ethics. Indeed, if happiness is defined as knowledge of the relationship – the union – of the mind with nature (with the whole, the totality of nature), this means, in a Spinozan context, that the reasons of ethics are to be sought in metaphysics. Happiness can then be identified with knowledge. *Felicitas* is *intellectus*, without reminder: and this suffices to

---
[1] *TdIE* 14; CWS I, 11.

attest the primacy of metaphysics over ethics. As for politics, it seems clear – in the path outlined here – that there can be no *societas* without moral perfection, i.e., without knowledge.

Yet, on closer inspection, this passage (the only one where Spinoza directly addresses this question) appears to be more complex and problematic. To begin with, everything that a human being can know about metaphysics – all that it is possible and necessary *to know* – can only be applied in the service of morality and is measured and constrained by the end goal of happiness: it is always the pursuit of happiness that pushes ahead and forges towards cognition, as much as it 'suffices for acquiring such a nature' (*quantum sufficit, ad talem naturam acquirendam*). The fact that happiness is here defined as starting from wisdom (from the knowledge of the bonds of mind '*cum tota Natura*') indicates that there is nothing different – logically antecedent and prior – to be grasped in metaphysics as opposed to ethics. There is no knowledge (*cognoscere*) without an inner impulse, a moral yearning. Moreover, human perfection will not be truly complete – it will not appear as such – unless it strengthens itself in a relative and connective dimension, and manages to extend itself onto 'others'. Built upon the dynamics of happiness, society presents itself as one of its own conditions, indeed the most important and *fundamental*. No real ethics (and no real metaphysics) exists without politics. This relationship truly encapsulates one of the most intricate knots in Spinozan philosophy.

A cursory look at the chronology of Spinoza's works already allows us to come to terms with this question. The son of Portuguese Jews transplanted to the Netherlands, Spinoza was born in Amsterdam in 1632 and died in 1677 of tuberculosis, an illness he had contracted twenty years earlier. None of his 'authentic' works were published during his lifetime or in his name: the *Principia Philosophiae Cartesianae* (*Principles of Cartesian Philosophy*, with the appendix of the *Cogitata Metaphysica*) saw the light, with his authorship made explicit, in 1663, but it merely contains a 'simple' (*breviter*) exposition of Cartesian philosophy, occasionally glossed with some barely veiled critical remarks. Indeed, this work includes the preliminary warning, explicitly commissioned by the editor of the work – Spinoza's friend Lodewijk Meyer – that a large number of the doctrines presented therein were rejected by the author as false, for he held 'a quite different opinion'.[2] The *TTP*, on the other hand, was published anonymously in 1670 in Amsterdam, yet ostensibly printed in Hamburg, Germany, '*apud Henricum Künrath*'. The rest of his works were published posthumously by his friends immediately after his

---

[2] *PP*, *Praef.*; CWS I, 229; see also *Ep.* XIII (to Henry Oldenburg); CWS I, 207.

death, both in their original Latin version and translated into contemporary Dutch.

Now, it seems that Spinoza never showed interest in politics before the 1670s, certainly not in any explicit manner, whether theoretical or practical/militant. His acquaintance with liberal circles and his probable (though not proven) friendship with the brothers Jan and Cornelius De Witt, leaders (the former in particular) of the Dutch republican 'party', seem to pose a question regarding his alleged indifference towards, and lack of familiarity with, the political scene. However, this partial involvement does not appear to have led to a direct engagement or, even less so, to any form of concrete participation in politics. After his excommunication and expulsion from the Jewish community of Amsterdam, his efforts to lead a solitary and private life became exemplary – efforts which were redoubled after the lynching of the De Witt brothers, who were considered by the Calvinist and monarchic-Orange faction to be the main culprits for the failures in the war that was raging with Louis XIV's France, during a popular gathering in 1672. Up until the time he spent preparing the *TTP* (roughly the years between 1665 and 1670) Spinoza's intellectual commitment ultimately seems to have been solely aimed towards ethics and metaphysics. These are the first three unfinished works (the already mentioned *De emendatione*, the fragments of the *Short Treatise* [*Korte Verhandeling*], and his *opus maius*, the *Ethica ordine geometrico demonstrata*, with at least three out of its five parts having been completed by 1670.[3] In short, in this respect Spinoza presents himself as a very different figure than Hobbes, a *totus politicus* thinker who published *De Cive* in 1642, *De corpore* in 1655, and *De homine* in 1658. However, these chronological elements do not entail the legitimacy (or the complete justification) of a transparent deductive articulation of Spinoza's ideal research path in a straightforward manner: from metaphysics to ethics to politics – a kind of geometric linearity, which would locate in metaphysics the strong promise of ethics and thus, in turn, be a sufficient condition for politics. In order to question the validity of this simple trajectory it is enough to acknowledge the fact, clearly and indisputably emerging from the chronology itself, that Spinoza interrupted (or otherwise slowed down, or partially left aside) the composition of the *Ethics* in order to work on the *TTP*, his first explicitly 'social' work. Although such a path does not completely rule out the plausibility of a 'deterministic' reading of his philosophical production (positing a metaphysics-ethics-politics thematic movement), it should at least caution us against considering this path as either obvious or

---

[3] See *Ep.* XXVIII (to Johannes Bouwmeester); CWS I, 396.

as something that can be taken for granted. In sum, even the simple order of the composition of Spinoza's works suffices to raise legitimate questions and problems in interpreting and reconstructing his intellectual development.

A text destined both to provoke scandals and cultivate enthusiasm (immediately after its publication, surely the former more than the latter), the *TTP* lifted its author – whose identification was all too quick and easy – out of his seemingly reserved and 'quiet' life, an outward performance carefully crafted to make him seem entirely devoted to 'pure' philosophical research. The *TTP*, however, exposed Spinoza to virulent public attacks from those who denounced him as an 'Impostor, one who was born to the great Mischief of Church and State', as the 'most impious Atheist, that ever liv'd upon the Face of the Earth', an 'impious author blinded by a prodigious presumption';[4] his book was 'full of curious, but abominable discoveries, the Learning and *Inquiries whereof must needs have been fetched from Hell*', in sum a volume 'to be condemned to eternal darkness'.[5] Indeed, it was now hard to doubt that the treatise had something to do with the political, cultural, and religious wars fought in contemporary Holland, and its publication shattered the prudent image – the vaguely Stoic demeanour, far removed from the hustle and the noise of the world – that Spinoza wanted to cultivate. Nonetheless, the mask of a wise man pursuing the immutable truths of reason, leaving to the common folk the degrading possibility of engaging in deadly clashes over passions and meaningless disagreements,[6] was ill-suited for the outraged citizen who, after the lynching of the De Witt brothers, expressed his intention to display a poster saying '*Ultimi barbarorum*' (the worst of barbarians). It is difficult to square the cautious and studious Spinoza who had declined the chair of philosophy in Heidelberg in order to pursue his own intellectual research in full freedom and solitude, with the fan of ink and charcoal drawing who enjoyed portraying himself as another Masaniello.

II

If we problematise the relationship between metaphysics, ethics, and politics – avoiding the neat and unidirectional procedures proper to simple

---

[4] See Musaeus 1674; Burman 1704; and Spizelius 1680 – all cited in Colerus 1994.
[5] See Blyenberg 1674 and Mansveld 1674, cited in Colerus 1994. For a complete survey of the historical texts engaged in a polemics with the *TTP*, see van der Linde 1961.
[6] See *Ep*. XXX (to Henry Oldenburg); *CWS* II, 14: 'I permit each to live according to his own mentality. Surely those who wish to die for their good may do so, so long as I am allowed to live for the true good.'

deduction – the life of the philosopher breaks out of the meaninglessness of its anecdotal nature, out of the banal enclosure of erudite curiosity, and somehow becomes both instrument and material for hermeneutic revision. When discussing ethics and politics (leaving aside mechanisms for an automatic metaphysical deduction), some urgent considerations concerning the 'epoch' we are dealing with inevitably emerge, that is, the importance of considering 'historical' imperatives, and not just because 'great philosophers have also been interesting and exceptional men'.[7] The challenges of history, to be sure, do not spontaneously dictate questions, nor do they offer mechanical solutions for moral or political thought. However, ethics and politics are usually involved in those historical challenges, at least to the extent that Plato and Aristotle could not avoid being involved with the crisis of the *polis*, nor Augustine with the decline of the Roman Empire, nor Machiavelli with the imminent ruin of Italy. How 'historical time' is related to 'thought' is clearly a wholly different and far more complex question, one that can probably be resolved only when dealing with genealogical and individualising procedures, beyond any abstract systemic generalisation and sheltered from any indistinct methodological universalisation.

'He appears to be living withdrawn into himself, always alone, as if buried in his study.'[8] When it comes to Spinoza's life, its 'strangeness' and 'isolation' has been a prevalent theme in biographical accounts. This is the profile of a thinker who was as lonely as his theories were profound and shocking. This is a representation that Spinoza himself endeavoured to corroborate, and which the very first biographers, followers and critics alike, accepted and amplified in their writings. Jarig Jelles, Spinoza's friend and correspondent (who shared with him both theoretical interests and a passion for the craft of lens polishing to which the philosopher had dedicated himself when he had to abandon his family business after his excommunication), briefly but emphatically sketches in his *Praefatio* to the *Opera Posthuma* the outline of a man who freed himself 'from all duties and practical occupations', in order to pursue a 'search of truth' so 'ardent' and 'boundless' as to remove him from 'the whole world', although also bringing to him fame and notoriety.[9] In his detailed and lively biography of Spinoza, of whom he was openly both a disciple and an advocate, Jean-Maximilien Lucas – a French libertine journalist and publisher, fiercely opposed to Louis XIV and who, perhaps for this reason, emigrated to Holland where he continued to conduct an energetic

---

[7] Hampshire 1951: 227.
[8] Kortholt 1701.
[9] Jelles 1677.

'anti-tyrannical' campaign against the Sun king[10] – insists on Spinoza's 'sweetness' and 'love of solitude', on his need for privacy and desire for peace: '[a]s he espoused no party he showed preference for none, he allowed to the liberty of its prejudices, but he maintained that most of them were a hindrance to Truth'.[11] Similarly, Bayle, who was among the first and most decisive critical interlocutors of Spinozan philosophy, asserts that '[h]e felt such a strong passion to search for truth that to some extent he renounced the world to be better able to carry on that search'.[12] Johannes Koehler (Colerus), Lutheran pastor in Düsseldorf and then in Amsterdam and The Hague (where he lived in the same house which twenty years earlier had hosted Spinoza), distanced himself from Spinoza, placing him among 'those, who die in despair, or in a final Impenitence', while still representing him, not without admiration, as bearing the virtues of serenity and measure, of sobriety and discretion.[13]

It is here that we are to look for the roots of that now-consolidated portrait of a shy and modest philosopher, a solitary and 'quiet' individual who cared little about the vicissitudes of his times because he was too concerned with that which lies 'beyond' time, wholly absorbed in the cultivation of his extraordinary and irrepressible vocation, *sub specie aeternitatis*. An isolated and cursed Spinoza: a sordid thinker plotting the perversion of truth and virtue in the darkness, according to his critics; a giant towering, unique and irresistible, above the confused upheavals and lacerating tumults of his time, according to his admirers. Although this image of the philosopher was definitively crystallised in the nineteenth century, it still projects a vividly romantic shadow on the most erudite of contemporary accounts, even as heated debates around various interpretive reconstructions continue to rage. Consider how Deleuze, in line with Nietzsche, wrote that '[t]he philosopher can reside in various states, he can frequent various milieus, but he does so in the manner of a hermit, a shadow, a traveller or boarding house lodger'.[14] Spinoza's life is elevated as a paradigm, epitomising *the philosopher* as such:

---

[10] See Freudenthal 1899 and Wolf 1927.
[11] Lucas 1927: 66.
[12] Bayle 1965: 294.
[13] See Bayle 1965: 294 and Colerus 1994. For some of the most careful modern reconsiderations of Spinoza's life see Freudenthal 1899; Dunin-Borkowski 1933–1936 (particularly the first volume); and Meinsma 1983. The shorter De Vries 1970 is useful as well. For a more recent account, with particular reference to the *TTP*, see Nadler 2001.
[14] Deleuze 1988: 4. My translation. Deleuze then proceeds to highlight links and connections between Spinoza and his time and environment, although he considers them irrelevant for what it pertains to the elaboration of his theoretical work.

grounded on the ascetic virtues of humility, poverty, and chastity, placed in the service of an extraordinary 'superabundance' of thought, an exceptional and unrepeatable theoretical productivity. Alienation from the world and *dis-integration* from any historical-political *milieu*: the *solitude du philosophe* becomes his own formative condition, his constitutive principle.

Since its inception, this approach has been particularly stoked by some 'stereotypes' or recurrent *topoi* in Spinoza's life, time and again repeated and amplified in order to underscore the Olympian detachment of the thinker from the uncertain movements of the world, his distance from the struggles of his time. I am here referring to and considering only the most frequently cited episodes: his excommunication, proclaimed by the synagogue of Amsterdam, and allegedly endured by Spinoza in order to preserve his intellectual freedom and to defend his own truth; his many movements across the country (from Amsterdam to Rijnsburg, a town near Leiden, and from there to Voorburg, and later to The Hague) prompted by his desire to 'be less distracted by his friends during his speculations', the same profound thoughts that once had him closed in his house for 'three consecutive months';[15] and finally his already mentioned renunciation of the chair of philosophy in Heidelberg, a post offered by the prince-elector of the Palatinate and declined because he considered it to be 'incompatible with his desire to constantly seek the truth'.[16] A closer investigation of these events – repeatedly attempted over the last few decades – seems to complicate the picture significantly, widening the spectrum of possible readings and plausible interpretations.

Let us begin with the excommunication, an episode that amounts to more than just noble philosophical grandstanding, or an elevated gesture of incorruptible coherence of thought. It has indeed been ascertained that the Jewish community of Amsterdam, far from being culturally uniform, was riven with tensions and internal differences. The 'Marranos' who composed most of this community – Jews forcibly converted to Catholicism in Spain and Portugal during Philip II's reign, and who later emigrated to Holland in order to flee from the persecutions and vexations endured in their homeland – were often moved by a multiplicity of philosophical and scientific interests, not always reconcilable with the traditional teaching of the rabbis, the latter's main concern being the rigorous preservation of the community's ideological compactness.[17] After all, in Amsterdam, there were those who

---

[15] Jelles 1677: 4. See also Lucas 1927, *passim*, and Bayle 1965: 294, 295.
[16] Bayle 1965: 295. See also Lucas 1927: 60, and Colerus 1994.
[17] On the Jewish presence in Amsterdam see Roth 1932 (esp. Chapter IX); Bloom 1937;

voiced open dissent against the orthodoxy, so radical as to question the very meaning of the Scriptures: the most infamous of these were Uriel da Costa (accused of heresy and expelled from the community for having denied both the immortality of the soul and the revealed word, accepting only the legitimacy of natural law), and Juan de Prado, who was first condemned to penance and later banished for having also argued that the soul dies along with the body, that God does not exist (save from his philosophical role), and that faith is useless.[18] Da Costa committed suicide in 1647, after submitting to the humiliation of public flagellation, to which he was condemned as a condition for being readmitted to the synagogue. Prado's trial took place in 1656, the same year as Spinoza's, indeed probably just a few days later. Prado's punishment was milder, because he accepted both the charges and the sentence. Spinoza, on the other hand, was immediately excommunicated because he refused any plea bargain.[19] If the love of truth and the heroism of the philosopher can be mobilised to explain his refusal to reach what for him was a hypocritical compromise (the stipend that, so it seems, the rabbis offered him in exchange for his silence and for his occasional attendance at religious events) it cannot also serve as an explanation for his overt hostility towards the trial and its motivations, and his refusal to take part in it. His was an explicitly confrontational gesture, which could be cast in an even clearer light if it was possible to confirm the hypothesis (often proposed but never corroborated) that Spinoza would have composed an *Apología para justificarse de su abdicación de la Synagoga* meant not simply to neutralise or alleviate the consequences of his excommunication, but which would also have anticipated some of his most subversive theses from the 1670s, including his critique of the idea that a religious controversy can have consequences in the sphere of civil society.[20] In any case, the discussions and the disagreements internal to the Jewish community always had a political

---

Yovel 1989 (esp. Chapter II); and Nadler 2001. Considering the brevity of this survey, meant as an introduction, I will omit a complete list of references. It would, however, be necessary to begin with general works on the history of the Jewish people, beginning with Baron's fundamental work (1973).

[18] On Da Costa and Prado see Gebhardt 1922 and 1923; Revah 1962 and 1959; Yovel 1989 (66–76 and 94–111); Nadler 2001. On this theme Signorile 1970 is also an extremely useful reference, in particular on account of its rich bibliography.

[19] Moving from an assessment of these different behaviours, Yovel (1989) tends to downplay the influence that Prado may have had on the young Spinoza, an influence that is conversely emphasised by Revah (1959). It should be remembered, however, that Prado too was excommunicated the year after Spinoza.

[20] See Bayle 1965: 294–5.

significance, since they involved both the hierarchy of the synagogue and the competence of the secular authorities.

After all, in the midst of the turmoil of seventeenth-century and premodern Europe, it was very difficult to occupy oneself with metaphysics and theology without also being implicated in the theoretical-practical dynamics of politics. The 'free Holland' of the time – the powerful Dutch 'golden age' – was no exception, as attested by the interlacing of religious and state pressures that characterised the two great opposing sides which, throughout the seventeenth century, dominated its community. These two sides had their most emblematic and significant representatives in the two major institutional figures of the country: the *stadthouder*, the prerogative of the House of Orange, positioned half-way between a monarch and a commander-in-chief of the army; and the *raadpensionaris* ('grand pensioner', 'representative') of the province of Holland proper, by far the strongest and most authoritative territory in the United Provinces of the Netherlands.[21] The Orange-royalist faction prevailing until 1650, when the twenty-five-year-old William II died unexpectedly and was succeeded by a feeble Regent, owed much of its stability to the support of the official Calvinist Church, and enjoyed the consent of the rabbis as well: the aspiration for royal absolutism and a centralised State is inseparable from the religious opposition to freedom of thought, to Catholic worship (the only form of publicly professed faith prohibited by the authorities), and to the proliferation of Christian denominations. Indeed, the idealistic lure of the fight for independence from Spain and, more generally, the bellicose attitudes of the monarchy, were wholly complementary to ancient 'anti-papal' resentments, while on the economic front open support for monopolies resonated with many vested interests that the Jewish community (but also the Reformed church) had in the East India Company. The monarchical 'party' could thus count on the support of the army, monopolistic interests, the most powerful religious organisations, as well as a significant segment of 'the people', which identified themselves with the monarchy for reasons of worship and social opposition to the rich 'middle-class', mercantile bourgeoisie. On the other hand, the republican side was characterised by a politics of containment and peace on the international scene, by its insistence on decentralised state organisation, and by the support it gave to the development of a liberal economy able to break an all-too-rigid and invasive concentration of economic power. Headed by Jan De Witt – who

---

[21] Important texts on the history of seventeenth-century Holland are Geyl 1951a, 1951b, 1964, and Huizinga 1968. On the institutional turmoil in the country see Wilson 1968; Droetto 1958: 29–33; and Negri 1981: 36ff.

became 'Grand Pensionary' and therefore the arbiter of the political life of the country as a whole – the republican faction accepted the support offered by the liberal bourgeoisie, which, especially in the most powerful province, was a rich, educated, and enlightened aristocracy, and which was further an object of interest and attention for many minoritarian religious movements, often headed by preeminent members of that very bourgeoisie: Arminians (Remonstrants), Mennonites, Socinians, and most importantly Collegiants (the most significant sect in mid-seventeenth-century Holland). These were '*Chrétiens sans église*'[22] who thrived in the shadow of the politics of tolerance advanced by the republican authorities, and yet who were openly opposed by the more structured and organised cults, whether on account of their mysticism, or on the grounds of their rationalism – and more generally, because of their refusal to recognise any form of ecclesiastical authority, in the name of natural law and freedom of thought.[23] Ultimately, the religious dimension always has a political meaning, because it is strictly linked to the struggle and the tensions proper to 'civil society'. Spinoza's excommunication, and his intransigent attitude, cannot be evaluated apart from this, according to which the theological and the political are always implicated, and reciprocally influence each other.

The *TTP* tried to disarticulate the narrower dogmatic and authoritarian form of this connection, promoted by the monarchical-orthodox side, while simultaneously delineating the boundaries of a possible alternative reconstruction, characterised by openness, freedom, and a new widespread element of 'reasonableness'. This text, then, cannot possibly be understood if considered outside of this historical context. Around 1665 Spinoza interrupted his writing of the *Ethics* and, for the first time, dedicated himself to a work that was directly engaged with the political, cultural, and religious conflicts taking place in his country. The secluded philosopher accepted the conflict, and exposed himself to the violent assault of theologians and politicians, with his 'unheard of' theses on God, the Bible, and democracy. He wrote about the impersonal and non-subjective character of the divine nature, devoid of intellect and will (or better, free from the limiting anguish of intellect and will); on Scripture as a work of sentiment and fervent imag-

---

[22] See Kolakowski 1969.

[23] Few essential bibliographical references are necessary here: on the interaction between theoretical work and political-religious conflicts, in addition to the historical reconstructions cited above, Solari 1930 is an important text; for an historical overview of Dutch society in this period see Dunin-Borkowski 1933–1936 (in particular the third volume). On religious sects Kolakowski 1969 is a classic reference. On De Witt see Rowen 1978.

ination, capable of arousing the useful certainties of faith, but alien to any authentic truth of reason; on the democratic *imperium* as a more complete solution to the political problem; and on the mutual connections between such a theological reinterpretation and his political proposal. The essay was published anonymously, but this does not suffice to place its author in the aseptic frame of the isolated philosopher, extraneous to the passions and the interests of its time. It would not have been hard for Spinoza to foresee how he could have been easily identified and viciously harassed, as indeed immediately happened. Moreover, the flimsy screen of anonymity does not explain why such a dangerous work was written and published in the first place.[24]

The theoretical outline of the *TTP* is far better understood if we consider how between 1665 and 1670 the clash between the pro-Orange monarchists and the republicans grew ever fiercer, how the hegemony of the latter quickly crumbled under the blows of new conflicts with England and France (eventually leading to the resignation and then murder of De Witt, the event that put a definite end to republican hegemony), and how this clash also took place on the intellectual level. Indeed, during this crucial phase of Dutch history, there was a proliferation of volumes, articles, and pamphlets aimed at strengthening, reforming, or downright revolutionising the relationship between reason and faith, religion and power, sectarian belonging and citizenship rights. Once placed in the context of this historical and environmental tapestry, Spinoza's excommunication stands out against the background of an intellectual and theological-philosophical controversy, with clear political and somewhat 'militant' aspects. This is the historical perspective that Spinoza's work, from 1670 onwards, intends to identify and examine, albeit *a posteriori*.[25]

---

[24] Besides, Spinoza acknowledges himself as the author in at least three of his letters: see *Ep*. XXX (to Henry Oldenburg); CWS II, 14–15; XLVI (to Gottfried Leibniz); CWS II, 395; and XLVIII (to J. Ludwig Fabritius); CWS II, 397.

[25] Political reading of the relationship between Spinoza and the De Witt brothers – the oldest proof of which can be found in Lucas 1927 – is offered by Gebhardt (1908), who was among the first interpreters to stress the politically engaged dimension of the *TTP*. Francès (1937) has criticised Gebhardt's theses (which were essentially repeated, among others, by Jaspers [1974]) by questioning the historical plausibility of a direct acquaintance between Spinoza and the De Witt brothers; along the same lines as Francès, see Droetto 1958, who reads the *TTP* as a 'neutral' essay on political philosophy. More recently, both Nadler (2011) and Rovere (2017) have expressed some doubts about the hypothesis of a friendship between Spinoza and the De Witt brothers; this is a hotly debated issue, and without reliable documental proof it is impossible to resolve it one way or the other. Personally, it seems to me that a friendship is most probable, especially if we consider the overtly political meaning of the *TTP*.

Having learnt as much of the human sciences as a philosopher ought to know, he was thinking of freeing himself from the crowd of a large city when they started to worry him. So it was not persecution that drove him thence, but the love of solitude in which, he had no doubt, he would find Truth. This strong passion, which gave him little rest, made him leave with joy his native city for a village called Rhinburg, where, removed from all the obstacles which he could only overcome by flight, he devoted himself entirely to philosophy.[26]

The theme of Spinoza's repeated movement within his country is another topic promptly employed by the first biographers as proof of his penchant for isolation, aimed at safeguarding his speculative solitude and avoiding, as much as possible, the annoyances of notoriety and of intrusive friendships:

[h]e was not content with having removed himself from all sorts of affairs; he also left Amsterdam because his friends' visits interrupted his speculations too much. He retired to the country, he meditated there at his leisure, and he worked on microscopes and telescopes there.[27]

Even if we avoid any simplistic reversal of this kind of narrative, it is easy to intuit how Spinoza's relocation from one place to another must often have been motivated by necessity, and at times even adopted as a security measure. For example, it is very probable that his leaving Amsterdam for Rijnsburg was motivated by both economic cause (such as the impossibility of carrying on his family's business because of the 1656 banishment),[28] as well as by the attacks from the local Jewish community he repeatedly endured. Those attacks, just before his excommunication, had created a heavy climate of hostility around him, which certainly contributed to the attempt on his life by a lone fanatic who stabbed him, the knife fortunately diverted by the vest he was wearing on that occasion.[29] It is also certain that he abandoned the village of Voorburg and moved to The Hague, in 1670, due to some very damning accusations and furious public denunciations, particularly by Calvinists, following the discovery of his authorship of the *TTP*. This is why the stereotype of the philosopher's life – his wallowing

---

[26] Lucas 1927: 56.
[27] Bayle 1965: 294.
[28] See Vaz Dias and Van der Tak 1932.
[29] Bayle 1965: 293; Colerus 1994.

in solitude, at the joyful service of pure theoretical investigation[30] – hardly remains plausible given the concrete problems of everyday existence, the clearly practical need for sustenance, and even his own personal safety.

Even less significant, finally, is Spinoza's refusal of the chair of philosophy at the University of Heidelberg, coming from the prince-elector of the Palatinate, Karl Ludwig. The episode can now be definitively archived as an example of how sometimes 'academic power is attested even on narrower and less far-sighted positions than political power'.[31] Written by the prince-elector's advisor, the theology professor Johan Ludwig Fabritius, the invitation letter addressed to Spinoza was composed in the sharp language of someone who hopes for a negative answer:

> [h]is Serene Highness, the Elector Palatine, my Most Gracious Lord, has commanded me to write to You, whom I had indeed not known until now, but who has been highly recommended to his Most Serene Highness, and to ask whether you would be inclined to take up [. . .]. I could not fail to comply with the command of this wisest of Princes.

Among the emoluments proposed was the annual salary offered to tenured professors as well as 'the most ample liberty to philosophise', with the implicit proviso that he would not abuse such freedom in order to disturb religion and 'established peace'. Fabritius closed his letter thus: 'I add this one thing: that if you come here you will live pleasantly a life worthy of a Philosopher, unless everything else turns out contrary to our hope and expectation.'[32]

It sounds more like a threat than an invitation, and indeed this was likely a provocation meant for a scholar whose subversive theses, in 1673 (the year this letter was sent), were certainly far more infamous and loathed than Fabritius formally acknowledged in his letter. Spinoza's negative response appears to be emblematic, pivoting around a fundamental impossibility, that of being able to commit himself always to reconcile intellectual freedom and respect for the publicly professed religion:

---

[30] 'He attributed most of the vices of men to errors of understanding, and, fearing that he himself should fall into such error, he buried himself still deeper in solitude, leaving the place where he was staying then in order to go to Voorburg, where he believed it would be more peaceful' (Lucas 1927: 58).
[31] Cristofolini 1987: 116. See also Droetto 1958: 26–9.
[32] *Ep.* XLVII (J. Ludwig Fabritius to Spinoza); CWS II, 396.

I think I don't know what the limits of that freedom of Philosophizing might have to be, for me not to seem to want to disturb the publicly established religion. In fact, schisms arise not so much from ardent zeal for Religion as from men's varying affects, or their eagerness to contradict one another. This results in their habit of distorting and condemning everything, even things rightly said. I have experienced these things already, while leading a private and solitary life. How much more would I have to fear them after I rose to an office of this rank.[33]

As is easy to discern, these are purely political considerations. And perhaps this also indirectly explains another impediment mentioned (but not specifically argued) in Spinoza's reply: that of reconciling philosophical research with the education of young people. Not a 'natural' incompatibility between objectively incompatible activities; nor, conversely, a subjective difficulty linked to lack of time or energies: teaching and research do not seem to be reconcilable for Spinoza since the State binds education to the protection of public morality, to the superintendence of the official religion. Spinoza's objections, in conclusion, are still clearly oriented towards the intertwining of theology and politics, which was thus emerging as a permanent challenge and a constant 'object' of his reflection.[34]

'I am a good Republican, and I always aimed at the Glory and Welfare of the State.'[35] Even the request, from the Prince of Condé, to be acquainted with the author of the *TTP* – the circumstances of which are still unclear – can assume a certain 'militant' meaning. Whether or not that encounter actually took place, and whatever the reasons which pushed Spinoza, not without hesitation, to accept the invitation and travel to Utrecht (the headquarters of the occupying troops during the Franco-Dutch war), what

---

[33] *Ep.* 48 (to J. Ludwig Fabritius); *CWS* II, 397.

[34] Early biographers recount the Heidelberg offer in fairly different ways: while Lucas (1927: 69) and Bayle (1965: 295) generically insist on Spinoza's need for speculative solitude, Colerus (1994) grasps the crucial political meaning of Spinoza's refusal: '[h]e perceived the difficulty, or rather the impossibility of reasoning according to his Principles, without advancing anything that shou'd be contrary to the Established Religion. He return'd an Answer to Dr. Fabritius the 30th of March 1673, and refused civilly the Professorship that was offered him.' Traditional interpretations of this episode (read as a paradigmatic example of the 'absolute solitude of the philosopher', bearing the cross of the 'purity of his truths', or again as the example of a 'choice for freedom and independence, aimed at the pursuit of truth'), can be found in Banfi (1969: 125) and Giancotti (1985a: 30). On Banfi, see the already cited Cristofolini 1987: 110–11.

[35] Spinoza, as quoted in Colerus 1994.

is certain is that he refused to dedicate one of his works to Louis XIV in exchange for life-long funding and accolades.[36] In the eyes of the republican faction's supporters, the Sun King was always a tyrant, as well as, in that historical moment, an aggressor of the Netherlands. The fact that he was also an enemy of the House of Orange was not enough to mitigate this judgment. Besides, Spinoza's old Latin teacher, the physician Franciscus van den Enden, who had been accused of atheism and libertinism and fled from the Netherlands to France, had been hanged for plotting against Louis XIV.[37]

To conclude. Each of the elements that have repeatedly been exploited to construct the image of an 'ascetic' and indifferent Spinoza, an image often inspired by what he presented himself to be, can be read in a substantially different way as soon as one offers – albeit very briefly, as has been done here – some contextualisation. Even the seal that Spinoza used to stamp-sign his documents could be interpreted as having a certain duplicity, so to speak. The motto *Caute* that appears under the engraving of a wild rose (the symbol of beauty) is perhaps more than an invitation to caution that would keep one distant from the world, suggesting indifference towards the reasons and the passions of the people and their time. That imperative is probably meant as a more precise and definite warning, an exhortation both flexible and contingent. *Caute* invites 'cautiousness', a virtue that, needless to say, has always had a political character.[38]

III

No reconstruction of Spinoza's life under the banner of a kind of militancy can suffice, on its own, to resolve quintessentially theoretical problems like that of the relationship between metaphysics, ethics, and politics in his

---

[36] Bayle's account, claiming to have heard that the Prince de Conde was at Utrecht, and asked Spinoza to come and see him (1965: 295), diverged from those of both Lucas (1927: 62–3) and Colerus (1994), who instead claimed that the meeting never took place, for contingent reasons.

[37] On Van den Enden see Meininger and van Suchtelen 1980. Signorile writes that: 'Van den Ende was no mere Latin teacher. [A] promising student in Louvaine, he joined the Jesuits only to leave the order shortly thereafter. He was an admirer of Vanini (who was executed as a heretic in Toulouse in 1619) and a rebellious and adventurous man, politically and socially engaged with the most avant-garde cultural and religious tendencies of his times, as well as a bitter critic of the traditions and conventions of his society' (1970: 10–11. My translation).

[38] On 'Spinoza's seal' (and the *prudentia*, entailed by the motto *Caute*, understood as both an individual and collective *virtus* that man can mobilise with respect to *fortuna* and the universal order of *causarum concatenatio*) see Mignini 1981b.

philosophy, or (strictly related) that regarding the links and dependencies between his various works. Such a reinterpretation widely attempted in recent decades can only have an indirect value, and be expedient to multiply questions, whilst prudently avoiding satisfaction with the first, more immediate, and perhaps more superficial, answers. These are the answers which have been offered many times in the past, starting from all-too-linear derivations or, vice versa, from too many unilateral premises of exclusion and non-communication. 'Life' itself warns us against simplifications when outlining the links between the most important Spinozan texts, thus preventing a hasty resolution of many questions. First of all, those concerning the links between the *Ethics* and the *TTP*, oftentimes interpreted, as it would seem easier to do, according to a 'from premise to consequence' scheme, according to which the *TTP* would be a kind of 'social' translation of the metaphysical and ethical precepts of his *opus maius*; or, conversely, assuming a distance and extraneity between the two works, an assumption suggesting that the second would have at best a marginal role, having no direct connection with the three parts of the first (although composed, in chronological terms, right in their middle). Or again, the relationship between the two works is occasionally resolved in a more dialectical and interactive way, according to which the 1670 additions modified something of the *Ethics*' contents, so that its fourth and fifth parts should be considered as more than a simple organic evolution of the first three. A further complication for these hermeneutic paths is the problem of the exact positioning of the last of Spinoza's works – the *Tractatus Politicus* – which he began writing at the end of his life but which was interrupted at the introductory lines of the eleventh chapter, where his analysis of democracy begins: the structural pivot and the speculative centre of his previous work. What are the links between the two texts? Is it the same thought, articulated according to different perspectives and approaches, or are we dealing with a (partially or wholly) *different* theoretical performance? And again, does this incomplete outcome simply indicate a shift of interests, as the author of the *Ethics* turned his whole attention to politics, or does the conclusive phase of his inquiry have an effect, perhaps somewhat retroactively, on his previous metaphysical and ethical systematisations?

On the historiographical level, these problems were diluted, at least until the first few decades of the nineteenth century, into a history of sweeping elisions and arbitrary discriminations, as anyone familiar with the secondary literature will know. And so it happened that, in the eighteenth century, the first Spinozan influence (an important albeit often indirect and seldom acknowledged one) left metaphysics in the background while privileging politics, so that in French culture – from Montesquieu to Voltaire, from Rousseau and D'Holbach to La Mettrie – the author of the *TTP* now became a brilliant explorer of the relationship between institutions and forms of power, now a champion of the fight against despotism and a defender of democracy, or again the most preeminent representative of modern materialism.[39] In the shadow of Hegel and early nineteenth-century German philosophy, on the contrary, an overpowering rediscovery of Spinozan metaphysics, interpreted in a strictly deterministic sense, relegated all of his political works to a wholly secondary level.[40] Between the nineteenth and twentieth centuries, this 'speculative' hegemony was broken by the emergence of two new research paths: an Anglo-Saxon one of essentially juridical orientation, reading Spinoza in a utilitarian key; and another one proper to the German school which, starting with the assumption of a neat discontinuity (if not precise contradictions and revisions) between the *Ethics* – now read naturalistically – and Spinoza's two political works, focused its attention on the latter two, studying their internal dynamics and relations.[41] In both cases the perspective that ultimately prevails is that of a 'liberal' Spinoza, hostile to the reason of State, mindful of the legal positivist dimension of democracy and of the safeguarding of individual rights and freedoms. A strict interweaving of metaphysics, ethics, and politics was instead proposed from the 1930s onwards, thanks mostly to the historiographical efforts of a small, yet theoretically very heterogeneous, group of scholars. Among the most important of these, Leo Strauss worked on what appeared to him to be the unsurmountable metaphysical-theological presuppositions of Spinoza's political thought, narrowing his polemical gaze on the democratic *imperium*: the most extreme and natural outcome of a precise rationalistic path aimed at the destruction of transcendence and theology.[42] Gioele Solari, for his part, postulated a strong continuity between the *Ethics* and the *TTP*, grounded on the challenges and tensions of its historical context: the 1670 work thus becomes the political precipitate of Spinoza's masterwork, baked in the furnace of the Dutch conflicts of the second half

---

[39] On Spinoza's presence in eighteen-century France, see Vernière 1954.
[40] For a wide-ranging reconstruction of the relationship between metaphysics and politics from the German Spinoza-Renaissance to the beginning of the nineteenth century, see Solari 1927: 195ff.
[41] For English-language works see, among many, Pollock 1880 and 1921; Duff 2012; and Vaughan 1925. For German ones see Gierke 1880; Menzel 1898 and 1904; and Meinecke 1957.
[42] Strauss 1965. See also Strauss 1947.

of the seventeenth century.⁴³ Their specific solutions aside (Strauss's theological and anti-modern approach against Solari's rationalistic and Kantian one), both scholars offered a new and precious methodological contribution to Spinozan scholarship. On the one hand their methods did not fragment Spinoza's intellectual experience, considering it as an essentially unitary, albeit dynamic trajectory and, on the other, they helped us to see the turmoil of that era as unavoidable background, an essential framework for the unique and original experience of the Dutch philosopher. The path was thus open for what is today, in the vast panorama of Spinozan scholarship, the most lively and interesting research avenue, producing the most stimulating ideas and the most significant insights. I am referring to that school of thought, primarily of French origin (but subsequently grown in Italy and South America as well), which considers metaphysics, ethics, and politics as reciprocally and profoundly implicated, under the pressure of the historical events that characterised Spinoza's life. According to this interpretative line, the stresses of his time kept Spinoza's thoughts in motion, and his philosophical and political outputs are indeed characterised by cross-reference and revision due to their constant mutual interaction.⁴⁴ The result is a reconstruction of Spinoza's thought as both unitary and in a constant process of becoming. This is at once a less geometrical and less dispersive approach as compared to many others. And, perhaps precisely for this reason, it is an interpretive strategy better able to synchronise itself with the manifold and mutable wavelengths of a variegated intellectual adventure.

As compared to these recent historiographical efforts, this book adopts the logic of *interaction* as a guiding thread. Yet it also tries to outline a somewhat different, broad hermeneutical picture by paying closer attention to a 'circular' dynamic between the essential components of Spinoza's life, starting from some fundamental assumptions. Here I can offer a preliminary and synthetic summary of those. The first assumption is that the real 'metaphysical foundation' of Spinoza's political thought is to be sought in the first book of the *Ethics*. The second is that the *TTP* is a not wholly coherent and consequent evolution of the *Ethics*, because of its militant structure, its programmatic nature as a manifesto of sorts, but is better understood as a

---

⁴³ Solari 1927 and 1930.
⁴⁴ See, in particular, Preposiet 1967; Matheron 1969; Mugnier-Pollet 1976; Tosel 1984; and Balibar 1985. Negri (1981, 1992) has greatly contributed to this French line of research. I will return to this tradition (which later spread to Italy and South America) and its peculiarities (often very diverse) below, offering a more precise and detailed analysis.

somewhat 'ideological' project, meant to be appreciated by one of the factions in the Dutch conflicts of the seventeenth century (and indeed meant to regenerate and consolidate the republican faction, which however turned out to be the losing side). The third assumption is that Spinoza's last and unfinished treatise (because of the defeat of the republicans) sketches the highest point of his political reflection, because it is more congruent with his metaphysical system. And finally, concluding the 'circular' progression of this approach, Spinoza's metaphysical system, far from being reducible to a mere premise for later work or to an unengaged theoretical speculation, holds, from the beginning, a precise political meaning and a very definite social intent. Deeply marked (even more decisively than is normally acknowledged) by the enigmatic notion of '*causa sui*', the metaphysics that inaugurates Spinoza's intellectual masterpiece was always injected with and intersected by a dynamic 'political' power destined to explicate itself, in various guises, in his later works.

Such an approach, to conclude, also attempts to avoid the risk of new and excessive forms of determinism in its analysis of 'philosophy' and of 'time'. It is paramount to always consider life and its vicissitudes. But in Spinoza and his work there is more than just an influence from the contemporary situation in the Netherlands. Within Spinoza resides the wider tension of an age and a civilisation, the very acute perception of a far-reaching historical transition of global importance. The constraints of the contingent, as always, press and challenge us. But a truly great theoretical gesture faces the immediate pressure of the facts and overcomes it, in order to reach beyond.

1
Metaphysics and Politics

Spinoza worked on the *Ethics* for about fifteen years, roughly between 1661 and 1674, including a partial interruption caused by his drafting of the *TTP*. In 1675 he intended to publish the book in Amsterdam, but he had to quickly give up his intent due to the fiercely hostile reaction of theologians and 'stupid Cartesians' who kept attacking his writings and opinions in order to avoid the accusation of being his sympathisers.[1] The new political climate, determined by the assassination of the De Witts and the defeat of the republican faction, must have contributed non-trivially to such a decision: in 1674, among other things, the *TTP* was officially condemned by the Court of the Netherlands, along with the *Philosophia S. Scripturae Interpres* by Meyer and Hobbes' *Leviathan*. The 'external' travails of the *Ethics* intersect immediately with the tensions and problems of its time. This is already enough to justify some scepticism towards the possibility of enclosing Spinoza's masterpiece within the aseptic confines of isolated research and pure thought.

This work, as is well known, consists of five parts, focusing respectively on 'God' (*De Deo*), on 'the Nature and Origin of the Mind', on 'the Origin and Nature of the Affects', on the 'Power of the Affects' as the cause of 'Human Bondage', and on the 'Power of the Intellect', the true source of 'Human Freedom'.[2] The most obvious difference, with respect to the preliminary attempts represented by the *KV* and the *TdIE*, can certainly be found in the complete and systematic structure of the work, as well as in its compactness, marked by a change of 'method': *Ethica ordine geometrico demonstrata*. Aside from the many differences pertaining to specific theoretical-conceptual problems, the first true novelty of Spinoza's *opus maius*, as compared to his previous

---

[1] Ep. LXVIII (to Henry Oldenburg); CWS II, 459.
[2] *Ethics*; CWS I, 408.

works, is its mathematical method: the geometric, Euclidean, demonstrative progress of the argumentation. This was probably a decisive element motivating Spinoza's interruption of his previous theoretical attempts and their global reworking. This methodological choice illustrates, perhaps better than any other, the passage from the first drafts to the definitive version of the masterpiece. This method, however, does not immediately imply a precise change of direction on a theoretical level. In this regard, it suffices to consider that such a methodological turn is wholly consonant with the general intellectual climate of Spinoza's age, with that 'enchantment of geometry' which conditioned, from the beginning of the modern period, much of sixteenth-century thought, from Galileo's mathematicism to Descartes' epistemic revolution, and its translation in the field of moral sciences by Hobbes.[3] A few decades later, even Vico – one of Descartes' first and unyielding adversaries – claimed to have employed geometric *ratio* when writing his *Scienza Nuova*. Spinoza, in sum, moves along a broad and rather generic path, tuned, so to speak, to a long-wave frequency, and not a very defined one.[4]

If the demonstrative procedure seems to link the *Ethics* to the founders of modern thought, the succession of its contents seems instead to distance it: where the 'moderns' *par excellence* (Descartes, Hobbes) begin with the human, Spinoza starts with God. This is a profoundly traditional starting point: medieval treatises, in both early and late Scholasticism, begin with God. Modern philosophy, on the other hand, begins with the 'cogito', the subject, and the State, only to reach God, if at all, consequentially as an extreme and external guarantee for the possibility of human science, or as the source of a primordial order, now disappeared and temporarily withdrawn from the world until its new, triumphant return. Conversely, Spinoza's philosophy is permeated by another, recurrent, 'principle', a different 'beginning': so it is in the KV (which pertains to 'God, Man, and His Well-Being'); in the CM (published as an appendix to the Cartesian PP), regarding 'Being and Its Affections', as well as God, its attributes, and the human mind. The same goes for the *Ethics*, the first part of which focuses precisely on *De Deo*. From these textual data, some important and landmark interpretations of Spinoza from the first half of the twentieth century reconstructed the profile

---

[3] Koyré 1957.
[4] For a useful synoptic picture of geometric *ratio* in seventeenth-century philosophy, see De Angelis 1964. Hubbeling 1964 is a useful source for the tensions and twists of the Spinozan method. That this method represents only the external and reassuring envelope in which wholly subversive theoretical principles are contained is Negri's thesis (1998): that which not only does not reduce, but rather emphasises the meaning of the turning point.

of an author far too influenced by medieval thought (either Christian or Hebrew), and radically extraneous from modernity. This is a historically paradoxical outcome (bracketing some indubitable virtues of these studies), according to which the philosopher who initiated the most devastating earthquake that shook the dogmatic certainties of the past would ultimately be re-assimilated by those very same dogmas.[5]

It is, however, indubitable that Spinoza begins with God. Indeed, the *Ethics* opens with one of the most oblique notions in traditional theology, that of *causa sui*. A '[b]izarre formula',[6] a concept enclosing some particularly complex implications, which was consolidated, in Western philosophy, through several semantical and theoretical stratifications from the Greeks to the Renaissance, from early to late Scholasticism.[7] Reflecting on this 'prominent expression' (*wichtiger Ausdruck*),[8] Hegel commented on both the extraordinary nature and the limits of a great tradition of thought, oriented to the logical-ontological principles of 'contradiction' and of 'mediation', yet prematurely inhibited and interrupted by the 'rigidity' and the 'immobility' (*das Starre*) of substance and its unaccomplished subjectivity. The concept of *causa sui*, therefore, is understood as the origin of that paradoxical condition according to which, in philosophy, one cannot but begin as a Spinozist, while it is impossible to end as one. Several interpreters have successively placed that idea in an almost perfect continuity with Descartes' thought, as a common and neat cut with the past. Among many, Leon Brunschvicg argued that:

> [e]verything, in Spinoza's work, reveals Descartes' decisive influence. The first of the opening definitions is that of *causa sui*: referring to his debate with Arnauld would suffice to convince ourselves that this is the crucial point where Descartes had broken away from the scholastic tradition, in order to bring the external and transcendent relation of efficient causality back to the intelligible form of the relationship between essence and existence. This transformation of causality, in turn, was meant to transform the notion of substance, towards immanence and spirituality.[9]

---

[5] See Dunin-Borkowski 1933–1936 and Wolfson 1934; but also Freudenthal 1887 before them.
[6] Rivaud 1909: 97. My translation.
[7] Freudenthal 1887: 119–20; Gentile 2019: 662; Giancotti 1988: 319–320n; Hadot 1976.
[8] Hegel, VG, 338.
[9] Brunschvicg 1927: 169. My translation. See also Brunschvicg 1904: 788ff, and 1971: 183ff.

According to this reading, Descartes would have introduced a new meaning of *causa sui*, which Spinoza would then have oriented towards the more consequential direction of immanence and 'spirituality'. But even when, as happens less frequently, the concept is revisited in an upside-down manner, in accordance with tradition, we end up with the perspective of a substantial homogeneity. As Piero Di Vona observes:

> [l]et us conclude that we should understand Spinoza's *causa sui* negatively. Spinoza undoubtedly studied Descartes' controversy with Caterus and Arnauld on this question, and the fact that Descartes, in order to avoid the stringent objections of the two theologians, was forced to understand the efficient causality of God with respect to his own existence only in an analogical sense could certainly not have eluded him.[10]

This wholly specular hermeneutical approach seems to suggest the necessity of a more transversal and less transparent exploration of both the Cartesian notion of *causa sui* and of its Spinozist repercussions. Here I will try to offer a re-reading of the first book of Spinoza's *Ethics* in the light of its inaugural definition. It should be immediately noted that I have no ambition to perform an *exhaustive* analysis of Spinoza's metaphysics: if anything, I am focusing on those peculiar metaphysical twists and vantage points from which we can better derive political implications. Either way, this is an uncommon approach, since the notion of *causa sui* is usually mentioned and then immediately put aside, without a real analysis, in order to avoid its complex implications in metaphysics and theology (the two fields where it has a direct effect and expression), and thus limiting its extension which cannot be truly limited to metaphysics and theology alone. Constrained within the relationship with Descartes, these interpretative paths abandon the notion of *causa sui* to a closed and isolated theoretical space, extraneous to political reflection. Conversely, it is precisely by starting from the multi-faceted projections of Spinoza's opening gambit that we may grasp, with steadfast clarity, the ground-breaking 'social' potential of the *Ethics*' theoretical edifice.

Non nimis improprie (Descartes)[11]

In Descartes we can undoubtedly find a *positive* version of the concept of *causa sui*: 'I did not say that it is impossible that something should be the

---

[10] Di Vona 1969: 221.
[11] Not wholly inappropriately (Translator's note).

efficient cause of itself.'[12] Descartes attempts explicitly to distance himself from the Aristotelian-Scholastic tradition, which clearly rejected any univocal and literal interpretation of the *causa sui*, because this would force him to admit some positive influence by virtue of which God would give himself existence, thus making himself an efficient cause of himself. This aporetic condition, since it contradicts the substantial and temporal heterogeneity of the cause with respect to its effect, was explicitly proscribed by Aquinas (in the wake of Aristotle): 'no case is known, nor is it possible, in which a thing is found to be the efficient cause of itself; for in that case it would be prior to itself, which is impossible'.[13] For late Scholasticism, then, *causa sui* is a merely analogical and 'negative' phrasing, a figure of speech used to indicate God's state of *non-dependency*, i.e. the First Cause's being *independent from any other cause*. According to Suárez, for example, God is 'from himself' or 'to himself' (*ex se vel a se*), in the sense that his essence contains (*claudit*) his very existence, excluding any precise origin, and every positive emanation: '[a]nd some holy fathers (*sancti*) recur to this way of exposition, when they argue that God is his own cause, or of his substance, or of his wisdom. [. . .] All these expressions are to be interpreted negatively.'[14] The deductions of reason are inadequate when facing the immediate divine identity of essence and existence, which unmoors the spatial and temporal coordinates within which the (all too human) causal logic necessarily unravels itself. Confronted with the inscrutable power (*potential*) of this identity, reason grinds to a halt, and can at best express itself by means of litotes, and the imperfect – and objectionable – technique of *non-assertion*.

Descartes starts from the status of reason. The natural light (*lumen naturale*) which assumes that nothing can exist about which one cannot legitimately ask a reason for its existence and, therefore, what its efficient cause is.[15] If indeed it were accepted that nothing can represent, by itself, what a cause is with regards to its effect, the causal chain would proceed to infinity, without the possibility of any ascent to the 'first cause'. Late Scholasticism, then, ends up in a contradiction when asserting God as being a 'first cause'

---

[12] *Resp*, 62.
[13] *ST*, I, q. 2, a. 3. See also Aristotle, *Met.*, V, 2, 1013a and *Phys.*, II, 194b–195b; also Suárez, *DM*, disp. I, sez. I, XXVII, v. II. Various commentators also noted the presence, in Thomas Aquinas – always following Aristotle – of a positive meaning assigned to the concept of *causa sui*: see *CG*, XV, p. 195; *SG*, I, 88, 4–5, p. 237; *ST*, I, q. LXXIII, a. I, 3. In these cases, however, the idea is more specifically targeting the conditions for the freedom of human and divine will. For Aristotle see *NE*, III, I, 1110a-b.
[14] Suárez, *DM*, disp. XXVIII, section I, VII, v. II.
[15] *Resp*, 63.

(when qualifying God by means of a causal determination, albeit merely in relation to things) but negating its status as a *causa sui*. The implicit meaning of the Cartesian discourse is that either reason must be considered completely powerless when referring to God – so that not even His being a 'first cause' can be asserted (the human can utter nothing at all) – or the possibility of defining God positively, as cause of himself, is to be considered (at least partially) legitimate. According to Descartes, Scholasticism remains ensnared in this problem when it resorts to the divine qualification of 'for itself', even if, as in Suárez, it is still assumed in a negative sense, univocally interpreted as an 'absence of cause'. This is a fragile artifice, since, if referring to an *ad rem* rather than an *ad verba*, it will become necessary to acknowledge that 'the negative rendering of the expression "derived from itself" proceeds merely from the imperfection of the human intellect'. Such an expression, therefore will also assume a positive meaning, 'sought from the truth of things'.[16] Thus Descartes seems to introduce, in the perfect divine immobility of being *for himself* (the essential nucleus, in the Aristotelian-Scholastic context, of God as an uncaused first cause [*causa prima incausata*]), the principle of a positive self-movement towards existence, demoting to *nugatoria quaestio* – i.e., to an obvious and useless simplification – precisely what Aristotle has instead identified as a rigorously unique component of the efficient cause: the heterogeneity of that which provokes a change with respect to the object that undergoes such change.

It is here, more than in any other, indirect and remote, source, that we should look for the origin of the Spinozist concept of *causa sui*. And yet these are only early and tentative formulations. Descartes, as Di Vona correctly argues, ends up reducing the idea to its recurrent analogical meaning, both because the objections he receives are rigorous and unsurmountable (at least from the purely logical-formal standpoint)[17] and because, as Deleuze has insightfully but cursorily highlighted, those objections hold within the 'system' to which Descartes still wants to belong.[18] Indeed, Descartes' entire theoretical approach, although formulated within a transitional frontier, still remains anchored to an apparatus that sharply separates human epistemic abilities on the one hand, and the inscrutability of the divine essence on the other. The *causa sui* is necessary in order for the *cogito* – a finite subject, immersed in mechanisms made necessary by its determinacy – to approximate, positively but only 'to some extent', God's true nature, his

---

[16] *Resp*, 63.
[17] Di Vona 1969: 217–22.
[18] Deleuze 1990: 147–8.

superhuman and inexpressible 'formal' cause, and his superabundance. The *causa sui* still capitulates to the '*exsuperantia*' of the divine essence. It is an *allusive* instrument of power: just as I can call efficient that cause which continuously creates and preserves me, 'there could exist something in which there is such a great and inexhaustible power that it never needs the help of anything in order to exist. Nor again does it now need a cause in order to be conserved. Thus, *in a manner of speaking*, it is the cause of itself.'[19] The causal argument can be applied to God only by means of approximations and hedging formulae like 'somehow' (*quodammodo*), 'it seems' (*videtur*), 'not wholly improperly' (*non nimis improprie*), 'as if by a cause' (*tamquam a causa*):

> because we perceive that his being derived from himself or his having no cause different from himself is itself derived not from nothing but from a real immensity of power, *it is wholly fitting* for us to think that God stands in the same relationship to himself as an efficient cause does to its effect, and thus that God is derived from himself positively.[20]

The causal argument holds only by analogy. This double aspect, both positive and 'weak', of Descartes' argument assumes a more precise form in the *Reply to the Fourth Set of Objections* under the pressure of Arnauld's admiring, deeply respectful and scrupulous questioning. Arnauld had proposed the distinction between cause and effect as inevitable and necessary, both in terms of their temporal heterogeneity (since the cause's influence is implicit in the notion of an effect, it follows that the former must naturally precede and anticipate the latter), and on the ontological level, that of essence and existence: the principle of efficient cause applies only to those entities whose existence does not depend upon their essence. Nothing, therefore, can give itself being if it does not already possess it, and in this sense the very idea of 'self-giving' becomes absurd. Arnauld had then ascribed the impossibility of positively conceiving God's infinite power to human epistemic limits. Reason, constitutively organised 'after the manner of created things', arbitrarily applies to God the principle of efficient cause: 'my answer to the person asking why God exists is that one should not reply in terms of an efficient cause. Rather, one should say merely that it is because he is God, that is, an infinite being.'[21]

Descartes' answer is twofold. On the one hand, he defends the legitimacy of human positive reference to God – in terms of the efficient cause – almost

---

[19] *Resp*, 62–3 (I have modified the translation; emphasis added).
[20] *Resp*, 64 (emphasis added).
[21] *Resp*, 127.

to the point of introducing, between this and the divine nature, a relationship of algebraic derivation, *more geometrico*:

> I think it is necessary to point out that there is a middle ground between an efficient cause properly so-called and no cause at all: namely, the positive essence of a thing, to which we can extend the concept of an efficient cause in the same way we are accustomed in geometry to extend the concept of an exceedingly long arc to the concept of a straight line or the concept of a rectilinear polygon with an indefinite number of sides to the concept of a circle.[22]

On the other hand, however, the oblique nature of this operation becomes even more evident: '[I have used] the analogy of efficient causality in order to explain those things that pertain to a formal cause, that is, to the very essence of God.'[23] In sum, Descartes defends the *positive foundation of analogy*: it is not arbitrary for the human to define divine substance by resorting to the efficient cause, if only because such cause (which, properly speaking, concerns only created things) will be neither extraneous nor external to the essence of God (on which all created things depend, as the efficient cause) and human reason. But the infinite nature of that essence is to be expressed in inevitably metaphorical terms. Now, even more than before, the term *causa sui* positively (if slightly improperly) indicates the immense and inexhaustible power of God. Once the identity of essence and existence is admitted (for logical-ontological necessity), the principle of efficient cause makes the infinite and omnipotent nature of God approachable. It allows the human, a finite and imperfect thinking substance,[24] to 'intuit', but never to 'understand' it: 'Nevertheless, all these modes of speaking, which are taken from the analogy of an efficient cause, are particularly necessary in order to direct the light of nature in such wise that we pay particular attention to them.'[25] The power of God is really the cause for which (the reason why) He needs no cause. Or, at best, he will be positively his own cause in a sense that escapes us, and that in any case will have to be quite different from the relationship he has with things – God *is*: '[n]owhere have I said that God preserves himself by means of some positive influence, as is the case with created things preserved

---

[22] *Resp*, 143
[23] *Resp*, 145.
[24] *Resp*, 65: 'And so, to begin with, I will declare here that the infinite qua infinite is in no way comprehended; nonetheless it is still understood.'
[25] *Resp*, 144.

by him'.²⁶ Descartes stops here: at the admission, of distant Augustinian ancestry, of God's 'being for a cause' as a mere human allegory for the unfathomable overabundance of his immense *potestas*.²⁷ He certainly adds to it the (mathematical) legitimacy of that allegory, yet he still interrupts his investigation well before a full and problematic collocation of the *causa sui* within the profound essence of the divine nature, taking care not to identify the necessary and causal procedure of reason with the infinite and omnipotent nature of God.²⁸ The power (*potentia*) of Descartes' God is neither voluntary nor arbitrary, neither mysterious nor, in a word, personal, *because* it is immediately identified with the *causa sui* and immediately implanted in the divine essence.²⁹ Rather, it is because the *causa sui* analogically, nonunivocally (and yet positively, for the human), expresses an essence-power that it truly remains unfathomable precisely because of its exorbitance with respect to the cause, and because it is not fully graspable by means of a causal definition. The nature of Descartes' God does not fully assume the stringent necessities (self-necessities) of being a cause; it does not assume as necessary and foundational (necessarily foundational) all the logical-ontological constraints entailed by being a cause. Its being a self-cause cannot be dissolved or identified within a precise determining-causal structure, such as to radically reposition itself and its relationship with the world.

Ultimately, Descartes still seeks a *sovereign* God, able (like Scotus' God) to *choose* causal logic, a God who would be able *absolutely* to impress a

---

²⁶ *Resp*, 141–2.
²⁷ Deleuze (1990: 162–3), observes that the Cartesian theory rests on 'three closely linked notions: *equivocation* (God is cause of himself, but in another sense than that in which he is the efficient cause of the things he creates; so that being is not affirmed in the same sense of everything that is, divine and created substance, substances and modes, and so on); *eminence* (God thus contains all reality, but eminently, in a form other than that of the things he creates); and *analogy* (God as cause of himself is not, then, grasped as he is in himself, but by analogy: it is by analogy with an efficient cause that God may be said to be cause of himself, or to be "through himself" as through a cause).'
²⁸ Brunschvicg (1927: 183ff), emphasises this geometric presence to the point of identifying it *tout court* with the divine essence. The whole context of such an answer actually seems to limit the mathematical-deductive procedure to an analogical approximation of the formal cause by means of the efficient cause. Conversely, Cassirer argues that truth and knowledge, implanted on the absolute foundation of God, are weakened, becoming the products of a creative activity whose free will has no limits (see Cassirer 1922: Book II, chapter I, section II).
²⁹ This is what Gueroult (1968: 40–42) hypothesises, in his subtle and complex interpretation; see also Gueroult 1953: 250ff.

cause without enduring it, making it speak without being spoken about. This approach is open to some peculiar political projections made explicit by Descartes himself, as will be seen.[30] Spinoza's project is the antipodes of metaphysical-political outcomes such as Descartes', for, beginning with the first book of the *Ethics*, he will instead aim to empty of meaning and foundation any possible symmetry between the kings and the gods.[31]

'Therefore it will be the cause of itself' (Spinoza)

'By cause of itself I understand that whose essence involves existence, or whose nature cannot be conceived except as existing.'[32] This, needless to say, is the *Ethics' incipit*, the very first definition in Spinoza's masterpiece. It is a truly privileged placement for a notion with a traditionally uncertain status, so often rejected or poorly tolerated, which, instead, now anticipates concepts and terms of a much clearer, and indeed golden, solidity: *substance, attribute, mode, God*. From the very beginning what strikes the reader the most is that no Spinozan formula, and not just in the *Ethics*, resembles the attenuating and allusive ones proper of traditional theological discourse – 'by *causa sui* I mean. . .', 'God is *causa sui*', 'the first cause of all things, and also the cause of himself', 'cause of himself, and all other things'.[33] God's being *causa sui* seems explicitly and apodictically to assume a precise and direct meaning, never 'as if' or '*tanquam a causa*' (and not even 'so to speak' (*ut ita loquar*), according to the literal wording of a passage by John Calvin which has also been referred to as a possible Spinozan source).[34] And compared to Descartes, then, the explicit shift of the concept from the plane of the essence to the less direct one of the divine properties appears evident:

> [f]or though *existing of itself, being the cause of all things, the greatest good, eternal,* and *immutable*, etc., are proper to God alone, nevertheless through those *propria* we can know neither what the being to which these *propria* belong is, nor what attributes it has.[35]

---

[30] See *infra*, the second part of this chapter.
[31] Already in CM, actually. But the theme is recurrent in Spinoza's works: see Caporali 2012: 11–27.
[32] *Ethics* I, Praef.; CWS I, 408.
[33] KV I, I, 10 (CWS I, 65); KV I, III, 5 (CWS I, 82). The only exception can be found in TdIE: see note 40 in this chapter.
[34] Di Vona 1969: 221.
[35] KV, I, VII, 6; CWS I, 89.

In Spinoza, this is a *topos*. On the other hand, in Descartes the *causa sui* tends explicitly towards the divine essence (it defines, in a positive but only analogical and allusive way, an indefinable substantiality). Spinoza decentralises every 'causal' notion towards a conceptually peripheral domain, the field of God's 'properties', 'actions' that are completely relevant to him but utterly mute as to His nature, and powerless to clarify 'what he is'.[36] These are direct derivations of its essence (concluding, 'from the given definition of any thing', a 'number of properties'), just as from a single premise multiple consequences may be derived.[37] It is therefore necessary to evaluate both the actual consistency of this relocation of the concept of *causa sui*, which usually is simply acknowledged without much analysis, and also to reconsider the first impression of its positive meaning, one suggesting that, in the shift from 'essence' to 'property', it immediately assumed a very serious connotation eluding any analogical cage and taking refuge directly in univocity. The possible logical-operative reasons for such a connection – for now only hypothetically accepted but that, if demonstrated, would allow us to delineate a new approach, not only with respect to the tradition but also to Descartes – should be pursued first of all, in relation to its object, in relation to the nature of God as it is gradually being structured throughout the first book of Spinoza's *opus maius*.[38]

---

[36] KV, I, II, 29; CWS I, 73; and see also I, III, 1 note a; CWS I, 80. On the various stratifications of the KV see Gueroult 1968: 473ff. and Mignini 1986: 13ff.

[37] *Ethics* I, 16 Dem. (CWS I, 425). On 'definitio-essentia' see *Ethics* I, 33 Schol. 1 (CWS I, 436); *Ethics* III, 4 (CWS I, 498); as well as *TdIE*, 95 (CWS I, 39). On the concept of definition in Spinoza see Neri 1992.

[38] In the wide-ranging panorama of Spinozan studies, the concept of *causa sui* is mainly approached on the basis of two different interpretative strategies, which we have already mentioned: one links it back to the traditional metaphorical dimension (Di Vona 1969: 217–22), or admits, at most, a substantial logical equivalence of its two possible meanings: see Dunin-Borkowski (1933–1936: I, 564), who speaks of '*kein Unterschied*' between the two meanings; and Wolfson (1934: I, 129), for whom in Descartes as in Spinoza the concept 'has both a negative sense and a positive sense'. (However, previously Freudenthal [1887: 120] had complained that the scholastic '*Herkunft*' of this concept had been ignored.) The other strategy, more widespread in recent studies, accepts the univocal and positive depth of the definition, but by and large it does not grasp its problematic nature, resolving it mostly in the immediate rational and operational transparency of the divine nature: among others, and of course each from their own particular perspective: see Hampshire 1951: 30–55; Hallet 1957: 10–11; Zac 1963: chapter I (in particular 20 and 31) and 1979: 17; Hubbeling 1964: 29, 128–9 and 1978: 49; Crippa 1965: 111–12, 117–18, 125; Deleuze 1990: 162–7 and 1988: 77–9; Gueroult 1968: 40–2, 250ff, *passim*; Negri 1981, 70–1, *passim*; Giancotti 1988: 31.

'By cause of itself (*causa sui*) I understand that whose essence involves existence, *or* that whose nature cannot be conceived except as existing.'[39] At this first level of analysis, that of its definition, the *causa sui* does not allow monosemic interpretations, between analogy and uniqueness. On the one hand, in virtue of its appearance as a *causa sui*, it seems to introduce the need for a decomposition between essence and existence, insinuating an unjustified mediation, a connection that is only postulated and not explained by the inscrutable compactness of its terms. This perspective would seem to be further strengthened by the overall structure of the definition. In it, as well as in subsequent definitions, parallels are drawn between the ontological ('that whose essence involves existence') and the logical-epistemological ('that whose nature cannot be conceived except as existing') dimensions of being a 'cause', or a 'cause-*ratio*'. On the other hand, when the *causa sui* is flattened onto an unspecified implication of existence into essence, it fails to indicate, in a certain and unilateral way, its own positive dimension. The notion of *involvere* seems already somehow to complicate the immediate and obscure indistinction of essence and existence (which was also proposed in CM: '*essentia in Deo non distinguatur ab existentia*'),[40] albeit not to the point of realising itself in an explicit relationship of determination, typical of every cause. At the same time, on the epistemological level, the spontaneous 'conceivability' of existence as a *causa sui* – its inability to conceive of itself otherwise than as existing – does not automatically disallow a metaphorical reinterpretation: it does not necessarily admit it, but neither does it necessarily exclude it.[41] The strength of the correspondence between 'cause' and '*ratio*' seems remarkably muted by its apodictic introduction, so that, on the one hand, it presents itself as a direct extension (to God and to its attributes) of the process from cause to effect with which Spinoza had reformulated, in his *Treatise on the Emendation of the Intellect*, the well-known Aristotelian-Scholastic principle of *vera scientia*, while, on the other, the actual nature of

---

[39] *Ethics* 1, Def. 1; CWS I, 408.
[40] CM I, 2; CWS I, 304.
[41] Nor can the reference to the antecedent in *TdIE*, 92 help to bring clarity: '[i]f the thing is in itself, or, as is commonly said, is the cause of itself, then it must be understood through its essence alone' (CWS I, 114), where the equivalence between '*in se*', '*causa sui*' and '*essentia*' does not seem substantially different from traditional representations, as clearly evidenced by the attenuating circumlocution ('*ut vulgo dicitur*'), used only once by Spinoza and by no means recurrent in the language of the Schools. It is precisely from this passage of the *TdIE* that Freudenthal (1887: 120. My translation) derives that 'Spinoza owes the term not only to Descartes, but also to the previous scholastic tradition.'

such an extension remains wholly implicit and utterly unmotivated.[42] While openly qualifying necessary existence, the *causa sui* does not immediately dissolve all the knots of its own univocity, because the terms it employs to describe existence are still not unequivocally distinct from the traditional ones: this is how the concept is characterised in the first part of his *Short Treatise on God, Man & His Well-Being* (*De Deo*), where it appears to introduce the necessary being of the attributes (which Spinoza provisionally calls 'substances of a single attribute'[43]) and, as a consequence, that of God.

A short trajectory of six propositions sets the stage for the first demonstration. From the definition of substance – its being and its being conceived 'in itself' and 'for itself' – Spinoza deduces in order: the 'incommunicability' between two substances with different attributes, the absence of a causal connection between things that have nothing in common, the impossibility of having more than one substance of the same attribute, and the impossibility of their mutual production. The conclusion, in the seventh Proposition is that:

> [i]*t pertains to the nature of a substance to exist*. A substance cannot be produced by anything else (by 6 Cor.); therefore it will be the cause of itself, i.e. (by Dem. 1), its essence necessarily involves existence, or it pertains to its nature to exist.[44]

Here too we find a certain conceptual duplicity. Spinoza explicitly and unequivocally states that the existence of substance is *causa sui*, but this position is determined by the obliqueness – the unnecessary univocity – of the first definition, cited *verbatim* in the predicates of the *involvere* and in the perhaps a little less generic yet still vague *pertinere*. Indeed, this obliqueness is now accentuated by the overall structure of the demonstration, by its 'negative', indirect, and *a fortiori* way of proceeding: it is the fact that a substance 'cannot be produced by anything else' which leads to the conclusion of a self-cause, of the necessary existence of substance.

The passages that follow offer cumulative – although not definitive – clues in favour of a univocal reading of the 'cause', beginning with Scholium 2 of Proposition 8, aimed at demonstrating the infinity of the 'substance of one attribute'. Here we find the explicit admission that 'that there must be, for an existing thing, a certain cause on account of which it exists' and that such

---

[42] *TdIE* 42, 84, passim; *CWS* I, 36–7. For Aristotle see *Phys*, I, 1, 184a.
[43] *Ethics* I, 8 Dem.; *CWS* I, 412.
[44] *Ethics* I, 7 Dem.; *CWS* I, 412.

cause 'must be contained in the very nature and definition of the existing thing [. . .] or must be outside it'.[45] This claim seems to echo Descartes, but without any reductive circumlocution, and the posthumous Dutch tradition, as Gebhardt reports, will significantly translate *'certam aliquam causam'* with 'een stellige oorzaak' (a positive cause), just as, after all, Spinoza himself had written in Latin in his epistolary.[46] And yet, even in this case, the apparently direct appeal to the *causa sui* does not suffice to prevent its sudden bending towards a still indistinct *pertinere* of existence into essence: 'since it pertains to the nature of a substance to exist'.[47] The picture does not change when it comes to articulating proofs for the existence of God, since, even before the *Ethics*, the choice of an *a priori* structure recurrently and surprisingly[48] invokes the concept of 'cause': '[s]ince God is the cause of himself', Spinoza explains in *KV*, 'it is enough that we prove him through himself'. Since I exist and nevertheless 'I do not have the power to preserve myself', Spinoza goes on to argue in one of the rare, explicit attacks on Descartes' *Principia*, I am 'preserved by another who has the power of preserving himself'.[49] The logical-demonstrative axis that, in Proposition 11 of the first part of the *Ethics* (and in its Scholium), supports the four fundamental proofs of the existence of God, draws from Proposition 7, and it is thus grounded on the notion of *causa sui* as well as on its unaccomplished positivity. This unitary thread, underlying all of Spinoza's arguments, should be briefly highlighted.

The first *a priori* demonstration, the *Grundnorm* of all others in its truly *fundamental* compactness, is constructed directly from the seventh Proposition, and it also borrows its indirect form, realising itself 'negatively', or *ad absurdum*: 'conceive, if you can, that God does not exist. Therefore (by A7) his essence does not involve existence. But this (by P7), is absurd. Therefore,

---

[45] *Ethics* I, 8 Schol. 2; CWS I, 415.
[46] See *Spinoza Opera*, ed. Gebhardt, II, 347 (*Textgestaltung*); *Ep.* XXXIV (to Johannes Hudde): *'Uniuscujusque rei existentis causam positivam, per quam existit, necessario dari debet'*; CWS II, 25.
[47] *Ethics* I, 8 Schol. 2; CWS I, 415.
[48] Surprisingly because, as we know, the causal procedure is normally reserved for *a posteriori* demonstrations.
[49] See *KV*, I, 7, 12 (CWS I, 90); *PP* I, 7 Dem. (CWS I, 252). In *KV* the option for the *demonstratio* a priori, made explicit since the first chapter, does not yet reach full autonomy from Descartes, also because, as has been noted by one of the most authoritative contemporary commentators on the *Ethics*, it is placed 'upside down' with respect to more mature positions, that is, before the treatment of the divine essence (see Gueroult 1968: 493ff). On the reversal of the post-Cartesian proof in *PP*, see again Gueroult 1968: 490–3 and Scribano 1990: xx–xxii.

God necessarily exists, q.e.d.'[50] The second demonstration is wholly complementary to the first one and it develops – *a fortiori* – around its being *causa sui*, since 'a thing necessarily exists if there is no reason or cause which prevents it from existing'.[51] The third demonstration is *a posteriori*, and again a *reductio*: because 'to be able not to exist is to lack power, and conversely, to be able to exist is to have power',[52] if only finite entities existed they would be more powerful than God, the absolutely infinite being; but this is clearly ('as is known through itself') absurd. It follows that either nothing exists or an absolutely infinite Entity exists necessarily: '[b]ut we exist, either in ourselves, or in something else, which necessarily exists. Therefore . . .'.[53] Finally, the fourth demonstration (added in the Scholium) also proceeds *a posteriori*: if the attributes cannot be produced by any external cause and if their existence must necessarily follow the internal perfection of their nature, 'so there is nothing of whose existence we can be more certain than we are of the existence of an absolutely infinite, or perfect, Being – i.e., God'.[54] The *causa sui* indicates the principle of necessary existence of substance, and it underpins all four demonstrations: it lies at the centre of the first one; it opens the way to the infinity of God in the second; it makes explicit, by supporting it, the accessory and subordinate structure of the third; and finally it binds God and his attributes in the fourth. Moreover, while proceeding along this demonstrative path, it accumulates other circumstantial elements of univocity: from the attention given, in the second proof, to a (positive) cause for the existence of substance in nature, to the claim that '[to] be able not to exist is to lack power, and conversely, to be able to exist is to have power',[55] which bolsters the third and fourth proofs, and that characterises being as the quantity of 'reality-power' contained in the nature of a thing: 'that the more reality belongs to the nature of a thing, the more powers it has, of itself, to exist'.[56] And yet the indirect development (a consequence of the structure of the seventh Proposition) of the four demonstrations – two *reductio* and two *a fortiori* proofs – does not allow us fully and completely to ascertain the positive value of the *causa sui*.

---

[50] *Ethics* I, 11 Dem.; CWS I, 417.
[51] Ibid.
[52] *Ethics* I, 11 Dem.; CWS I, 418.
[53] Ibid.
[54] See *Ethics* I, 11 and Schol.; CWS I, 417–18.
[55] *Ethics* I, 11 Dem.; CWS I, 418.
[56] II, 52–4. *Ethics* I, 11 Dem.; CWS I, 418.

Causa rerum

Having deduced the indivisibility of God (in Propositions 12 and 13), Spinoza proceeds to state his uniqueness:

> *Except God, no substance can be or be conceived*. Dem.: Since God is an absolutely infinite being, of whom no attribute which expresses an essence of substance can be denied (by D6), and he necessarily exists (by P11), if there were any substance except God, it would have to be explained through some attribute of God, and so two substances of the same attribute would exist, which (by P5) is absurd.[57]

It is hardly necessary to stress how, here, Spinoza performs a first great split with tradition. The uniqueness of substance, of God-Nature-Substance, is the key to the whole Spinozist system, and the first critics of his work could not but immediately notice it.[58] From this notion the coordinates for a criterion of truth are immediately drawn: *cogitatio* and *extensio*, like all the infinite attributes of a single substance that are unknown to man, are elevated to the status of 'attributes of God, or . . . affections of God's attributes'.[59] The reach of causal knowledge – the logical-ontological significance of the *causa-ratio* – is located in this gathering of both thought and extension within one, infinite *substantia*. This takes place in the *tautological* simplicity of a circular motion, by means of which demonstrative knowledge could lead to a God which is, by its very nature, always-already its true source, its first metaphysical root.[60] This 'circular' nature of the criterion of truth is immediately meant to settle the issue of the *res singulares*.

'Whatever is, is in God, and nothing can be or be conceived without God (*nihil sine Deo esse, neque concipi potest*)'.[61] Proposition 15, along with its Scholium, plays a strategic role in the conceptual architecture of the first part of the *Ethics*. Not only because, as has been rightly and authoritatively

---

[57] *Ethics* I, 14 and Dem.; CWS I, 420. See also *KV* I, I, 2–19; CWS I, 66–71.
[58] See Leibniz, *RIS*, 122–3; Bayle 1965. On Leibniz and Spinoza see Morfino 1994.
[59] *Ethics* I, 14, Cor. 2; CWS I, 420.
[60] Moreau (2021: 207) writes, in reference to *TdIE* and to the *Ethics*, that 'the system is founded exclusively on its own architectonic. In the space of this architectonic, the system produces its own beginning.' All that Moreau's extensive research intends to demonstrate is that alongside this path of the '*philosophia*' there is a 'philosopher's beginning', for which the role of 'experience' is fundamental.
[61] *Ethics* I, 15; CWS I, 420.

stated, it concludes the deduction of the divine essence,[62] but also because its overall articulation indicates precisely and synoptically the conceptual pathways taken by the second part of *De Deo*. The '*nihil sine Deo esse, neque concipi potest*' – the statement that the being of things, and its conception, resides within God and begins with it – paves the way to the construction of a very peculiar relationship between the one only substance and the various *res*, i.e. its 'modes', its positive *expressions-modifications*. At the same time, this connection illustrates the nature of God, clearly and unequivocally targeting the anthropomorphic image of God and the authoritarian, personal, and creationist nature of substance. This attack begins with the Scholium, which is aimed at demolishing a central quality of the Jewish-Christian God, his misunderstood immateriality. This conception would not admit any allegedly 'unworthy' *res extensa* within the divine nature: an absurd and paradoxical claim which, while postulating the infinity and omnipotence of God's nature, also forces it to undergo the effects of something external to it.[63] The nature of substance and the derivation of things from it, systematically intertwined but distinct and indeed distinguishable, these two paths converge in the final movement of the *De Deo* when they recognise and mirror themselves into the new and provocative image of a new 'power' (*potentia*).

Both the existence and the 'conceivability' of *res* are 'within' God. Spinoza takes this assumption to its extreme consequences, up to its coincidence with the very structure of the God-things articulation, identified as a causal and necessary link of 'deduction', *from essence to property*: from the necessity of the divine nature 'there must follow infinitely many things in infinitely many modes'.[64] Similarly, from the definition of each thing the intellect infers a plurality of properties which follow necessarily from the thing's very essence; 'it infers more properties the more the definition of the thing expresses reality, i.e., the more reality the essence of the defined thing involves'.[65] The very same necessity that binds the definition to its 'properties' also involves substance qua *natura naturans*, as a holder of infinite attributes, in relation to itself qua *natura naturata* as a set of finite and infinite modes (of 'that which is in another through which it is also conceived').[66]

[62] Gueroult 1968: 222–3.
[63] *Ethics* I, 15 Schol.; *CWS* I, 421.
[64] *Ethics* I, 14 and Dem.; *CWS* I, 420. See also *KV* I, I, 2–19; *CWS* I, 66–71.
[65] *Ethics* I, 16 Dem.; *CWS* I, 425.
[66] *Ethics* I, Def. 4; *CWS* I, 409. According to Giancotti (1988: 14–21), the methodological turning point of the *Ethics* is given by this theoretical assumption: if the *TdIE* still proceeds on an 'analytical' basis (the only one admitted by Descartes), the *Ethics*

This is the obligatory and pressing meaning that makes God the cause of all things: an efficient cause, 'absolutely the first cause', and 'immanent, not transitive'.[67] He is also a 'free' cause, but this is a geometric freedom, which implies the necessity of a *lex*, the regularity of a norm: '[t]hat thing is called free which exists from the necessity of its nature alone, and is determined to act by itself alone'.[68] This is enough to confuse the consolidated and edifying understanding of a concept-term, to derail it from the traditional, reassuring (and anthropomorphic) tracks it has followed for millennia. And it is no coincidence that it is precisely from here that the derivation from God to things goes to intersect inevitably with the true nature of substance. Freedom cannot exclude necessity, an ontological keystone inherent in the relation of cause, but only compulsion: a free cause (already an achievement of the KV) 'which is not one which can both do and not do something, but only one which does not depend on anything else'.[69] To accept that God could avoid things that derive from his nature would be like claiming that 'God can bring it about that it would not follow from the nature of a triangle that its three angles are equal to two right angles', while 'from God's supreme power, or infinite nature, infinitely many things in infinitely many modes, i.e., all things, have necessarily flowed' just as 'from the nature of a triangle it follows, from eternity and to eternity, that its three angles are equal to two right angles'.[70] Freedom, therefore, is to be conceived 'not in a free decree, but in a free necessity', as Spinoza clarifies when responding to one of the many requests for clarification about this subject.[71] A surprising conceptual juxtaposition is thus fitted into the gears of the Spinozist metaphysical system. This link between substance and mode – geometrically structured on the 'causa-ratio', and *free because necessary* – aims to wither the metaphysical-political idea of a God conceived in the image and likeness of man, as arbiter

---

adopts instead a synthetic-deductive procedure (also used by Hobbes) as the only method that, starting intuitively from the 'first cause' to then derive 'from this idea the ideas of its effects', proves able to ground and build the system of science.

[67] *Ethics* I, 16, Cor. 3; CWS I, 425.
[68] *Ethics* I, Def. 7; CWS I, 409; on the modality of being-cause of God see *Ethics* I, 16, Corr. 1–3; 17 Corr. 1–2; 17 Schol.; 18; CWS I, 424–8. For a comparison with the analogous treatment in *KV* I, I, 3, as well as with Heereboord – its closest reference – see Gueroult 1968: 243ff.
[69] *KV* I, I, 8; *CWS*, 83.
[70] *Ethics* I, 17 Schol.; CWS I, 426. Here there is an evident Cartesian echo which, however, significantly widens the geometric comparison from the field of the necessary existence of God to that of the derivation of the modes from the one substance (for Descartes see *Disc*, 314–15, and *Princ*, I, 14, 28).
[71] *Ep.* LVIII (to G. Hermann Schuller); CWS II, 427.

and emperor, the God dreamed by the prophets and by the common people, a God 'now angry, now merciful, now longing for the future, now seized by jealousy and suspicion, indeed even deceived by the devil'.[72] This would be a God with eyes, with hands and feet, with right and left coordinates, a God who likes and dislikes, who hears and makes statements by means of miracles, a king and a legislator, a depository of a naive and imaginative power different from that of nature, active only where it was extraordinarily forced to stop its course.[73] But the free necessity of the causal-rational deduction also demolishes the God (again, a *personal* and *sovereign* deity) described by the most subtle and refined categories of theologians and philosophers: 'the actual intellect, whether finite or infinite, like will, desire, love, etc., must be referred to Natura naturata, not to Natura naturans'.[74] Strictly speaking, God neither 'wants' nor 'understands'. The modes of thought (of the *absoluta cogitatio*) – intellect and will – have the same relationship with the nature of the one substance as motion has with stillness: *omnia naturalia*, in need of a cause that determines them to exist and operate.[75] Moreover, the admission of possibility and of contingency has no foundation in the face of the cause of all things (in the same sense, remember, in which the definition is in relation to its properties). If all things are in fact necessarily deduced from the intimate essence of God, to hypothesise them as being different, to think that they 'could have been determined to produce an effect in another way', would mean, absurdly, to accept the idea that 'God's nature could also have been other than it is now'.[76] God's alleged freedom and will are '*magnum scientiae obstaculum*', because they lead many to erroneously postulate the existence of an 'end', of a 'direction', for the eternal and infinite action of substance: 'if God acts for the sake of an end, he necessarily wants some-

---

[72] It is so in *Ep*. XIX (to Willem van Blijenbergh); *CWS* I, 358. On the topic see also *KV*, II, XXV (*CWS* I, 145); *Ep*. LXXVI (to Albert Burgh) (*CWS* II, 473–4).

[73] Among the many possible references, see *CM* (which on this topic is in a transitional position between the old and the new), I, 6 and II, 3 (*CWS* I, 311–15 and 319–21); *Ep*. LIV (to Hugo Boxel) (*CWS* II, 413–16); *Ep*. LXXV (to Henry Oldenburg) (*CWS* II, 470–3); as well as, of course, the whole first part of the *TTP*.

[74] *Ethics* I, 31; *CWS*, 414.

[75] Ibid.; and see the aforementioned *Ep*. LIV (to Hugo Boxel): 'For if someone asks them whether the divine will does not differ from the human will, they answer that the one has nothing in common with the other except the name. [. . .] I too, not to confuse the divine nature with the human, ascribe to God no human attributes, such as will, intellect, attention, hearing, etc. I say, then, as I said before: the world is a necessary effect of the divine nature, and was not made by chance' (*CWS* II, 414).

[76] *Ethics* I, 33 Dem.; *CWS* I, 436.

thing which he lacks'.⁷⁷ Final causes are, at most, efficient causes: relative determinations within the perennial movement of the modal chains. God truly has no 'meaning'. Nor does he have any 'quality'. He is 'perfect', of course; but, as Spinoza will put it at a later time, '[b]y reality and perfection I understand the same thing'.⁷⁸ Perfection – this is continually repeated – is the 'same reality', or 'the very essence of the thing'. Perfection is the 'power of acting'.⁷⁹

*Eo sensu*⁸⁰

The geometric-deductive relationship on the basis of which substance stands together with its modes leads to important consequences, pertaining to its very nature. The impossibility, for the one and only substance, to admit *accidentes* makes God's *causam esse* necessary, i.e. it makes his being a cause not an option but an integral part of his essence. And yet this does not imply that the whole constitution of the divine nature exhausts itself in this causal function. It remains to be clarified whether the relationship involves the 'whole' of substance – substance 'in itself' and as such – or if it rather concerns it only with reference to the modes, as the engine for the existence of *res singulares*, that is, if the causal-rational relationship can leave space to unexplored residues, to unfathomable substrates in the essence of the substance – perhaps to new margins of will and decision, oriented, with respect to its connection with things, towards an unknown 'not yet', an unknowable 'before', or an unfathomable 'below'. It remains to be clarified, in short, if substance's being *causa sui* implies the same exact regularity, the same geometric normativity of its being *causa rerum*.

'God must be called the cause of all things in the same sense in which he is called the cause of himself.'⁸¹ Confined, in an apparently parenthetical way, to the Scholium of Proposition 25, this claim should certainly not be excessively emphasised, but neither should it be resolved in heterogeneity, as the explication of two different ways of being a cause: an analogical one,

---

⁷⁷ *Ethics* I, App.; *CWS* I, 442.
⁷⁸ *Ethics* II, Def. 6; *CWS* I, 447.
⁷⁹ See *Ethics* II, 1 (*CWS* I, 448); *Ethics*, III, DA (*CWS* I, 542–3); *Ethics*, IV, Praef. (*CWS* I, 545); *Ep.* XIX (to Willem van Blijenbergh) (*CWS* I, 358–9); as well as the first attempts in *TdIE*, 12 (*CWS* I, 10); *PP* I, 7 Lem. 2 Dem. (*CWS* I, 252); CM, I, 6 (*CWS* I, 315). There are useful considerations on the 'reality-perfection' relationship in Vincieri (1984: 91–109). On the nature of the Spinozan God see Giancotti (1985b).
⁸⁰ In the same sense (Translator's note).
⁸¹ *Ethics* I, 25 Schol.; *CWS* I, 431.

addressed to God, and a univocal one, focused on things. Let us briefly look at the overall structure of the second part of the *De Deo*: divine causality (Propositions 16–18); eternity of attributes and of God (Propositions 19–20); modes (Propositions 21–25); the reduction of the intellect and of the will to the condition of modes, and the consequent necessity (neither arbitrariness nor subjectivity) of divine 'production' (Propositions 26–33); and the power of God (Proposition 34). The argumentation proceeds thus: 1. God-things, through the causal relationship; 2. the infinite essence of the substance; 3. the modes' being *in alio*, both for essence and for existence; 4. *Potentia*, introduced in its true nature through the analysis of *intellectus* and *voluntas*, a sort of long parenthetical remark that recalls the Scholium of Proposition 15 and sets the stage for the *Appendix*, against the final prejudice and its causes. But then what was affirmed in the Scholium to Proposition 25 should be given a central role, connecting the analysis of the relationship between God and things with the fullest and more precise identification of divine power (*potentia*). Let us consider the structure of the Proposition as a whole. Its statement affirms that 'God is the efficient cause (of things) not only of their existence, but also of their essence'; the proof leans on Axiom 4 (according to which knowledge of the effect depends on that of the cause, and implies it) and on Proposition 15 (all that is, is conceived by God – and necessarily so). In the Scholium it is said that this Proposition follows even more clearly from Proposition 16 which, as we have seen, argues for the necessity of the derivation of infinite things, in infinite ways, from the divine nature, on the basis of the same geometric link in virtue of which the intellect draws the property of a thing from its definition:[82] 'and in a word, God must be called the cause of all things in the same sense in which he is called the cause of himself'. Divine substance is *causa sui* in *the same sense* in which it is also the *causa efficiens* of things: the immediate identity of essence and existence – simply posited in the already mentioned Proposition 20, in a way that, if evaluated in isolation, does not yet allow the total resolution of the divine nature into the cause: 'God's existence and his essence are one and the same'[83] – is now explicated as a *self-cause, identical to the cause of things*. That is, it is given a meaning according to which it functions as the efficient cause of the essence and of the existence of modes: '[t]his will be established still more clearly from the following corollary. Particular things are nothing but affections of God's attributes, or modes by which God's attributes are expressed in a certain and determi-

---

[82] *Ethics* I, 25 Dem. and 25 Schol.; CWS I, 431.
[83] *Ethics* I, 20; CWS I, 429.

nate way.'⁸⁴ The *causa sui* explains the God-Nature-Substance's identity of essence and existence through the necessity of 'slicing' or 'expressing' itself, of its positive self-production 'in a certain and determinate way' through things. And indeed the passages that follow turn to the two fundamental articulations of this single and unitary structure (*'ad operandum'*) of reality: God's determination of things *'in alio'* (including the modes of the intellect and of the will)⁸⁵ and substance's free necessity (a necessity inherent in its very essence): '[t]hings could have been produced by God in no other way, and in no other order than they have been produced'.⁸⁶ Towards the end of the *De Deo*, the *causa sui* is shown to recapitulate *in potentia* the whole nature of substance:

> God's power is his essence itself. For from the necessity alone of God's essence [*necessitas Dei essentiae*] it follows that God is the cause of himself and of all things. Therefore, God's power, by which he and all things are and act, is his essence itself.⁸⁷

The key lies in this *necessitas Dei essentiae* which now leaves no residue, and excludes from essence any solution other than the necessity of the *ratio/causa*. The equation 'cause of itself = cause of all things' has no unknown values because it results in an active energy, an operative 'virtue' fully deployed and without unexpressed surpluses of essence. The conceptual shift, away from the Aristotelian-Scholastic notion of power (*potentia*) – according to which the *eminence* of the cause with respect to the effect keeps a space of indeterminate possibility (the unfathomable arbitrariness of the will, in the Christian version, including the Cartesian one) open onto the *actual*⁸⁸ – is now clear and wholly definitive. 'To be able not to exist is to lack power, and conversely, to be able to exist is to have power':⁸⁹ as we have seen, ever since its first appearance in the *Ethics*, power (*potentia*) is presented as being an act, the whole of *being there*, the totality of *existere*. *Posse* does not mean 'to have the possibility to', but rather 'to have the power/strength of'. The compactness of the *esse* excludes chance and the flexibility of contingency in favour of persistence and the constancy of determination. The positivity

---

⁸⁴ *Ethics* I, 25 Schol. and Cor.; CWS I, 431.
⁸⁵ See *Ethics* I, 26–32; CWS I, 431–5.
⁸⁶ *Ethics* I, 33; CWS I, 436.
⁸⁷ *Ethics* I, 34 and Dem.; CWS I, 439.
⁸⁸ On the classical notion of 'power' (*potentia*) see Fütscher 1933. The CM, II, still adhered to the idea of the 'eminence' of a 'creator' God.
⁸⁹ *Ethics* I, 11 Dem.; CWS I, 416.

of the cause makes power (*potentia*) 'actual from eternity and will remain in the same actuality to eternity';[90] without gaps, beyond becoming and the 'derivation' of things, and without blind spots in its continuity: 'God's power is nothing except God's active essence.'[91] The identity of *causa sui* and *causa rerum* thus resolves the eternity of substance into a mechanism of power (*potentia*), realising it in the necessity of its actualisation, in its determinative essentiality.

From Metaphysics to Politics

Martial Gueroult was probably correct when he explained that the semantic shift that the concept of *causa sui* undergoes in Spinoza with respect to Descartes moves it from a 'definition' to a 'property' of God, a move needed to keep divine power at bay, so to speak, so as not 'to subordinate its essence to its power, and to make it an arbitrary power high above all rational and natural necessity'.[92] A too immediate contact between the *causa sui*, essence, and power (*potentia*) would readily expose substance to the contagion of traditional authoritarian and anthropomorphic conceptions of the divine. And yet, this interpretative strategy can only grasp one layer of the problem. Indeed – from its definition and the still undefined function that it performs in the first part of *De Deo*, to the power-essence of the substance – the *causa sui* moves from *proprietas* to (the conquest of) *essentia*. The initial shift avoids shortcuts that might lead to traditional conceptions of power (*potentia*), but the whole development of the first book goes far beyond the simple process of deriving the cause 'from definition to property'. The essence of God-Substance, its nature as an absolutely infinite entity 'consisting of an infinity of attributes, of which each one expresses an eternal and infinite essence',[93] does not deductively imply regularity, nor the necessity of its causal-productive structure. On the contrary, its being a cause (an expressive-productive energy) is what realises its unity – articulated in the God-attributes-modes assemblage, *natura naturans*, and *natura naturata*. And, in the end, it is precisely power (*potentia*) that permits the elimination of any personal or arbitrary residue from substance, gathering its nature – all of nature – within its actuality. Unlike Descartes, Spinoza conceives *essentia*

---

[90] *Ethics* I, 17 Schol.; CWS I, 425–6.
[91] *Ethics* II, 3 Schol.; CWS I, 449.
[92] '[À] subordonner son essence à sa puissance, et à faire de celle-ci un pouvoir arbitraire élevé au-dessus de toute nécessité rationelle et naturelle' (Gueroult 1968: 41).
[93] *Ethics* I, Def. 6; CWS I, 409.

as eluding the dimension of the unfathomable (the inscrutable omnipotence of the will) precisely because it is maintained and governed by the cause. This movement of *causa sui* – going from 'property' to 'essence' – is nothing other than its own gradual acquisition of a univocal value. The positive aspect of the *causa sui* can only be conceived in the context of an articulation which, within substance, becomes a constitutive and decisive part of substance itself. Only its self-production as a *causa rerum* unravels the 'seriousness' and the non-allusiveness of the *causa sui*. And only then such a *proprietas* becomes *essentia*: it identifies it, it wholly resolves it into itself. This is when it establishes its 'forms'. No form-quality can necessarily recall or determine its cause; instead, it is the movement of the cause that unleashes the forms, a movement that must necessarily 'take shape'. The problem of the 'form' – the great Spinozan knot of attributes – lies entirely within the relationship between substance and its modes.[94]

Deriving from the cause the circularity of *essentia* and *proprietas* necessarily implies the circularity between substance and the *res*. A few years after writing the *Ethics*, Spinoza explains again this crucial node of his metaphysical edifice – '[f]rom this it follows that the power by which natural things exist, and so by which they have effects, can't be anything but the eternal power of God itself'.[95] '*Ipsissima potentia*',[96] because 'the universal power of the whole of nature is nothing but the power of all individuals together',[97] and *potentia* is the *ipsissima essentia*: '[w]e could also show the same thing from the fact that the power of nature is the divine power and virtue itself. Moreover, the divine power is the very essence of God.'[98] *Causa sui–causa rerum, essentia, potentia*: nothing 'deeper' agitates the heart of substance.

---

[94] Perhaps this makes the quarrel between the opposing interpretations unsolvable, for they see in the attribute ('what the intellect perceives of a substance, as constituting its essence' [*Ethics* I, Def. 4; *CWS* I, 408]) a pure cognitive breakdown operated by the intellect or an actually realised dimension of substance. Hegel, as we know, spearheads the first group (followed, among others, by Erdmann 1848; Pollock 1880; and Wolfson 1934). Fischer (1909) is one of those in the 'realist' camp, also frequented by Robinson (1928) and Gueroult (1968: 428–68). For extensive reconstructions of the debate, please refer to the aforementioned Gueroult, as well as to Sportelli 1995: 27–60.

[95] *TP* II, 2; *CWS* II, 507.

[96] *TP* II, 3; *CWS* II, 507–8.

[97] *TTP* XVI, 4; *CWS* II, 282.

[98] *TTP* VI, 7; *CWS* II, 154. Spinoza's substance is distinguished from the Plotinian One, which determines the world but absolutely transcends it, as the one who is 'beyond Being' (*Enn*, V, 5 and 6, 872–3). On Spinoza and Plotinus see Deleuze (1990: 169–86), who moreover dissolves the complexity of the '*causa sui*' by conceiving the attribute as a sort of 'middle term' between substance and modes. But far from resolving the

The effect (the infinite chain of effects) occupies the whole constitution of the cause, because the cause is nothing other than itself, it is nothing but a cause. And from this follows the full *homogeneity of being*. There can be no difference of *substance* between God and his modes. And yet – and this is the crucial point – a difference remains: between what is in itself because cause of itself and what is 'in another'; between what is an absolute affirmation and what is a partial negation of *existentia*.[99] There is a gap without '*proportio*',[100] which cannot be measured, because it is decided by the *genus* of existence: cause of itself, caused by another.[101] The *causa sui* of substance is bound to the cause of the modes '*eo sensu*' and not '*quatenus*' – not *inasmuch as*. It thus delineates an unthinkable ontological primacy of determinations over the determinant, of the caused over the cause. And yet, once again the *causa sui* subsists, alone and in its entirety, through its being the cause of 'other': a circularity of origins, an unresolved duplicity of *beginnings*.[102] Or rather: the impossibility of reducing the eternal and perpetual continuity of *potentia-essentia* to the logic of the 'principle', to force it to punctuality, to an *eventuality* (to the contingency of an 'event', of a decision). Besides, the nature of this *potentia-essentia* is identified with its own uninterrupted repositioning, its own incessant relocation as a productive and determining act. An authoritarian will is foreign to the *non-initiating* essence of Spinoza's power (*potentia*), which is completely identical to the 'free necessity' of its continuous beginning, of its eternal act of determination.

The fully causal nature of substance frees the relationship between God and things from the anthropomorphic (voluntarist and personalistic) link of 'creation', hence the abandonment of every 'eminence', of every hierarchy, in favour of the compact and *perfect* unity of being: radical immanence. There is no mystery: '[a]s for your contention that God has nothing formally in common with created things, etc., I have maintained the complete opposite of this in my definition.'[103] The primacy of being as power (*potentia*).

---

foundational tension of the cause, the uncertain nature of the attribute seems to reside *within* it.

[99] *Ethics* I, 8 Schol. 1; CWS I, 412.
[100] *Ep.* LIV (to Hugo Boxel); CSW II, 415.
[101] *Ep.* XII (to Lodewijk Meyer); CWS I, 202.
[102] The complexity of this movement is partly sacrificed where the *causa sui* simply becomes the 'Seins und Erkenntnisgrund' of the *natura naturans*, completely extraneous to the 'kausalmechanische Wirkungen' of the *natura naturata*. See Kather 1994.
[103] *Ep.* IV (to Henry Oldenburg); CWS I, 172. On the problems of interpretation relating to the passages in which Spinoza seems to affirm the absolute heterogeneity of cause and effect see Giancotti's considerations (1988: 347–9n); according to him, in

The reciprocal call between God and the world (the infinite and the finite, the one and the many, equality and difference, order and disorder) within the positive continuity of being. Substance (the infinite, the one, etc.) is not transcendent, it is not located 'beyond' its modes (the finite, the many, etc.); substance is always wholly present within its modes. But this is only possible in virtue of the 'cause'. This is the primacy of the cause, of the productivity of the cause/power (*potentia*). An identification of being with the activity of the cause; power (*potentia*) as a structure of being: '[n]othing exists from whose nature some effect does not follow'.[104] In the beginning there is the uninterrupted *facere*, the eternal *operari* of God-Nature-Substance (God-Nature-Substance *qua* eternal *operari*). Spinoza does not proceed backwards, *cosmologically*, from things-effects to a first cause, a *first being* that, as such, would overflow out of the nature of a cause, unbinding itself from its own necessity – whether the 'unmoved mover' which has no fault/responsibility for its causal function, or a creator God who *wants* that function, who chooses and decides it, without exhausting itself in it. Spinoza's substance is nothing but a cause and therefore, inevitably, it is *causa sui*. But it is the cause of a 'self as a cause': therefore, this *causa sui* is necessarily identical to a *causa rerum*, a *causa sui eo sensu*, just as a cause is understood as the cause of *some-thing*, a cause of *things*. Dense with ethical and political potential, this is perhaps the original and most complex device – the buttressing mechanism, so to speak – that supports the entire Spinozist metaphysical system.[105] Because this is how the irreducible difference and the absolute unavoidability of the *res* with respect to substance as *a whole* – the whole essence-power of substance (the self-causing and causing of other) – is posited. The commonality persists while continually recalling the difference. On the one hand there is no transcendence, no concealment (but the inevitable, mutual summoning of the opposites). On the other there is the intangible and

these contexts, Spinoza would temporarily assume the thesis, not his own, of a 'creative intellect'.

[104] *Ethics* I, 36; CWS I, 439.

[105] Terrenal (1976) considers the *causa sui* as a rationally non-deducible presupposition of the Spinozan argumentative mechanism. However, transforming it into a 'primitive intuition of the *ens perfectissimum*', he employs it to recuperate a rather traditional image of God (something that seems to me to be untenable). Even the considerations of 'value' introduced by Armour (1992: 113–15) seem extraneous to that mechanism, where the question is resolved in terms of a tension towards the moral perfection of 'the Whole'. The many merits of Macherey's 'lecture minimale' and 'purement littérale' in his five volumes of commentary on the *Ethics* do not exclude that sometimes, as in the specific case of the *causa sui*, there is a risk of diluting the density of Spinoza's argument. See Macherey 1998: 31–3.

ungraspable priority of productive *facere*, which excludes any *con-clusion* of substance from determination (even an infinite chain of determinations), placing it beyond the logic of opposites: beyond the one (which makes sense only in relation to the many), and beyond order (which applies only in relation to disorder). Substance, then, will never be revealed as being simply the 'sum of its parts', but neither will it ever be able to transcend (or annihilate) the parts. Compared to Descartes' thought, the Spinozan equation preserves a 'beyond' – although it nails it to the things. Such a beyond is immediately and automatically reconducted, forever and entirely, to the things.[106] Therefore, this is not, in Hegelian fashion, the collapse of the finite into the rigid and immobile *Grund* of an identity.[107] It is even less the dialectic of a subject who, immediately posited, would be alienated from itself, only to then recompose itself as an Absolute, by way of *negation and overcoming*. Being essentially a power (*potentia*), Spinoza's substance is not properly a 'subject', and it has no 'purpose'; it has neither a 'terminus' nor a 'goal'.[108] If anything, to use twentieth-century terminology, it is a *being* that is beyond *being-there* just as it can never be 'given', and that, conversely, cannot but reveal/manifest itself as a '*being-there*'. A *being* whose essence is wholly and uniquely enclosed within the need to 'give itself', to *be-there*. We inhabit (and therefore do not exhaust) the force of a *Sein* that transcends us, but that is always, fully and without residue, active within us, its 'things'.

Why this tension? Why is the circle of *facere* at the heart of being and of metaphysics as a whole? Why is this circle given, referring to the non-deductibility and the impossibility of *potentia*, or even to the movement of its own positing, of its own self-deducing as the essence of substance? It is hardly necessary to recall that none of the great argumentative strategies of the seventeenth century inevitably implies either a naive 'realism' – a linear

---

[106] Useful considerations have been made by Bunge (1959), who sees the Spinozan system as moving away from Descartes' one-way mechanism, starting from this intrinsic causal connection, which continually refers to the necessary relationship and to the interacting connection. Yakira (1994) distinguishes the use of the notion of the *causa sui* in physics from its use in metaphysics: problematic and contradictory in the first case but not in the second, where the principle is transferred from the *outside* – from the otherness-exteriority of the cause-effect relationship – to the *inside*, the interiority-homogeneity of an 'expressive' substance, which is expressed in 'its' modes; however, the need for this expression – the conclusion of the substance in this causing-itself/causing-others – remains unsolved.

[107] Hegel, VG, 361. For a reconstruction of the origins of Spinoza's Hegelian interpretation, see Morfino 1997.

[108] See, albeit with some excessive interpretative simplification, Macherey 1979, in the wake of Althusser 1978.

relationship between reality and knowledge – or reason's firm grasp, totalising and self-legitimising, an element about which many orthodox reconstructions have far too often complained. Indeed, this is not so for Descartes' and his *méthode*, which still finds its ultimate mooring in God, an Anselmian God, conceivable as infinite and perfect inconceivability, and for this reason recognised as not only necessarily existing but also as necessarily true and 'undeceiving', such as to guarantee the certainty of science and of the simplest and most obvious human beliefs. A God capable, therefore, of being an *external* foundation for reason and its mathematical procedures. It is also not so for Hobbes, the 'nominalist' whose rigorous science of ethics and politics is set in motion by the indefinability of passions, the obscure naturalness and the *pre-dominant* physicality of fear, an exterior fear, always pressing the epistemological conversions of the *verum* and of the *factum*, always incumbent on the (never permanently) resolved rational transparency of human constructions. And the same can be said about Galileo's scientific system, the most solid mathematical system of the seventeenth century, wherein the 'experimental' artifice complicates the possibility of a simple grasp, an instantaneous superimposition of geometric *ratio* onto the motions and the phenomena of nature. The *functionality* and the *productivity* of reason do not immediately imply its complete 'truth'.

> [a]nd if even once I found that the fruits which I have already gathered from the natural intellect were false, they would still make me happy, since I enjoy them and seek to pass my life, not in sorrow and sighing, but in peace, joy, and cheerfulness. By so doing, I climb a step higher.[109]

It should not be forgotten that Spinoza's metaphysics begins with the *Ethics*, indeed it is the first movement of a book about *ethics*. '*Coup de dés qui abolit le hasard*', the dice roll that abolishes chance: perhaps it is here that we find the root of the complex mechanisms of the *causa sui*.[110] The articulation of being *qua* cause-power (*potentia*) does not destroy the finite – as the Hegelian critique maintains – nor can it be traced (as Schopenhauer wanted) to a simple dogmatic substitution of the Jewish-Christian God with Nature, so as to preserve the awe of the mystery.[111] Irreducible to any preliminary simplification, the *causa-ratio* – the causal-rational essence of

---

[109] *Ep.* XXI (to Willem van Blijenbergh); CWS I, 376.
[110] See Breton (1979: 149) who, following Plato (*Rep*, X, 604c), overthrows Mallarmé's motto: 'Un coup de dés jamais n'abolira le hazard.'
[111] See WW, 787, and SG, III, 2, 135–6.

nature-substance — still makes nature-substance accessible and intelligible to humans as an operational *vis*, a productive energy that involves them in the double, structural function of both actors and recipients, of both subjects and objects of actions and passions, beyond any superhuman titanism or any superstitious subordination of the human. This *participatory presence* within the universal enables humans to best grasp their particular condition, a decisive presupposition for their 'perfection' and for reinforcing their presence in being. It is here that we find the most implicit and yet the most powerful circularity of beginnings, that is, the most radical immanence. It is here that we find the ethical *ratio* of metaphysics. And here, finally, we understand its crucial civil projection, its specific political value.[112]

---

[112] On the ethical-practical purposes of the *De Deo* see Macherey's insightful observations. According to him, this preliminary Spinozan reflection on the *rerum natura*, expressed in the 'sharp rapidity' of his thirty-six propositions, represents 'the initial stage of an approach which pushes beyond while still being inscribed into what its author has chosen to call *Ethics*, so as to clearly show that the meaning of his philosophical enterprise is not only in its telling the truth about the world but in finding the means to change life, from a perspective that puts theory at the service of a practice, and precisely of an ethical practice' (Macherey 1998: 14, 7. My translation). Between 'experience' and 'luck', the 'peculiarity of Spinozism' consists, for Moreau, in the creation of 'a way of approaching reality that introduces pre-philosophical preoccupations into the very heart of the system' (2021: 567).

2
Towards a Political Order

The Imagination of Order (Premise)

'For Kings are not Gods, but men, who are often captivated by the Syren's song.'[1] Approaching the end of his brief existence, Spinoza once again, albeit from an inverted perspective, states a cardinal point of his entire system of thought. Of course, strictly speaking, the aphorism about kings that 'are not gods' (and who therefore often end up lured by the songs of too many sirens) only serves, at the beginning of the seventh chapter of the *Political Treatise*, to introduce the theme of the superior stability of the law with respect to the one who governs, thus confirming the principle of the greater reliability and of the objective virtual-rational impartiality of righteous institutions, as compared to the inevitable passional/individual weakness of the *rex*.[2] This is a topical subject in the Aristotelian tradition, successively re-employed, and variously reconceived, in many contexts within modern political thought. But this affirmation is really emblematic, well beyond its literal context, because it represents the reciprocal of the repeatedly emphasised distinction between *Dei potentia* and *humana Regum potentia* which, together with his metaphysics, defines much of the new Spinozist dislocation of theology and politics: '[s]uch is the absurdity into which they have fallen, through confusing the divine intellect with the human and frequently comparing his power with the power of Kings'; '[f]urther, they very often compare God's power with the power of Kings'; 'not to confuse God's power with

---

[1] *TP* VII, 1; *CWS* II, 544.
[2] 'Now that I've explained the fundamental principles of a Monarchic State, my intention is to demonstrate the same things in this chapter, in proper order. The most important point is that it's not at all contrary to practice for these laws to be so firmly established that not even the King himself can repeal them'; *TP* VII, 1; *CWS* II, 544.

the human power or right of Kings'; 'they imagine God as corporeal and as maintaining a kingly rule'.³ This persistence of the image, this continuous merging aimed at reaffirming a difference, should suggest great caution when reducing Spinoza's political dimension to a simple product of his time, a sort of practical commitment devoid of significant connections with theoretical work, a noble and generous battle to be sure, yet fundamentally detached from important and profound philosophical speculation. On the contrary, the insistent distinction drawn between 'kings' and 'gods' suggests a much more stringent logic and internal consequential ties, just as a certain novel conception of the *divine* implies and involves a new and different conception of the *imperium*.

In the meantime, such an image consciously shatters the Cartesian equation between personalism and voluntarism, and goes straight to the heart of substance: to its energetic/causal essence, to the *libera necessitas*, which excludes any subjective characteristic belonging to the *intellectus* and to *voluntas*, thus proposing an utterly different idea of God to the one established by two thousand years of Jewish-Christian culture. *Deus sive natura* resolves itself in the infinite fullness of being, in the continuity of its own action-perfection, in its self-realising as a *causa sui* not unlike, and indeed identical to, the cause of everything else. *Substantia* thus frees itself from the cage of 'meaning', unbinding its eternal *operari* from the inevitably extrinsic constraint of any 'final' reason and from the prejudice of the existence of an 'end', capable of orienting the world's processes. A prejudice that derives only from the particular condition of human beings, aware of their own appetites but unaware of the causes that determined them.

The *ordo* is also part of this. *Connexio rerum*: conceived as a *causa-potentia* (a concatenated *operari* of beings, a circularity of beginning), order loses its noble and strong function of the structure of things, of that which assigns a *meaning*, a *goal*, or a *direction*. Like any other quality proper to a 'purpose' (the good, love, beauty, or substance's own uniqueness), even *ordo* abandons the sunny regions of *essentia*, to withdraw into the most inaccessible and obscure paths of the *modus imaginandi*, of the confused concepts of human beings who so often 'firmly believe, in their ignorance of things and their own nature, that there is an order in things'.⁴ We consider *res* to be well-ordered

---

³ See, respectively, CM, II, 3 (in a context that still admits the existence of an intimate and inscrutable 'divine will') (*CWS* I, 321); *Ethics* II, 3 Schol. (*CWS* I, 449); *TTP* VI, 58 (*CWS* II, 165).

⁴ *Ethics* I, App.; *CWS* I, 444. On the positive use of the term 'ordo' as a causal relationship see *TdIE*, 15ff. (*CWS* I, 11–13), CM I, 3 (*CWS* I, 307); CM II, 9 (*CWS* I, 333),

when they appear to us arranged in such a way that, when representing them through the senses, we can easily imagine and remember them. And since this *imaginationis facilitas* is particularly pleasing to us, we prefer order to confusion, as if it were something objectively existing in nature: '[t]hey also say that God has created all things in order, and so, unknowingly attribute imagination to God'.[5] In reality, *ordo* and *confusio* mirror each other, and they are both inadequate to grasp the essence of the universe, to whose productive structure 'neither beauty, nor ugliness, neither order nor confusion'[6] can be attributed. In this way Spinoza separates the two traditionally converging dimensions of the classical-Christian notion of 'ordo'. In both Aristotle and the Stoics, serial/causal and teleological/final forms of succession overlap, since they are seen as derivations of a single, underivable *arché*: the cause that can exist without its effects, for the latter will be disposed '*suo loco*'[7] on the basis of their greater or lesser proximity to the 'principle', which will remain intact, untouched, and aloof. Dovetailing with this pagan version, Christian theology reinterprets the '*ardua questio*'[8] of order starting from the perfect immobility of the *Ego sum qui sum*, the God who changes things without changing himself, on the basis of a relationship of creation by 'likeness' that establishes, among the *res*, a precise order of 'forms', an unquestionable hierarchy of correspondences and differences, of perfections and imperfections. An '*ordo finium*'[9] which, according to Augustine, proceeds from the *Verbum*, from the Platonic 'likeness' of God with himself, whose explanatory methods exceed the understanding of human reason.[10] The Spinozan decomposition is made possible by questioning the nature of this *arché*. *Vis*, power: the ability to cause oneself as well as to cause others. On the one hand the 'principle' is never given without its effects, for it is nothing but the act of determining effects and producing consequences (it is both and necessarily 'other' and 'not-other'). On the other, all things inherit

---

and especially *Ethics*: I, 33 and Schol. 1 and 2; II, 7 and Cor.; III, 2 Schol.; IV, 62 Schol. (*CWS* I, 436–9, 451, 494–7, 581–2). There is another meaning linked to this one, equivalent to 'method', the deductive procedure able to adequately grasp causal relationships: *TdIE*, *passim*; *Ep*. XV (to Lodewijk Meyer) (*CWS* I, 215–16); *Ethics* I, 8 Schol. 2 (*CWS* I, 412ff.), *passim*. On the substantial equivalence of the positive notion of '*ordo*' with that of '*necessitas*' see Hubbeling 1964: 27–33.

[5] *Ethics* I, App.; *CWS* I, 444.
[6] *Ep*. XXXII (to Henry Oldenburg); *CWS* II, 18.
[7] Cicero, *De Off*, I, 40. For Aristotle see *Met*, V, 11, 1018, and V, 19, 1022b.
[8] St. Augustine, *DO*.
[9] St. Thomas, *ST*, I, II, q. 109 a. 6.
[10] See Gilson 1949, as well as Mignini 1989.

from the principle the same status and the same nature of 'modes', since they are all equally consequent from (and necessary for) the cause: from the law of determination to which the latter is constitutively subjected. The essentialist progression of ends is thus supplanted, 'in nature', by a universal connection of forces, by the (egalitarian and quantitative) *enérgeia* of persistence within existence.

No conciliatory reading – whether connecting Spinoza to Scholasticism, to Renaissance Platonism, or to the Kabbalah – can repair this dissolution of the pre-modern solidarity of theology and politics. The interruption of the universal circulation of *ends*, and the precipitation of meaning in the narrow and decentralised horizon of human imagination, exclude any direct foundation and any linear derivation of a political relationship from the 'cosmos', i.e. from the order that *Summum Numen* imposes on the universe. The *vis* of God-Nature-Substance disrupts all ontological hierarchies: the *natural* and unchangeable subordinations that are rigorously arranged for progressive purposes and gradually oriented to perfection, according to their greater or lesser proximity to the omnipotent will of the creator.[11] *Conservatio* rather than *imago Dei*. But Spinoza's solution takes a path that is (at least partly) different from the modern 'representative' model of the political relationship, as well as from the secularised strategy that aims towards a new metaphysics of the political order, emblematically and enigmatically thematised through the figures of the 'subject' and of the '*pactum*'. The Spinozist perspective implies something altogether different also with respect to the 'mortal God' and to the superb, contingent, powerful, and determined mechanism borne out of the ruins of the '*ordo universalis*'.

'Spinoza [. . .] supplies the connecting link between Hobbes and Rousseau';[12] '[h]e was an important link in the chain that leads from Hobbes to Locke'.[13] The homogenising effect of the hermeneutic commodity chain smooths over all differences and particularities; and of course the highest price is paid by those intermediate 'links' of the chain, now reduced to 'pre-someone' or 'post-something' – that is to say, substantially devalued. And yet, albeit implicitly and unintentionally, the fact that multiple comparisons are possible and that many different similarities hold true also illustrates the complexity of a philosophical position, and the impossibility of its straight-

---

[11] On the medieval concept of order see Vasoli 1970 and Simson 1988; about the cosmological and philosophical-political influences exerted on it by Neoplatonism, see Cassirer 1961.
[12] Vaughan 1925: 125.
[13] Hubbeling 1964: 103–4.

forward resolution or reducibility to another. And so, the overabundance of comparisons made between Spinoza and other philosophers becomes the best testimony of the complexity of his thought. The metaphysics and the physics of *conatus* (that is, the theoretical arrangement which, as we shall see, makes the *conatus* the crucial link between physics and metaphysics) keep Spinoza away from the teleo/theo-logical perspectives which were prevalent in the ancient world. The mechanical, inertial principle of the *conservatio* replaces all other identifying qualities of the human: his/her (Aristotelian) natural sociality, the *appetitus societatis*, the goal/fulfilment that defines him/her within a nature that is either positively *reified* (substantiated), or *desertified*, as in the case of Christianity, always in favour of the human as the only earthly 'substance', the only creature that truly is 'analogous' to the creator. The character of 'mode' of every *res singularis*, i.e., the expression of its very essence (an effort/tension *towards* existence) within the inevitability of *determinatio* and of the expressive-causal intersection, holds open the *conatus*'s fundamental dimension of natural relationality, thus setting it apart from the unilateral deduction which prevails in modern political philosophy. It is a deduction, resolved in the *in-dividuum*, in the nuclear reality of the 'subject', impenetrable to further decompositions and articulations. For Spinoza it is *vis* – the *agere* as substance – that innervates the nature of various forms of *ex-sistence* by generating, via productive connections, the 'self' of every single human being, and by occupying its whole essence through the constant mobility of determination – and the continuous instability – caused by the relationship. This is an essence that, in turn, recalls and identifies, in a circular manner, the essence of substance. Hobbes and Locke, but also Rousseau and Kant, construe the individual as the sole and fulfilled foundation of the *vis*: a perspective which implies the need to give a face to such a force, to postpone its dating according to the particular configuration that the *res* (which comes *before* force) assumes in each author: negative/destructive, positive/proprietary, ethical/natural, or rational/moral.

It is precisely from this complex resolution of the Spinozist system that some fundamental premises of the problem of politics are articulated, premises relative to the sources of both the *conatus* and of *societas*, to the exact focus of natural right, and to the space where the 'artifice' (of each human being's *operari*) and the absolute universality of *necessitas* can be recomposed. These are core presuppositions which remain unchanged throughout Spinoza's major works, and which can therefore be addressed synchronously, almost like a background that is common to all the different – or at least partially different – conclusions which Spinoza seems to reach in his reflection on the nature of the *imperium*, as they evolve from the first to the second of his political treatises.

The *Conatus*

'Each thing, as far as it can by its own power, strives to persevere in its being.'[14] The *res* are 'modes' which express, within the finite, the *Dei potentiam* by means of which God exists and acts; not the eternally accomplished cause/self-expression of substance, but a need, an impulse towards one's own being/existing: a 'force for persevering in its being' (*'conatus in suo esse perseverandi'*). A 'certain and determinate mode' (*'certo et determinato modo'*)[15] of the *conatus* corresponds to the infinite power-essence of God: '[t]he striving by which each thing strives to persevere in its being is nothing but the actual essence of the thing'.[16] According to the 'actualising' ontology of the cause, from every existing *res* some consequence follows, 'from the given essence of each thing . . . some things [effects]' must inevitably spring. This inevitable process is imposed by the *vis*, which encapsulates the whole reality of the thing:[17] '[t]he striving by which each thing strives to persevere in its being is defined by the thing's essence alone'.[18] The human, being a mode that participates in the infinite attributes of *cogitatio* and of *extensio*, is *essentially* neither *mens* (will, freedom) nor *corpus* (motion, rest). Its tension towards existence and its progression within *permanence* are the crucial sparks of *in-dividuation*, the beating heart of every single 'determined unity', of every single and actually existing human being. Not a quality but an energy, operating at the core of the mode; not just another 'entity', a more or less obscure substrate, a new 'substantialising' arrangement *à la* Descartes. Rather, individuation is the aseptic neutrality, the irresistible intrusiveness, and the universal pervasiveness of a power (*potentia*). The *vis* does not reach its conclusion in any form. The qualities give a face to the *conatus*, but they do not adjudicate it. Mind and body speak of it, they 'express' it well within its essential conditions and subordinate to its peremptory impulses.[19] *Mens* and

---

[14] *Ethics* III, 6; CWS I, 498.
[15] *Ethics* I, 57 Dem.; CWS I, 528.
[16] *Ethics* III, 7; CWS I, 499. On the frequent use of '*vis*' as a synonym of '*conatus*' see *Ethics* II, 45 Schol.; *Ethics* III DA; *Ethics* IV, Praef.; *Ethics* IV, 3; as well as, earlier, CM, II, 6; CWS I, 481, 545–6, 548, 325–6.
[17] *Ethics* III, 7 Dem.; CWS I, 499.
[18] *Ethics* IV, 25 Dem.; CWS I, 558.
[19] 'We can consider man from different points of view, but what founds his unity is always the *conatus*, expression of the life of God' (Zac 1963: 128. My translation).

corpus are nothing *other* than power. They are will (*voluntas*) when 'related only to the Mind'; appetite (*appetitus*) when both are comprehended, so that they are related 'to the Mind and Body together'; and desire (*cupiditas*) when they are 'with consciousness of the appetite'.[20] The essence of the mode is power (*potentia*), unfolded and determined *in mente* and *in corpore*. It is a force/appetite from whose nature 'those things that promote his preservation'[21] necessarily follow. An effect that has a power (*potentia*), a determination that determines, a consequent that produces consequences.

Firmly built upon this causal foundation, the Spinozist *conatus conservandi* differs from any of its previous formulations, which at best display some linguistic or semantic similarities to Spinoza's concept. Compared to its classical renditions, the latter is defined in far more extensive terms, well beyond its configuration as a rule, as a principle that merely pertains to the 'lower' forms of life, the *low-lying* areas of existence, whether only animate beings, as in Stoicism, or even plants and minerals as in Augustine (and then, with some obvious complications and variations, in the Renaissance and in Descartes).[22] The metaphysics of the cause implies, under the same conditions, a relationship of absolute difference and absolute identity between substance and the modes, that is, one that excludes any 'natural' diversity between 'entities' and any hierarchy, evolution, or gradation among determined forms of being. Functioning as a kind of law of universal gravitation towards existence, the *conatus* does not differentiate between humans, things, and animals. The *vis* is not limited, as in Aristotle, to the regulation of the most immediate and elementary functions of human nature: its vegetative and impulsive/perceptive aspects, teleologically placed 'on hold', *pre-disposed* to different 'fulfilments'. *Mens* and *corpus* are at the service of one and the same force. Even the most sophisticated abilities and the most complex operations of the mind respond to the law of the *conatus*, and tend towards its maximum 'empowerment': towards its strengthening within being and the accumulation of 'life'. By making any gap within the nature

---

[20] *Ethics* III, 9 Schol.; CWS I, 500; II, 147–8. 'We are at the mercy of these affective states. Indeed, this is an understatement. We are they [...] The *I* is nothing but the play and conflict of affective states' (Rensi 1993: 103. My translation).

[21] *Ethics* III, 9 Schol.; CWS I, 500. See also *Ethics* III, DA; CWS I, 542–3. On *cupiditas* and *potentia* cf. Sportelli 1995.

[22] The most thorough survey of the sources of the concept of *conatus* can be found in Wolfson 1934: II, 195–208, where he considers the Aristotelian tradition, the Stoics, and Cicero (for which see also Carnois 1980), Augustine, Thomas, Duns Scotus, Dante, Telesius and the 'other philosopher of the Renaissance', as well as popular Jewish wisdom.

of the modes impossible, and by eliminating every 'stratification' (either ascending or descending) in the sphere of essences, the *conatus* breaks with the ancient and approaches the modern, heading towards the Hobbesian elaboration of this concept, seen as a 'continuous' and quantitative force.[23] However, the metaphysical device of cause/power (*potentia*) also implies a profound difference with respect to Hobbes' position. *Causa sui* and *causa rerum*: Spinoza's theoretical mechanism posits a 'foundational relationality' of the mode, so that its irreducible individuality is defined through a 'bond', an unavoidable and binding 'constraint' of constitution. A connection that unleashes *vis*; a conjunction that exists and persists for the whole *duration* of the 'thing', for the whole duration of the existence and persistence of the force. A connection between the 'self' of determination and the 'other' of substance: a formative duplicity that realises the mode. Rich in ethical and political consequences, this 'relativised' version of the *conatus* will ultimately appear different from the one – more unidirectional and 'negative' – proposed by Hobbes, the philosopher of fear and of war (*bellum*).[24]

The human-mode is 'part' of the infinite power of God, since substance is the cause of itself in the same sense in which it is the cause of things. This is why *cupiditas* presents itself, first of all, as a positive *vis* 'in itself': no *res* can preserve itself in function of another, nor can it hold within itself the principle – the *ratio* – of its own disintegration – to the extent that, were it not destroyed by an external agent, it would continue to exist for an indefinite time.[25] As the expression of an essence that does not imply necessary existence, the *conatus* will still be an impulse, an appetite, a desire for something; it will be an 'effort', induced and forced by its own striving nature, pushing it to project itself *in alio*, to seek its own confirmation and progress. The *conatus* is a *quid*, positive in itself: it is a compulsion towards its own conservation and progression within being. But this very nature – which does not include necessary existence and which indeed arises precisely from its absence – inevitably pushes the mode's effort towards the other, because

---

[23] On the *conatus* in Hobbes (to which we will return later in this chapter), see *Lev*, I, 6 and *De corp*, III, 15.

[24] The idea of the *conatus* as a strategic dimension of 'affirmation and resistance' of the man-mode is at the core of the remarkable work by Bove (1996).

[25] See *Ethics* III, 4; CWS I, 498. On the debts of the modern Hobbesian and Spinozan notion of the '*conatus*' with respect to Galileo's physics, see Jacob 1974; Filippi 1985: 82ff.; and Messeri 1990: 155–61. More generally, on the relationship between Galilean physics and Spinozan metaphysics ('the physics of Galileo, this new science about which Spinoza tried to construct a metaphysics...'), see Zac 1963: 48–52. My translation.

the 'in itself' of the *res* exists and persists only *in alio*: 'from the necessity of our nature', and 'we are a part of nature' under the same conditions.[26]

The whole essence of the human pulsates within *cupiditas*. Nothing else defines it 'from the outside', as it were. There is no 'purpose' within *conservatio*, for no external 'objective' organises its power. There is no goal at the end of force's path; there is only the end of a mode. From *utilitas* to *felicitas*, from *bonum* to the *perfectio*: it is only starting from non-negotiable positivity, from the irreducible 'self-justification' of the *conatus*, that the effective scope and the real consistency of every other horizon – of human *operari* – can be measured: 'everyone should strive to preserve his own being as far as he can'.[27] Pursuing one's advantage (*suum utile quaerere*) amounts to preserving one's being (*suum esse conservare*), with neither residues nor hidden overtones.[28] No one 'neglects to seek his own advantage, *or* to preserve his being' unless forced by factors extraneous to his essence (*a causis externis coactus*):

> [b]ut that a man should, from the necessity of his own nature, strive not to exist, or to be changed into another form, is as impossible as that something should come from nothing. Anyone who gives this a little thought will see it.[29]

This '*ipsum conatum proprium esse conservandi*'[30] is also the *fundamentum virtutis*, the first and only foundation of virtue. Indeed, *virtus* is not distinguished from the very power (*potentia*)/essence of the human – which is defined by *vis* alone – through which the human strives to preserve his or

---

[26] *Ethics* IV, App., 1; G II, 266; CSW I, 588. Those found in KV, I, 6 are somehow 'preparatory' materials for the doctrine of the *conatus* as it appears in the *Ethics* and in the political treaties, in which the tendency of all things towards the maintenance and conservation of their own being is presented as divine *providentia*, distinct, according to a classic Scholastic partition, in 'general' and 'particular': '[t]he universal is that through which each thing is produced and maintained insofar as it is a part of the whole of Nature. The particular Providence is that striving which each particular thing has for the preservation of its being insofar as it is considered not as a part of Nature, but as whole. This may be explained by the following example. All man's limbs are provided and cared for, insofar as they are parts of man: That is universal providence. The particular is that striving that each particular limb (as a whole, not as a part of man) has to preserve and maintain its own well-being'; CWS I, 84. See also the commentary on Descartes in *PP* II, 14; CWS I, 277.

[27] *Ethics* IV, 18 Schol.; CWS I, 555.
[28] *Ethics* IV, 20; G II, 224; CWS I, 557.
[29] Ibid.
[30] *Ethics* IV, 18 Schol.; CWS I, 554.

her own being: the more one succeeds in it, the more this will be *virtute praeditu*, and the *happier* one will be, since *felicitas* consists solely in 'being able to preserve [one's] being'.[31] *Bonum* is 'what we know to be useful to us' while *malum* is that which 'prevents us from being masters of some good',[32] so that 'we call good, or evil, what is useful to, or harmful to, preserving our being'.[33] It follows that 'we neither strive for, nor will, neither want, nor desire anything because we judge it to be good': on the contrary, 'we judge something to be good because we strive for it, will it, want it, and desire it'.[34] Good and evil do not indicate anything positive about the nature of things as such, they are not compositional realities with respect to the *res*, but only '*cogitandi modos*', extrinsic notions, which 'we form because we compare things to one another'.[35] The universal chain of causes excludes good and evil from the *necessitas* of any determination. It is only our mental constructions, the ever-changing 'ideal' archetypes of humans (their artificial *exemplaria*), that externally superimpose moral/final qualities to essence-power (*potentia*), thus postulating a spurious distinction between the *res* and its *conatus*.[36] Completely arbitrary with respect to the things themselves, those mental constructions ultimately refer to our own *conservation* – their only real motive. Such is the only 'good' and the only admissible 'final cause' of our being: 'a human appetite insofar as it is considered as a principle cause, of some thing'.[37] The purpose of 'perfection' is the same, beyond our deductive and comparative mental operations (in light of which *perfectio* and *imperfectio* are pure 'modes of thinking, i.e., notions we are accustomed to feign because we compare individuals of the same species or genus to one another').[38] Perfection, as we have already seen, designates the reality of the *res*, its *agendi potentiam*: 'the essence of each thing insofar as it exists and produces an effect'.[39] Perfection, otherwise said, is *conservatio* and *perseveratio* within existence. It is impossible to distinguish between the *res*

---

[31] See *Ethics* IV, 18 Schol.; *Ethics* IV, 20 Dem.; *Ethics* IV, 22 Cor. On the identity of *virtus* and *conatus* see Zac 1977.
[32] *Ethics* IV, Deff. 1 and 2; CWS I, 546.
[33] *Ethics* IV, 8 Dem.; CWS I, 550.
[34] *Ethics* III, 9 Schol.; CWS I, 500.
[35] *Ethics* IV, Praef.; CWS I, 545.
[36] *Ethics* IV, Praef.; CWS I, 545. See also KV, I, 10 and II, 4; on the 'error of opinion' that disarticulates *res* and *conatus*, see CM, I, 6 (against the '*bonum metaphysicum*'); CSW I, 92–3 and 102.
[37] *Ethics* IV, Praef.; CWS I, 544.
[38] Ibid.
[39] See *Ethics* II, Def. 6 e; *Ethics* IV, Praef.; CWS I, 447 and 545–6. But see also *Ethics* III, DA; *Ep.* XXXVI (to Johannes Hudde); CM, I, 6; *PP* I, Def. 8.

and the *conatus*. Force occupies the whole essence, the whole constitution of the 'thing'. The 'in itself' of the mode, the positivity of power, subsumes every form and every purpose of determined being, resolving them in the punctual simplicity of one's nature of *sese conservandi*, of one's own *pro-jected* essence, which strives to persist in (its own) existence. No opposition can arise between the *conatus*, on the one hand, and the mind or the body, on the other, for indeed they are a necessary expression under the ('modal') aspect of thought and extension. Nor is there any 'meaning', any direction or goal that can impose autonomous rules (superordinate and independent, presumed and imaginary *auto-nomoi*) to the *appetitus*, to the impulses of *conservatio*. Virtue, the good, happiness, and perfection: these are all *epiphanies* of power; *figures*, human incarnations/representations of essence-power (*potentia*).[40]

---

[40] Body and mind are not merged by means of any relationship of *fundamental* determination, which would position one element as the constitutive principle of the other. Spinoza is strongly against a bond of superiority of *mens* over *corpus* which, variously articulated, animates much of the classical Greek tradition and every strand of Christian thought, from the Platonic vision of the violent and unnatural character of this union (*Phaed* and *Rep*., I), to the Aristotelian-Scholastic conception, which identifies within it a teleological dynamic, 'from form to matter' (Aristotle, *DA*; Aquinas, *SG*, II, 50ff.). The mind does not *in-form*, it does not give shape to the body, because the form and the matter of both depend on their respective attributes, without any possible confusion of *genus*. Here we find an explicit criticism of Descartes who, after transforming the body and mind into two autonomous substances, proposes yet another hierarchical unity among them, seeking surreptitious justifications in God and in the 'pineal gland': new esoteric bonds and new occult qualities, right in the *vir philosophus* of clear and distinct thought (*Ethics* V, Praef.; CWS I, 596–7). Spinoza translates the two Cartesian substances into modes of the one *substantia*, being causally dependent on two of its infinite attributes. This arrangement supports the distinction, continually referring to an indissoluble, mutual identity: expressions of the same mode-human, mind and body become, in fact, declarative variants of the same 'thing', different but so merged in it as to form a single *whole* (KV II, 19, 9; CWS I, 131–2); *Ethics* III, 2 and Schol; CWS I, 494–7). 'The object of the idea constituting the human Mind is the Body, or a certain mode of Extension which actually exists, and nothing else' (*Ethics* II, 13; CWS I, 457). The essence of the human mind is an 'idea', a modal affection of thought, wholly coinciding with a 'thing', a modal affection (*its own* peculiar modal affection) of extension. The entry into 'duration' of a particular modification of *extensio* does not 'determine' but rather 'corresponds' to the entry into existence of its awareness, of its idea, whatever that may be, of itself; a certain *modificatio* of the attribute of extension is not 'other' than a certain idea within the attribute of thought. Without any reversal, without any new overlap, this ontogenetic parity is, in itself, an original and scandalous rehabilitation of the body. Among the many studies on the 'body' in Spinoza, see Jaquet 2001 and 2018.

Ultimately, the *conatus* expresses, above all, the *individuality* of the mode, its necessity and its unrepeatability which derive from its relationship with substance, whose structure of '*causa sui eo sensu causa rerum*' implies the irreducibility of the *res*, the impossibility to eliminate the *id* and to dissolve it into something else. The mode is, so to speak, 'necessary' for substance: it is entailed by its very essence, i.e., by its being a cause, which is the sole essence of substance. And yet, being an induced effect, *vis* – the intimate nature of the 'thing' – also expresses, inevitably and perpetually, the thing's self-positing into 'something else'. Within the 'in itself' of *the conatus*, however, its characterisation as 'caused' – that is, as being produced, from the movement of the cause/power to the positive of existence and persistence – is always implied. There is a correspondence between the double relationship inscribed in the infinite determination of things by substance (substance produces things, but only because it is essentially necessitated – freely self-necessitated, by its very nature – to produce them), and the double determination operating within the finitude of the modes: 'in itself', because they are always bound to substance, and implicit within the law of production which substance obeys and in which it is fully resolved, but also '*in alio*', since they are *forced* to exist, they are *identified* in a 'strife' or 'appetite' that, as such, has to constantly proceed out of itself in order to affirm itself.

The hard core, the *in se* of the mode, does not exclude its subordination (its being an 'effect') which in turn allows it to be and to exist *in alio*. The various *res* do not draw their existence from their own nature, but rather are born, preserved, and die within the infinite causal chain of beings: 'we can never bring it about that we require nothing outside ourselves to preserve our being, nor that we live without having dealings with things outside us'.[41] *Indigere* is the force that organises the *conatus*: 'need' is an integral and constitutive part of strife/power (*potentia*). Only an arrogant humanism, destined to continually fold itself into its opposite, would preach the dream of a complete autonomy, of our absolute mastery of both ourselves and things. These are anthropocentric mirages, developed when one of the many *res singulares* is seen as *the* end, as *the* purpose of nature. Vain, presumptuous hallucinations of a 'substance' fantasised as ready to become a means, an instrument for the action of a 'mode'. This is a paradoxical reversal of the relations between cause and effects, where the 'thing' – the product, that which is caused – becomes a 'cause of the cause', a motive for and an engine

---

[41] *Ethics* IV, 18 Schol.; *CWS* I, 556.

of the cause itself.⁴² Humans transform their particular appetites into absolute 'objectives' of nature and, in order to elevate themselves as masters of the universe, they invent an all-powerful Father, a condescending lord, a benevolent prince, guarantor of their wholly imaginary supremacy. The result is that 'nature and the Gods are mad as men'.⁴³ In reality, substance does not operate in view of an end, because 'that eternal and infinite being we call God, or Nature, acts from the same necessity of nature from which he exists'.⁴⁴ The human is not made in the image and likeness of God any more than any other mode, any other effect of the same cause, is. No 'mode' has any unconditional *imperium* on nature. On the contrary: there is an insuperable dependence of the '*res singularis*' on the chain of causes: '[w]e see then that because man is a part of the whole of Nature, depends on it, and is governed by it, he can do nothing, of himself, toward his salvation and well-being'.⁴⁵ This condition directly refers to the Spinozan decomposition of another *idolum* of Western thought: that of an imaginary *voluntas* (whether Platonic, Stoic, or Christian) which would be independent from the principle of causal determination. Like the human body, which is not an absolute extension, but is rather determined through motion and rest, 'so also the human Mind, or Soul, is not thought absolutely', since it is inevitably regulated 'according to the laws of thinking nature'.⁴⁶ The ontology of the cause, which excludes pure, absolute *cogitatio* from the essence of man, also denies any real consistency to *voluntas* and to free will:

> [t]he will cannot be called a free cause, but only a necessary one. The will, like the intellect, is only a certain mode of thinking. And so each volition can neither exist nor be determined to produce an affect unless it is determined by another cause, and this cause again by another, and so on, to infinity.⁴⁷

---

⁴² See Bodei 1991, 59–60. My translation: 'The Renaissance model of "man" as a "microcosm", to be harmoniously embedded in the whole and capable – despite its smallness – of embracing it, ends with Spinoza. [...] Rather, Spinoza considers mankind and every single individual to be only a part of the universe, inseparable from its processes, yet without the faculty to fully mirror it. Man must therefore adapt both to the marginal role attributed by modern astronomy to the planet on which he lives, and to the idea of the inevitable and anonymous necessity that governs all events.'
⁴³ *Ethics* I, App.; CWS I, 441.
⁴⁴ *Ethics* IV, Praef.; CWS I, 544.
⁴⁵ KV II, 18, 1; CWS I, 127.
⁴⁶ PP, Praef. (by L. Meyer); CWS I, 229–30.
⁴⁷ *Ethics* I, 32 and Dem.; CWS I, 435.

Being a 'certain and determined' modification of thought, the mind cannot be understood as a free subject of its own actions, it cannot have the uncontaminated freedom of wanting or not wanting, but is always 'determinari debet a causa'.[48]

The will (*velle*) – like understanding (*intelligere*), desire (*cupere*), or love (*amare*) – is not a concrete faculty (*facultas*) but an abstraction, a universal name (*nomen*) which we assign through comparison with the particulars: *voluntas* does not actually affect this or that volition, no more than *lapideitas* affects a single stone, or than the generic concept of human being affects the individuals Peter and Paul, or than 'albedo' affects this or that empirical instance of 'white'.[49] Being an *ens rationis*, and not a real faculty, *voluntas* has no power over actual volitions which, in order to exist, require a cause and therefore 'cannot be called free' but only 'tales, quales a suis causis determinantur'.[50] Being unaware of the impossibility of reconstructing the infinite movement of the cause due to the objective non-existence of a motionless starting point of its eternal *operari*, and to the limited and finite constitution of the mode, humans will become 'conscious of their own actions' but also 'ignorant of the causes by which they are determined'.[51] It happens, then, that the infants think they freely desire milk, the angry toddler desires revenge, the shy child seeks to hide, the drunkard is convinced to spontaneously say things that, were he sober, he would have preferred to have kept silent, and that the *delirans* or the *garrulus*, like many others, consider themselves acting 'ex libero mentis decreto', while they are actually

---

[48] *Ethics* II, 48 and Dem; CWS I, 483 See also KV, II, 16; CWS I, 121–5.
[49] See *Ethics* II, 48 Schol.; CWS I, 483–4, and *Ep*. II (to Henry Oldenburg); CWS I, 164–8. On the '*universalia*' see *Ethics* II, 40 Schol. 1 and 2; CWS I, 475–8. As a further example of the 'nominalism', borrowed from the Occamist tradition, which Spinoza shares with Hobbes, commentators have repeatedly referred to a short passage from the KV, in which, against Platonists and Aristotelians, it is explicitly said that universals 'are nothing', while only particular things exist because they 'have a cause' (CWS I, 87). For Hobbes see EW, I, 5, 1–6, and the first part of *De corp*, I, 1–6.
[50] *Ep*. II (to Henry Oldenburg); CWS I, 168. See also *Ethics* II, 40 Schol. 2; CWS I, 477–8), and *TdIE* 85: 'This is the same as what the ancients said, i.e., that true knowledge proceeds from cause to effect – except that so far as I know they never conceived the soul (as we do here) as acting according to certain laws, like a spiritual automaton' (CWS I, 37). On this much discussed definition of the action of the soul '*quasi aliquod automa spirituale*', see Cremaschi 1979.
[51] See *Ethics* I, App.; *Ethics* III, 2 Schol; CWS I, 440 and 496. This sort of 'unconscious' dimension of Spinoza's theory has been repeatedly compared to Freud's ideas: see, among others, Burbage-Chouchan 1993, which also contains numerous bibliographical references.

compelled by their impulses.⁵² To have a healthy mind is no more in our power than to have a healthy body.⁵³

To be 'in another' is a fundamental characteristic of the *id*, of the way that a mode is a 'self'. And precisely for this reason any *res* finds an insurmountable obstacle to its realisation (to the indefinite determination of its strength) *in alio*: '[b]ut human power is very limited and infinitely surpassed by the power of external causes. So we do not have an absolute power to adapt things outside us to our use.'⁵⁴ Both the mode's condition of possibility

---

⁵² *Ep.* LVIII 58 (to G. H. Schuller); *CWS* II, 427–30. *Ethics* III, 2 Schol.; *CWS* I, 494–7. On Spinoza's criticism of free will see Siwek 1947.

⁵³ *TP* II, 6; *CWS* II, 509–10. In this way, Spinoza reinterprets Hobbes's mechanicism and nominalism within a wider and all-encompassing metaphysical system. In the first place, he accepts Hobbes's critique of the classical-scholastic (Platonic, Aristotelian-Ciceronian, Thomistic) conception of the will as 'quae quid cum ratione desiderat' (Cicero, *Tusc*, IV, 6,12) and its substitution with the principle of causation, which transforms the *voluntas* into the final act of a necessity-bound chain into the impulse closest ('last appetite') to the decision: 'the last act of him who deliberates' (*De Cive*, II, 14: *EW* II, 23; *Lev*, VI: *EW* IV, 272). The Hobbesian assumption that freedom does not consist in the indifference of the option (that is not 'freedom from necessity'), but rather in the possibility of doing or not doing without impediments (namely freedom from constraint: 'Liberty is the absence of all the impediments to action that are not contained in the nature and intrinsic quality of the agent', *EW* IV, 273; and see *Elements*, I, 12: ed. Tönnies, 61–3; *De Cive*, IX: *EW* II, 120–1; *Lev*, II, 21: *EW* IV, 196), is then transferred from man to substance, i.e. in a purely anti-Cartesian direction, which eliminates from the essence of God the fictitious *facultas* of his desire for the mechanical and self-necessary *facere* of the *potentia*. God is not a cause because it 'wants' to be so, but it is God precisely because it is cause of itself as well as of things: *libera necessitas*, a freedom that necessarily implies doing things, substance's own reification as things. Hence, finally, the criticism of Descartes' distinction between intellect and will. By revisiting the Augustinian and Anselmian tradition of *voluntas* as the general (and not necessarily rational) origin of the action, Descartes differentiated the unlimited – active and judgmental – realm of the will from the circumscribed, passive, and receptive one of the intellect (*Med*, IV, and *Princ*, I, 35). This is a position to which Spinoza's metaphysics of power (*potentia*) is opposed, denying the existence of '*universalia*': just as in the essence of substance the faculty of an abstract and undifferentiated will is not given – rather there is an *automatic* device of production of God-things – in the same way there is no *single will* in natural beings, but the individual volitions act (and are acted upon), inevitably marked by the infinite causal chain of the modes. Plural and determined wills, quite identical, in their essential status, to the individual 'ideas', they both are judgment and evaluation procedures, necessary activities of affirmation and denial. On the equation of *volitio* and *idea*, of intellect and will, see *Ethics* II, 49 Dem. and Cor.; *CWS* I, 484.

⁵⁴ *Ethics* IV, App. 32; *CWS* I, 593–4. On the 'social' nature of the *conatus* and on the insuperability of passions see Crippa 1965: 86–7, 95, *passim*.

and its constraint can be found in *ea*, '*quae extra nos sunt*'. Indeed, it is also the mode's mortal danger: '[t]here is no singular thing in nature than which there is not another more powerful and stronger. Whatever one is given, there is another more powerful by which the first can be destroyed.'[55] Taken singularly, and considered from the standpoint of its being 'in itself', the strength of the *conatus* – the nature of the *res* – does not imply a finite time of existence, because the essence/definition of each thing affirms and does not deny, poses and does not remove, the thing itself.[56] And yet the modes are, properly speaking, neither eternal (the 'eternity' that characterises existence because of the '*causa sui*' of substance) nor immortal. The time of things is the *un-defined* temporality of 'duration', i.e. things persist in an actuality that requires external causes, but that will nevertheless always be interrupted by them.[57] Such an actuality will always end up broken, shattered *ab alio*. The other is both an affirmation and a negation of the mode; for the *res singularis*, it represents a horizon of both life and death.

Nothing Is More Useful to Man

Spinoza writes, in a passage that should be quoted in full,

> [t]here are, therefore, many things outside us which are useful to us, and on that account to be sought. Of these, we can think of none more excellent than those that agree entirely with our nature. For if, for example, two individuals of entirely the same nature are joined to one another, they compose an individual twice as powerful as each one. To man, then, there is nothing more useful than man. Man, I say, can wish for nothing more helpful to the preservation of his being than that all should so agree in all things that the Minds and Bodies of all would compose, as it were, one Mind and one Body; that all should strive together, as far as they can, to preserve their being; and that all, together, should seek for themselves the common advantage of all. From this it follows that men who are governed by reason – i.e., men who, from the guidance of reason, seek their own advantage – want nothing for themselves that they do not desire for other men. Hence, they are just, honest, and honorable.[58]

---

[55] *Ethics* IV, Ax.; CWS I, 547.
[56] *Ethics* III, 4 and 4 Def.; CWS I, 548–9.
[57] On 'duration' see *Ethics* II, Def. 5 (CWS I, 447); *Ethics* III, 8 and 8 Dem. (CWS I, 499); *Ethics* II, Def. 5 and *Ethics* III, 8 and 8 Dem. (CWS I, 447 and 499).
[58] *Ethics* IV, 18 Schol.; CWS I, 556.

At first sight, the demonstrative procedure that follows and supports this fundamental lynchpin of the fourth part of the *Ethics* seems to favour a direct, linear, and transparent concordance of *ratio* with that which is useful '*omnium commune*'. This is in the name of a clear incompatibility and a rigid incommunicability with the affections/passions, a process that, if confirmed, would place Spinoza's thought in agreement with other anthropological-political paradigms of his age. A more careful analysis, focused on highlighting conceptual tensions, and on revealing all the complex implications of the metaphysics of the cause, would show how the Spinozist argumentative system actually turns out to be much more complex and obliquely outlined than it might seem at first sight.

[m]ost of those who have written about the Affects, and men's way of living, seem to treat, not of natural things, which follow the common laws of nature, but of things which are outside nature. Indeed they seem to conceive man in nature as a dominion within a dominion. For they believe that man disturbs, rather than follows, the order of nature, that he has absolute power over his actions, and that he is determined only by himself. And they attribute the cause of human impotence, not to the common power of nature, but to I know not what vice of human nature, which they therefore bewail, or laugh at, or disdain, or (as usually happens) curse.[59]

Considering how for thousands of years – from Greek philosophy to Roman common sense (and both subsumed in the last segment of the Stoic tradition), up to the entirety of Christian thought – the passions had been object of condemnations and anathemas, this passage, from the preface to the third book of the *Ethics*, is both notorious and scandalous. Just as it excludes the existence of 'miracles' from the domain of substance, the metaphysics of power does not leave any space for deviations, 'vices' or 'defects' (it does not allow 'faults' or 'moral degenerations'), in the domain of the mode. The infinite power of causal determination proceeds only through *necessitas* and its 'properties'.

Not even *passio* eludes this rule. Hatred, anger, and envy all derive from the same natural 'virtue', from which all other singular *res* spring forth:

and therefore they acknowledge certain causes, through which they are understood, and have certain properties, as worthy of our knowledge as

---

[59] *Ethics* III, Praef.; CWS I, 492.

the properties of any other thing, by the mere contemplation of which we are pleased. Therefore, I shall treat the nature and powers of the Affects [. . .] just as if it were a Question of lines, planes, and bodies.[60]

With Hobbes, and above all with Descartes, Spinoza shares the notion of '*scire per causas*', the extension of the deductive method to the knowledge of 'affects'. However, the metaphysical foundation and the entire system of the *Ethics* places this investigation on a completely different ground, even with respect to those that are closer and contiguous to it.[61] There is no difference, no hierarchy of substance, between the mind and the body; no Cartesian possibility of absolute control, no unconditional lordship of the soul over the passions. There is only a harsh training applied to the mind and the body in order 'to moderate and restrain the affects' (*in moderandis affectibus*).[62] An itinerary that moves and keeps the whole structure in continual fibrillation: the double conformation, both *in itself* and *in the other*, of the mode. 'By affect I understand *affectiones* of the Body by which the Body's power of acting is increased or diminished, aided or restrained, and at the same time, the ideas of these affections.'[63] *Affectus* does not, as it would for Descartes, come into conflict with *mens* (the luminous stage of *ratio* and *voluntas*), or with the *corpus* (the obscure background, muddy motility of the *pati*);[64] rather it involves the mode in its entirety, in the unity of its constitution and in the duplicity of its expressive forms. 'Being affected' is its destiny, its essence as *conatus-cupiditas*, of something *caused that causes*. Nothing can avoid being 'affected' since nothing exists without *affections*: it is impossible to exist without being affected, being provoked by states of mind, pains, and feelings, according to the Cartesian meaning of these terms. But, for Spinoza, it is also impossible to exist without being 'gifted', without being 'provided with', as per the classic Latin meaning of the term.[65] In the continuous and uninterrupted causal sequence of the modes, 'being affected' amounts to 'being disposed to' (*disponi*), meaning both determining and being determined, 'imprinting' and 'being imprinted'.[66] *Affectus* is a shared root, the common matrix of both 'actions' and 'passions':

---

[60] *Ethics* III, Praef.; CWS I, 492.
[61] For Descartes see *Pass*; for Hobbes: *EL*, I, 4; *De Hom*, XI and XII; *Lev*, I, 6.
[62] *Ethics* III, 56 Schol.; CWS I, 527
[63] *Ethics* III, Def. 3; CWS I, 493.
[64] See *Ethics* III, Praef.; *Ethics* III, DA.
[65] See, for example, Cicero, *Tusc*, 4, 37, 81: 'Therefore, as all those who enjoy good health', or 'therefore the wise man too will be so disposed towards a friend'.
[66] *Ethics* II, 14; CWS I, 462.

I say that we act when something happens, in us or outside us, of which we are the adequate cause, i.e. when something in us or outside us follows from our nature, which can be clearly and distinctly understood through it alone. On the other and, I say that we are acted on when something happens in us, or something follows from our nature, of which we are only a partial cause.[67]

Through the notion of 'adequate cause', which implies the '*clare & distincte*' perceivability of the effect (starting only from the cause, from the sole nature of *its* cause),[68] Spinoza traces a clear and precise first line of demarcation between the actions and the passions of human beings (and of modes in general). This is a fundamental distinction, indeed a decisive one for the fate of power (*potentia*); yet not a divarication so wide as to erase the common imprint of their shared origin, or to extinguish the same source that feeds both of the opposite determinations of the *affectus*. Up to the mode's disruptive and apparently contradictory impossibility of avoiding being acted on: '[w]e are acted on, insofar as we are a part of Nature, which cannot be conceived through itself, without the others'.[69] As a *naturae pars* the human is unable to accept any 'changes except those which can be understood through his own nature alone, and of which he is the adequate cause'.[70] Nor should this be simply considered a negative possibility: a 'risk' that humans *might* not be able to overcome their passions. This impossibility is inescapable, because it is inscribed in the very genome of the mode, it is congenital to its very essence of *conatus* and *cupiditas*: '[f]rom this it follows that man is necessarily always subject to passions, that he follows and obeys the common order of Nature, and accommodates himself to it as much as the nature of things requires'.[71] 'Very limited',[72] and 'infinitely surpassed by the power of external causes',[73] this is a fact, an irrepressible condition, in stark opposition to the prospect of an 'ethics' and a politics of *action* and of control over

---

[67] Ethics III, Def. 2; CWS I, 493. Despite the different conception of modes and of substance, and considering different relationships between soul and body, a similar, preliminary division can be found in the aforementioned Descartes, *Pass* I, 1.
[68] *Ethics* III, Def. 1: 'I call that cause adequate whose effect can be clearly and distinctly perceived through it. But I call it partial, or inadequate, if its effect cannot be understood through it alone' (CWS I, 492).
[69] *Ethics* IV, 2; CWS I, 548.
[70] *Ethics* IV, 4; CWS I, 548.
[71] *Ethics* IV, 4 Cor.; CWS I, 549.
[72] *Ethics* IV, App. chap. XXXII; CWS I, 593.
[73] *Ethics* IV, 3; CWS I, 548.

passions, such as to lead man and society to the highest *beatitudo*. Being modes, we are infinitely 'exposed' to external causes: we cause and we are caused, we use and we are used; we are not outside of nature so that ours could be considered, with respect to nature itself, an *imperium in imperio*. We are affected by nature's infinite, and for us insuperable, determinations. And yet, despite this first immediate evidence, we are neither devoted to failure nor doomed to renunciation. Spinoza seems to pose a distinction and, at the same time, to argue for both the necessity and impossibility of its overcoming. These two pull in opposite directions, or they could even be considered as contradictory: actions can take place, being situations in which the power of the mode is an adequate cause, i.e. the only cause of its effects (and this, indeed, remains the real goal of the mode, the only path towards power (*potential*)). But the passions cannot be overcome, and passivity cannot be avoided. Once again, the problem refers to the essential dimension and the delicate identity of the modes: we are active or passive depending on whether 'our nature' acts as an adequate cause or as a partial cause, but 'our nature' always implies a 'self' and an 'other', in the depths of one's own essence. Activity, then, does not consist in the annihilation of all passions, but in this more complex movement of the mode out of its comfort zone. Likewise, being passive, the mode can never eliminate all forms of activity and presence: even when passively enduring something we still 'are', and for this very reason we are a 'cause'; 'to be' always means 'to be active'. It indexes the acting (*agere*) of a power, the action of a *conatus* which, in a precise and determinate manner, pursues itself into existence.[74] Now, given that a rela-

---

[74] Among the three primary affects, being 'active' even when we are the only partial cause of the acts we perform appears to be more relevant for those passions, deriving from desire (*cupiditas*) and joy (*laetitia*), which are capable of strengthening our *conservandi potentia*. Beginning with those that can become 'actions' when, having overcome external vicissitudes, they are produced by our being 'modes' as an adequate cause: self-love (*philautia*, joy that arises when man contemplates himself and one's power to act), glory (a *laetitia* accompanied by the idea of a particular action, which we imagine as praised by others), or 'favor' (love 'toward someone who has benefited another'), *Ethics* III, DA 25, 30 and 19; CWS I, 536, 538 and 535. Passions such as these, far from disappearing in the dimension of an adequate production, are vivified and definitively strengthened with its conquest, turning precisely into 'actions'. However, these are passions that testify to an intense operative participation of the mode even when they remain passions, even when inadequate knowledge and feeling prevail. On the other hand, unlike those deriving from joy, the affects determined by sadness (*tristitia*) always weaken the *conatus* and can never be transformed into actions, i.e., they are among the 'more passive' (so to speak) of the *passions*. And yet even sadness will still appear to be a (frustrated) effort of the *vis*, a misplaced attempt of

tionship can only be established between modes that participate in the same attributes (since the causal movement proceeds directly, within each attribute, through the 'qualitative-expressive' channels of the cause), nothing can be either 'good' or 'bad', i.e., nothing will be able to increase or decrease our power of acting without having anything in common with us.[75] Nor will this 'something in common', as such, ever be harmful or indifferent to us, because this would blatantly contradict the *conatus*'s very nature, in virtue of which no one holds the principle of his/her own negation or limitation within him/herself, just as no one can be destroyed if not by an external power.[76] And therefore: '[i]nsofar as a thing agrees with our nature, it is

> *conservatio*, a retreat of the *conatus* in which it itself participates – that moves, indeed, from the *conatus* itself. In short, even in this case, it is not a simple 'being acted upon'. And then hate (*odium*) – the first and most semantically extended expression of sadness ('*sadness with the accompanying idea of an external cause*') – is resolved in the effort 'to remove and destroy the things he hates', *Ethics* III, 13 Schol; CWS I, 502; 'envy' is still hate 'insofar as it is considered so to dispose a man that he is glad at another's ill fortune and saddened by his good fortune', *Ethics* III, 24 Schol.; CWS I, 507; anger is presented as a kind of desire 'by which we are spurred, from Hate, to do evil to him we hate', *Ethics* DA 36; CWS I, 539; revenge appears as the attempt 'to return an evil done us', *Ethics* III, 40 Cor. 2 Schol.; CWS I, 518. Among these types of passions, even the most 'inner' and wearisome ones require an irrepressible core of 'self' and of strength: from humility, which implies the contemplation of 'his own lack of power, or weakness', to scorn (*abjectio*), which still requires 'thinking of one self' (although 'less highly than is just, out of Sadness'), *Ethics* III, DA 26 and 29; CWS I, 536 and 538. Some agency of the *conatus* is felt even when external causes overwhelm it, up to the extreme negative gesture, the act against nature by definition, the total erasure of oneself: a human commits suicide either 'because he is forced by the command of Tyrant (as Seneca was) to open his veins, i.e. he desires to avoid a greater evil by [submitting to] a lesser; or finally, because hidden external causes so dispose his imagination, and so affect his Body, that it takes on another nature, contrary to the former, a nature of which there cannot be an idea in the Mind', *Ethics* IV, 20 Schol.; CWS I, 557. There is a presence of 'life' even in 'death': to *choose* '*maius malum minor vitare*'; to *assume* '*aliam naturam priori contrariam*', albeit under the pressure of a devastating imagination. The impossibility to reflect and manage if not life, at least its strength. The inability to reflect on and to manage death except from the perspective of life. Thinking about death is still a living and doing, even if it weakens the *vis*: 'A free man thinks of nothing less than death, and his wisdom is a meditation on life, not on death', *Ethics* IV, 67; CWS I, 584. *Vitae meditatio*: not a superficial exorcism, a false knowledge (a *paranoia*) about death; rather, the ontology of the full and the living, from which alone – and always – the *not-being-any-entity* of death (nothingness) can be identified and 'seen' (positioned, empowered, positivised). On the nature of the passions in Spinoza see Brugère and Moreau 1999, Vinciguerra 2015: 159–74.

[75] *Ethics* IV, 29; CWS I, 560.
[76] *Ethics* IV, 30; CWS I, 560.

necessarily good',[77] for it is destined to increase our power. But as long as they are victims of the turmoil of passions, human beings 'cannot be said to agree in nature'.[78] Indeed, in this case 'they can be contrary to one another' because, since affects draw nourishment not so much from humans but rather from the power of those external causes that arouse *affectio* within them, the affects will be as numerous (and as varied and different, indeed often opposite to one another) as the external objects. Without even considering how often humans, like every single individual, are 'affected differently by one and the same object'.[79] It follows that they 'must ... always agree in nature' only if they attend to 'the guidance of reason'. This is the only way for humans to be 'active' (they will act having themselves as the proximate cause of their own actions) and they 'must do only those things that are good for human nature, and hence, for each man'.[80] In the structure of this reasoning there is no gratuitous *altruism*, nor any novel or disguised 'social' finalism. Nor is there any heterogenesis, no invisible hand, which would tortuously lead the results away from the path of intentions or elevate weaknesses to the level of strengths, complicating the 'vices' up to the level of 'virtues'. 'When each man most seeks his own advantage for himself, then men are most useful to one another';[81] the relationship is direct and immediate, because Spinoza's *virtus* never strays from the pursuit of the useful (the specific preservation of every individual), which alone can increase individual power, pushing – *for this very reason* – towards a life lived according the laws of one's own nature. This linearity, indeed this direct proportionality, is made possible by the inexhaustible character of the *bonum commune*, the *summum bonum* reached by those who, through concordance, are best able to cultivate their force: 'to know God'.[82] Reason highlights the non-perishability and the non-exclusivity of its own 'good': to draw on substance, the source of the modes, the power (*potentia*) that impresses itself onto everything without consuming itself, without for this reason diminishing its intensity but indeed reflecting itself onto the power of things – being their cause while necessarily corresponding to its own being the cause of itself. This is how substance finds itself within the universal bond of *energetic* determination, which makes the *res* both absolutely identical and irremediably

---

[77] *Ethics* IV, 31; CWS I, 560.
[78] *Ethics* IV, 32; CWS I, 561.
[79] *Ethics* IV, 33 and 34; CWS I, 561 and 562.
[80] *Ethics* IV, 35 and Dem.; CWS I, 563.
[81] *Ethics* IV, 35 Cor. 2; CWS I, 563; and see *Ethics* IV, 20; CWS I, 557.
[82] *Ethics* IV, 36 Dem.; CWS I, 564.

different from their full, inexhaustible source. The 'knowledge of God', therefore, would not be a sort of mystical overcoming or ecstatic disguise of the 'sociological' argument which, often recurring in the history of political thought, pointed to the scarcity of goods and to the limited nature of material resources as the cause of conflicts and of social subordinations.[83] To climb along the impervious upward path towards the *beginning* means, for the mode, to strengthen body and mind, to understand itself: a movement of self-grasping capable of comprehending its peculiar nature, what makes it both irreducible and interdependent, singular and connective. Up to *amor Dei*, that two-sided 'love of God', i.e., the love shared by things through substance, in which they both exist and con-sist (*erga Deum amor*), and the love of the substance, expressed in the *res singulare* as the 'idea of God' (*amor Dei intellectualis*), that elevates the modes towards *beatitudo*, the apex of their power.[84] To know the particular from the universal means to discern the arcana of their identical nature, of their very same power (*ipsissima potentia*). At the same time, it also means to 'participate' in the universal, to become 'part' of it: to merge into a totality whose essence requires the *pars*, for it is always completely enclosed within the parts, without ever really breaking down, without ever really *de-composing* into them. 'To comprehend': to recognise oneself (and to love oneself) as existing within God-Nature-Substance, the cause identical to us under the same conditions that place it 'beyond' us, thus making it 'other' than us. A journey that gives the *res* their maximum extension, freeing them from the superb hallucination of an absolute, fanciful substantiality, or that of a fictitious and privileged centrality in the order of things:

> [w]hat do the common people not foolishly claim for themselves, because they have no sound concept either of God or of nature, because they confuse God's decrees with men's decisions, and finally, because they posit a nature so limited that they believe man to be its chief part![85]

---

[83] On the Hobbesian approach to this theme see the following paragraph.
[84] *Ethics* V, 23; CWS I, 607. It also gives them 'a certain eternal necessity', probably detectable in the *necessitas* of things, in the inevitability of 'change', in the 'inversion' of substance into entities. Intertwined with the theory of *amor Dei*, this idea of a 'certain eternity' of the modes is articulated in the final part of Spinoza's *opus maius*, starting from *Ethics* V, 15. And, whatever their interpretative strategy might be, all scholars highlight its shadows and its uncertainties: see Brochard 1974; Baensch 1927; Hallet 1930; Rice 1969–1970; Steinberg 1981; Rodis-Lewis 1986; Di Vona 1995.
[85] *TTP* VI, 5; CWS II, 153.

Pressed by *conservatio*, by the pursuit of their own profit, humans find *in se & extra se* a number of means that actually allow them to satisfy this irrepressible impulse: 'eyes for seeing, teeth for chewing, plants and animals for food, the sun for light, the sea for supporting fish'.[86] They therefore become accustomed to considering their own benefit as the universal purpose of nature, and to see things as mere *media*, tools to achieve their goal. Aware of not having themselves created these means, they end up construing one or more imaginary rulers of nature (*naturae rectores*), which would have thus ordered them:

> [a]nd since they had never heard anything about the temperament of these rulers, they had to judge it from their own. Hence, they maintained that the Gods direct all things for the use of men in order to bind men to them and be held by men in the highest honor. So it has happened that each of them has thought up from his own temperament different ways of worshipping God, so that God might love them above all the rest, and direct the whole of Nature according to the needs of their blind desire and insatiable greed.[87]

However, the light of reason dispels the darkness of superstition. Once the teleological spell is broken, and the mirage of 'purpose' is eliminated, there no longer is a mirroring *resemblance* between God (Nature) and the mode: a new causal and metonymic bond has supplanted the ancient and remissive binds of the *image*. The first and immediately noticeable effect of this oblique condition of the human is its loss of centrality within the universe. Once the illusion of affinity – resolved in *conatus* and in the mode – is dispelled, the human being discovers itself as a segment of a nature without order and without measure, or in any case endowed with a *constantia* whose code of regularity, in the infinity of its articulations, inevitably eludes its grasp:

> [f]or I do not think it right for me to mock nature, much less to lament it, when I reflect that men, like all other things, are only a part of nature, and that I do not know how each part of nature agrees with the whole to which it belongs, and how it coheres with the other parts.[88]

---

[86] *Ethics* I, App.; CWS I, 440.
[87] *Ethics* I, App.; CWS I, 441.
[88] *Ep.* XXX (to Henry Oldenburg); CWS II, 16.

The impossibility of reaching a complete understanding of the infinite interconnections of the cause can lead towards two consequences, different from each other yet not wholly divergent. The first is the acquiescent one of '*imbecillitas*',[89] of human fragility: 'because man is a part of the whole of Nature, depends on it, and is governed by it, he can do nothing, of himself, toward his salvation and well-being'.[90] Hence the inconstancy of its judgment, as well as the *alea*: the uncertainty and the risk that are inherent in most human actions.[91] This is the path of passion and of human servitude which, however, still responds to the logic of power and of *conservatio* (not being substantially different from the *conatus*), even if in a weak and confused way. The other path involves, more productively, the constitutive relationality of the mode, the 'structural' duplicity of the *vis*, a path of self-preservation and self-perseverance, while nature is always and inescapably proceeding *in alio*. This is the path of 'action' which proceeds from the awareness of our fragility and of the insuperability (at least a certain insuperability) of our limits and of our passivity. As a 'part' of the infinite power (*potentia*) of God, the force of the mode is both positively self-determined, for its own preservation, and an essence which draws its existence from the *other* of substance. But the infinite and universal power of this *other* does not in turn include anything, except 'the power of all individuals together'.[92] Conceivable solely in virtue of the mechanism of the cause, the human *in itself* is constructed in relation to the whole of the modes. Indeed, in relation to *all* the modes, and according to a (serious) *ecological* perspective which, grounded on the reciprocal determinations of the *res*, naturally allows humans to 'preserve or destroy'[93] everything according to their purpose and their advantage, while also admitting a reciprocal natural potential that things exercise over them. Freed from any anthropocentric prejudice, this perspective excludes any form of absolute *potestas* over nature,[94] inviting us to look at it, even when it is necessarily used or consumed, with the respect and the prudence which is due to the *whole* from which every *individual* (with no distinction of *mode*) draws both its power and its impotence.[95]

---

[89] *TdIE* (R, 120); *CWS* I, 127.
[90] *KV* II, XVII, 1; *CWS* I, 127.
[91] See respectively *Ethics* III, 51 Schol.; *CWS* I, 522–3 and *TTP* XV, 38ff.; *CWS* II, 280–3.
[92] *TTP* XVI; *CWS* II, 282; 'But the universal power of the whole of nature is nothing but the power of all individuals together.'
[93] *Ethics* IV, App. 26; *CWS* I, 592:
[94] *Ethics* IV, App. 32; *CWS* I, 593.
[95] It is here that Deleuze (1988: 125) sees the beginning of an 'ethological' rather than

In any case, the more actively the constraint of determinacy is applied to the single individual, the more it reconnects it to homogeneous entities, i.e., those that are expressions of the same *genus*, of its own particular *essence*. The duplicity of the cause thus comes to assume, for actually existent humans, the face of the other: *homo homini deus*.[96] This is no mere moralistic and edifying analogy, aimed at a quietist rebuttal of those inverted and noisier images which only appear to be more realistic and innovative. Nor is it a fully resolved transparency, a kind of pacifying anthropological simplification. We are instead dealing with a univocal assertion, a strict *metaphysical-natural* 'truth': *ratio* knows the relation, the fact that the mode can give itself (preserve itself, remain and progress within existence) only within the relative. These are the authentic foundations of *societas*, with respect to which any other 'advantage' (security, economy, freedom) appears as a mere consequence, a simple descriptive extension. Peace and security would certainly elude the 'monastic life' of a single man 'burdened daily with sleep, often with illness or grief, and in the end with old age'.[97] Nor would anyone be able to procure what they need most: both strength and time would not suffice if the individual 'alone had to plow, to sow, to reap, to grind, to cook, to weave, to sew, and to do the many other things necessary to support life'.[98] These are purely argumentative expansions, corollaries around the true essence of the *conatus*: an *effort*, a naturally interactive *id*, a caused that causes. Demonstrative accumulations on the duplicity of the mode: to speak of the *solus* is a pure expository convenience, just as the term 'monastic life' is an oxymoron. There is no single individual without a relationship. No self without the other.[99]

And this fact is accompanied by all the extraordinary, irrepressible implications and *affective* complications that it *alone* already entails, because to acknowledge this connection also means admitting the insuperability of the passions. By accepting and welcoming the other within the intimate and most hidden foundation of the self, reason is able to mitigate and to restrain the passions, but never to annihilate or to completely eradicate them (a ruinous, and indeed *ir-rational* ambition). The power of reason includes its own self-limitation, as well as its ability not to construe itself as

a 'moral' perspective in the *Ethics*: 'a composition of fast and slow speeds, of capacities for affecting and being affected on this plane of immanence'.

[96] See *Ethics* IV, 35 Schol.; CWS I, 563.
[97] TP III, 11; CWS II, 522.
[98] TTP V; CWS II, 143.
[99] On Spinoza's 'transindividual' anthropology see Balibar 1990 and 2020; more generally see Balibar and Morfino 2014.

a 'pure' reason: yet another reified, impoverished, and simplified version of substance, which would be far from the vital ganglia of the origin, from the problematic registers of the beginning.

It is not enough. When can *concordia*, that is born of reason, be affirmed? Always and never:

> [s]till, it rarely happens that men live according to the guidance of reason. Instead, their lives are so constituted that they are usually envious and burdensome to one another. They can hardly, however, live a solitary life; hence, that definition which makes man a social animal has been quite pleasing to most. And surely we do derive, from the society of our fellow men, many more advantages than disadvantages. So, let the Satirists laugh as much as they like at human affairs, let the Theologians curse them, let Melancholics praise as much as they can a life that is uncultivated and wild, let them disdain men and admire the lower animals. Men still find from experience that by helping one another they can provide themselves much more easily with the things they require, and that only by joining forces can they avoid the dangers that threaten on all sides – not to mention that it is much preferable and more worthy of our knowledge to consider the deeds of men, rather than those of the lower animals.[100]

The relative nature of the *conatus* implies sociality, but this cannot be given in a unitary fashion, either though reason alone or purely through the passions. It cannot be given by reason because a life lived according to reason, as we have just seen, cannot be considered as a static alternative to the passions, finding in the *other-than-itself* (i.e. in the *self-other* circularity) the inextricable duplicity of the mode, the manifestation and the 'phenomenology' of the unavoidable tension that relates all *res singulares* to their cause. Indeed, the true strength of this life lived according to reason lies in this awareness, and its supremacy in the ability to produce power. Mostly because the only permissible form of rationality (the one that encompasses and capitalises on the passions) is not itself a universally achievable result, a 'for the most part' (*plerumque*) that could be inscribed in the causal chain of human determinations. Rather, its nature is that of a second kind of knowledge: located between imagination (the only form of knowledge exposed to error and to the passions, formed in the mind on the basis of our body's empirical encounters with external objects, through the dim experience (*experientia vaga*) of the senses and of signs) and intuition (which, by means

---

[100] *Ethics* IV, 35 Schol.; CWS I, 564.

of the intellect 'proceeds from an adequate idea of the formal essence of certain attributes of God to the adequate knowledge of the essence of things'). Reason is the understanding of 'common notions', of that which can be found in both the part and in the whole, a conversion of the plurality of things into the unity of their shared properties.[101] On the level of society, therefore, reason captures the 'common' element of conservation, the unitary and egalitarian human dimension: the *conatus* as the shared generic essence of human beings, and their belonging to a *genus*. And yet this important convergence can only emerge from the intersection and the contamination with the particular, the encounter with the *actual and specific existence* of the individuals and of their relationships. This is an arduous emergence, which laboriously unfolds within the magma of desires, the tangle of impulses and instincts, of frequent imaginations and rare intuitions; an interweaving marked by *time*, by unavoidable difference, and by the irreducible *discontinuity of existence* that the chain of causes imposes on the modes' being. And then: 'everyone is born ignorant of everything',[102] although they must live and preserve what is within them, 'according to the laws of appetite'.[103] The presence of substantial *life differences* and of compromising inequalities of *duration* means that it is rarely possible (and only by a few) to think of a rational society. What is actually given is a *mostly* rational society, or at least one wholly different from the imaginary and impossible world of 'pure reason'. *Plerumque* (i.e., for the most part, and most people) one lives under the dark and *envious* banner of immediate stimuli, the narrower and *bothersome* domain of the affects-passions. But nevertheless (*at nihilominus*) '[t]hey can hardly live a solitary life'; and yet (*tamen*) '[m]en still find from experience that by helping one another they can provide themselves much more easily with the things they require, and that only by joining forces can they avoid the dangers that threaten on all sides'.[104] Even when affirming the *passio*, a minimal level of concordance and action remains inescapable, on pain of the very existence of the *pati*. Pure reason is never given, but neither is it possible to have a completely naked form of suffering. Taken individually, the three tracks along which the Spinozan approach proceeds can be seen as bringing it closer to different segments (both ancient and modern) of political thought. But if considered together, they outline a new and original physiognomy of thought: a) the highest and most powerful response to the

---

[101] *Ethics* II, 40 Schol. 2; CWS I, 477–8.
[102] *TTP* XVI, 7; CWS II, 283
[103] *TTP* XVI, 6; CWS II, 283.
[104] *Ethics* IV, 35 Schol.; CWS I, 564.

human need for perseverance and conservation – a life lived according to reason – includes an inevitable contamination with the passions; b) social dynamics are in any case limited to the more restricted and limiting areas where *patire* prevails; c) this fact, in any case, does not undermine the existence of society (*communis societas*) and it does not prevent people from experiencing more advantages than harm from it, so much so that most people consider to be pleasing 'that definition which makes man a social animal'.[105] The relative imprint and tension (between *in se* and *in alio*) of the *conatus* make it impossible to draw a dynamic of mutual exclusion between *actio* and *pati*. The unavoidable reciprocity and, at the same time, the reciprocal irreducibility of the 'self' and of the 'other' hold firm the essential priority of *conservatio* by preventing the possibility that a different 'nature' of the mode might more or less implicitly take its place: neither passions, which weaken it, nor reason, which strengthens and reinforces it. It is from the notion of *jus naturale* that it is possible to assess the first and most precise 'political' outlines of this particular aspect of the Spinozan system.

Natural Law

As Spinoza explains: '[b]y the right and established practice of nature I mean nothing but the rules of the nature of each individual, according to which we conceive each thing to be naturally determined to existing and having effects in a certain way'.[106] Although the subject of various reinterpretations, the Spinozan notion of *jus naturale* is actually very simple in its bare essentiality:

> [b]y the Right of nature, then, I understand the laws of nature themselves, or the rules according to which all things happen, i.e., the very power of nature. So the natural Right of the whole of nature, and as a result, of each individual, extends as far as its power does. Hence, whatever each man does according to the laws of his nature, he does with the supreme right of nature. He has as much right over nature as he has power.[107]

Like the good, virtue, and happiness, *ius* is also nothing other than *potentia*, 'i.e., the very power of nature'.[108] This is a famous and corrosive equation

---

[105] *Ethics* IV, 35 Schol.; CWS I, 564.
[106] *TTP* XVI, 2; CWS II, 282.
[107] *TP* II, 4; CWS II, 508.
[108] *TP* II, 4; CWS II, 508.

which aims to completely reabsorb within the *conatus* and the determination any other 'velleity', every other character of the law, every distinction or tension which is virtually opened the moment in which we speak of *jus* and not simply of 'nature'. The 'brutal simplicity'[109] that the concept of *jus* assumes in Spinoza's works undoubtedly differentiates it from the classical, Stoic-Ciceronian, and then Christian tradition, which instead places the *jus naturae* within the substantial order of ends, thus endowing it with a rational essence and a moral consistency.[110] If anything, the 'absolute pleonasticity' ('*die ganze Überflüssigkeit*')[111] of the Spinozan idea makes it contiguous to one of its clearer, and more radical, modern stipulations: that of Hobbes. Contiguous but by no means identical: for the former is characterised, in its most intimate features, by the more complex value – a more complicated structure – assigned to the *res singularis*.

The *jus-potentia* derives immediately from the 'in itself' of the mode, from the necessary function that it performs with respect to the essence of causal (self-)determination of substance:

[b]ut the universal power of the whole of nature is nothing but the power of all individuals together. From this it follows that each individual has a supreme right to do everything it can, or that the right of each thing extends as far as its determinate power does.[112]

The 'power of all individuals together' leaves no surplus to 'universal power'.[113] '[T]he power of natural things' is nothing but the 'the very power of God':[114] and this is why the mode – the effect – is an unavoidable and indispensable element for the constitution of substance, for its essence *qua* cause. It follows that individual right is valid in and of itself, without any *external*

---

[109] Matheron 1969: 292. On the equation *jus* = *potentia* in Spinoza see Walther 1985.

[110] On connections and differences between ancient and modern naturalism see Strauss 1953; Passerin d'Entrèves 1954; Piovani 1961; Fassò 1964 and 1983.

[111] Geismann 1989: 416. Droetto looks at the Galilean and Grozian connotations of this concept: '[t]he equation *tantum juris quantum potentiae*, represents the definitive and unreserved extension to the moral world of the principle of "quantification", which Galileo had formulated for the physical world and that Grotius had adopted in his work on "juridification", limited to the case of the "just war"' (1958: 67. My translation).

[112] *TTP* XVI, 4; *CWS* II, 282.

[113] *TTP* XVI, 3; *CWS* II, 282

[114] *TP* II, 3: 'From this fact – that the power of natural things, by which they exist and have effects, is the very power of God – we easily understand what the Right of nature is'; *CWS* II, 507.

subordination, without depending on anything else. 'That each thing strives to persevere in its state, as far as it can by its own power':[115] this is the governing principle of the law, the first *institutum*, the strongest and supreme natural law. And it is based, as it is explicitly stated, 'not on account of anything else, but only of itself'.[116] The fact that the right/power (*potentia*) of the effect is not *substantially* different from that of the cause (indeed, it is the same), implies the necessity and the positivity of its determination to be and to operate in a *certain way*: '[e]veryone exists by the highest right of nature, and consequently everyone, by the highest right of nature, does those things that follow from the necessity of his own nature'.[117] And then it will be due to their natural *jus* that a big fish will eat smaller ones, and it will be impossible to make legal distinctions 'between men and other individuals in nature' or between rational human beings and the fools and the madmen. To think that the latter must adhere to the principles of *sana ratio* would be like claiming that a cat should live 'according to the laws of a lion's nature':[118]

> [w]hatever anyone who is considered to be only under the rule of nature judges to be useful for himself – whether under the guidance of sound reason or by the prompting of the affects – he is permitted, by supreme natural right, to want and to take – by force, by deception, by entreaties, or by whatever way is, in the end, easiest. Consequently, he is permitted to regard as an enemy anyone who wants to prevent him from doing what he intends to do.[119]

The term *licet* does not indicate a duty or an obligation, but it refers to being able, or being capable of performing an action: the *jus & institutum naturae* neither commands nor prohibits anything, 'except what no one desires and no one can do',[120] and neither is it the right of the strongest, 'justified' by a force that would actually be both alien and antecedent to the attribution (and the very logic) of 'right' and 'wrong'.[121] *Naturmacht*[122] is the fullness of the *jus naturale* of every single thing, defined by its own particular determination of power.

---

[115] *TTP* XVI, 4; CWS II, 282–3.
[116] *TTP* XVI, 4; CWS II, 282–3.
[117] *Ethics* IV, 37 Schol. 2; CWS I, 566.
[118] *TTP* XVI, 5 and 7; CWS II, 283.
[119] *TTP* XVI, 8; CWS II, 284.
[120] *TP* II, 8; CWS II, 511.
[121] Geismann 1989: 416.
[122] Fischer 1909: 464 ff.

And yet, 'as long as human natural right is determined by each person's power, and belongs to that person, there's no human natural right'.[123] The more a natural right is seen as the unique possession of one individual, the more it means nothing: although grounded onto itself and identical with its own essence-power, the right of the mode would be nothing without all the other *res* – without their own 'rights' and their own powers. The necessity of the effect does not exclude its subordination, its determination as an effect, which makes it exist *in alio*. Things do not derive existence from their own nature; rather they are born and preserved within the infinite causal chain of the modes:

> [e]very singular thing, or any thing which is finite and has a determinate existence, can neither exist nor be determined to produce an effect unless it is determined to exist and produce an effect by another cause, which is also finite and has a determinate existence; and again, this cause also can neither exist nor be determined to produce an effect unless it is determined [. . .] and so on, to infinity.[124]

The mode is structurally exposed to connections, to the point that, as we have seen, it finds its condition and its boundary, its presupposition and its own peril always *in alio*: in nature, another *res* that would be 'more powerful by which the first can be destroyed'[125] is always necessary. This is the (posthumous and indirect) revenge of the small fish: there is no complete *auto-nomy*, not even for the big fish. The Hobbesian principle, according to which no one in nature can be so physically or mentally powerful as to live in absolute safety and without fear, is reinterpreted here in terms of the mode's constitution: a necessary effect of the essence of its principle (the causal nature of substance), but still an *effect*, a determined and interdependent[126] *operari* which might either fear or enjoy its constraints, but that will never be able to posit itself outside of them.[127] These are the presuppositions of the very particular 'civil' solution which, in the context of the modern age, is outlined by Spinoza.

---

[123] *TP* II, 15; *CWS* II, 513.
[124] *Ethics* I, 28; *CWS* I, 432.
[125] *Ethics* IV, Ax.; *CWS* I, 546.
[126] Will return to this aspect of Hobbes shortly.
[127] On this dimension of interdependence of the Spinozan *jus naturae* see Balibar 1990: 72–8; Breton 1979 is also useful (163–75, in particular 170).

Locke too, against the teleological and hierarchical structures of the cosmos, asserts the egalitarian impulses of *conservatio*: the first natural power of the human consists in '[doing] whatsoever he thinks fit for the preservation of himself and others within the permission of the law of nature ... the fundamental law of nature being the preservation of mankind'.[128] In this case, however, the *conatus* is far from assuming the shape of a composite relational dynamic, as entailed by Spinoza's metaphysics of the cause. With Locke, the *jus naturae* is once again construed from an anthropocentric – creationist and teleological – perspective:

> [w]hether we consider natural reason, which tells us that men, being once born, have a right to their preservation, and consequently to meat and drink and such other things as nature affords for their subsistence; or revelation, which gives us an account of those grants God made of the world to Adam, and to Noah and his sons; it is very clear that God, as King David says (Psalm cxv. 16), 'has given the earth to the children of men,' given it to mankind in common.[129]

Being a manifestation of divine will – created for human beings just as it introduces the notion of natural equality against the despotism of the past – the *jus naturae* exceeds the immediate and quantitative givenness of power (*potentia*), in order to assume a precise and positive configuration, the mandatory dimension of a rational substantiality and of a merely individual content. Natural law, then, does not count as an actual 'licence', as an effective 'power' of force, but is rather a synonym of reason, homologous to the natural light:

> [t]he state of nature has a law of nature to govern it, which obliges every one; *and reason, which is that law*, teaches all mankind who will but consult it that, being all equal and independent, no one ought to harm another in his life, health, liberty, or possessions.[130]

The rational-natural *lex* prescribes the complete and intangible independence of the individual, who holds 'an uncontrollable liberty to dispose of his person or possession'. Of course, God wanted the human to be unfit

---

[128] T2 IX, 128 and XI, 135; ed. Peardon, 72 and 77.
[129] T2 V, 25; ed. Peardon, 16. For a survey of the theological-Calvinist influences on Locke's political thought see Dunn 1959.
[130] T2 II, 6; ed. Peardon, 5.

for solitude and thus He 'put him under strong obligations of necessity, convenience, and inclination to drive him into society, as well as fitted him with understanding and language to continue and enjoy it'.[131] But society is precisely an object of 'fruition', a benefit available to human beings. Sociality – above all the great 'natural community of the human race'[132] – *follows* the linear and complete deduction of individuality. 'It is not good that the man should be alone':[133] *first* there is Adam, *then* his solitude is recognised as something to be avoided. This is how a seventeenth-century Englishman rereads the book of Genesis: the tale of a *self-made man*, in both the narrowest and most elevated sense of the term. The conatus subsides in 'the great foundation of property'[134] (and of the value of work). *Conservatio* is simplified by becoming substantial. A 'self' without, and untethered to, any *other*: a bourgeois, winning solution.[135] And the passions are reduced to an inessential eventuality, a subordinate alternative, a negative interference that emerges at the moment of sociality, a phase which is ontologically posterior to the unilateral determination of the individual human being. Once the fundamental quality of the individual is obtained in a positive way (without contradiction), then the 'possibility' of an irrational-passionate disturbance, when living among others, emerges. Although 'the law of nature be the law plain and intelligible to all rational creatures' it is still admissible that some degenerates 'biased by their interest' and unaware of the law 'for want of studying' would be unwilling to recognise it 'as a law binding to them in the application of it to their particular case'.[136] It is a very likely possibility, but it remains just a possibility. Hence the three-tiered paradigm, the tripartite subdivision that leads towards the political order (and which translates the Christian parable that goes from *integrity* to *redemption* going through *fall* into the language of secularised thought): a) humankind's purely rational essentiality, a circular deductibility, through reason – at least by he 'who takes the trouble to consult it'[137] – of the complete and compact nature of the *in-dividual*; b) the possibility of negative interference at the level of social relations, a disturbance of reason caused by the passions' limiting and contradictory interventions; c) the opportunity for a readjustment, through a convergence

---

[131] T2 VII, 77; ed. Peardon, 44.
[132] T2 IX, par. 128.
[133] *Genesis* 2:18–24.
[134] T2 V, 44; ed. Peardon, 27.
[135] On the *conatus* in Locke and in Hobbes, as a keystone for the modern-individualistic overcoming of the conceptual of law as related to social classes, see Semerari 1992.
[136] T2 IX, 124; ed. Peardon, 71.
[137] T2 II, par. 6.

of the free and rational wills of many individuals towards the constitution of a civil environment that might compensate for the uncertainties and the three 'deficiencies' of the state of nature, by means of 'an established, settled, known law', 'a known and indifferent judge', and a 'power to back and support the sentence when right, and to give it due execution'.[138] Aside from superficial and ultimately insubstantial similarities, the distance between the Englishman's and Spinoza's ideas appears to be truly unbridgeable. For Spinoza, the relation is both an integral part and an unavoidable determination of the mode, a mode which is always irreducible *to* the other and always – continuously and inevitably – constituted *in* the other. This tension within the structure of the *conatus* does not force us to see the passions as the stumbling block, the accidental pitfall on *ratio*'s path. However, since the beginning of its deduction and of its own 'individuation', the mode is still organically exposed to *pati*, even when it wins, even when reason prevails.

For the most part, within society, the passions rule. Nonetheless (*nihilominus*) the preponderance of the passions does not exclude the presence of reason, nor does it annihilate any form of 'action'. Indeed, it could not do so even on the logical-hypothetical level of *projection* and *calculation*, on pain of the very persistence of that *conatus* that even the passions, albeit confusedly, intend to safeguard (on pain of the very possibility of calculation). Some superficial similarities notwithstanding, Spinoza's approach is also irreducible to Hobbes' ideas on the physiognomy of the *jus naturae*. At the beginning of the fourteenth chapter of the *Leviathan*, the latter writes:

[t]he right of nature which writers commonly call *jus naturale*, is the liberty each man hath, to use his own power, as he will himself, for the preservation of his own nature; that is to say of his own life; and consequently, of doing any thing, which in his own judgement, and reason, he shall conceive to be the aptest means thereunto.[139]

The evident congruence with Spinoza is not obscured by the insistence on 'liberty' and 'arbitrariness', aimed here at stressing the difference between *jus* (which indicates the possibility 'to do, or to forbear') and *lex*, which instead 'bindeth to one of them'.[140] In Hobbes, *voluntas* assumes a deterministic character that considerably restricts the meaning of such an articulation, tracing it back to exquisitely functional and explanatory domains (to

---

[138] *T2* IX, 124–6; ed. Peardon, 71. On contractualism in Locke see Cavarero 1987.
[139] *Lev*, I, 14; *EW* III, 116.
[140] *Lev*, I, 14; *EW* III, 117.

registers of function and explanation). Here too, as in Spinoza, *jus*'s heart beats on the anomic rhythm of *conatus* and *conservatio*:

> [e]very man hath right to protect himself [. . .]. The same man therefore hath a right to use all the means which necessarily conduce to his. But those are the necessary means with which he shall judge to be such [. . .]. He therefore hath a right to make use of, and to do all whatsoever he shall judge requisite for his preservation.[141]

In the bare state of nature considerations of 'right' and 'wrong' do not apply, but rather everyone is free 'to do what he would, and against whom he thought fit, and to possess, use, and enjoy all what he would, or could get'.[142] Moreover, Hobbes also argues that the *conatus* leads to the natural equality between human beings. Another well-known passage from the *Leviathan* reads:

> [n]ature hath made men so equal, in the faculties of body, and mind; as that though there be found one man sometimes manifestly stronger in body, or of quicker mind than another; yet when all is reckoned together, the difference between man, and man, is no so considerable, as that one man can thereupon claim to himself any benefit, to which another may pretend, as well as he.[143]

In terms of bodily energy, 'the weakest has strength enough to kill the strongest, either by secret machination, or by confederacy with others, that are in the same danger with himself', and as for the faculties of the mind, no one believes in the existence of wiser people than him- or herself, and this, paradoxically, demonstrates 'a greater equality amongst men, than that of strength'.[144] Starting from here, however, i.e., from a common acknowledgement of the *conatus* and of its egalitarian nature, the two theoretical projects end up on clearly diverging paths. That is because, for Spinoza, there is equality between 'modes', i.e., between beings that are always related and intersecting. Hobbes, on the other hand, thinks of an equality between 'monads', atomic individuals whose essential character does not lean towards the positives of reason and of *proprietas*, as happens in the edifying Lockean

---

[141] *De Cive*, I, 10; *EW* II, 10.
[142] *De Cive*, I, 10; *EW* II, 10.
[143] *Lev*, I, 13; *EW* III, 110.
[144] Ibid.

version, but rather deviates towards the more disenchanted and realistic side of passions and aggression.[145] The equality among monads is an 'equality of hope in the attaining' of one's ends. From this comes 'diffidence' and (therefore) conflict: in its highest, most devastating and implacable *spatial* ('of every man against every man') and *temporal* (not only the limited and contingent moment of 'combat', but the indefinite and indefinable duration of the will to fight) extension.[146] A truly epochal watershed, leading towards modernity, the Hobbesian critique of natural sociality – of the existence of a *finis ultimus* and of the consistency of a *summum bonum* that would go beyond the *conatus* of individuals – produces natural conflict. This is an inevitable outcome for Hobbes, for at least two orders of reasons, which are supported by two different logical structures:

[a]nd therefore if any two men desire the same thing, which nevertheless they cannot both enjoy, they become enemies; and in the way to their end, which is principally their own conservation, and sometimes their delectation only, endeavour to destroy, or subdue one another.[147]

On the one hand, there is scarcity of goods: an 'evident' but empirical and contingent argument, plausible yet not 'true' – neither binding nor necessitating – since it is impossible to exclude the existence of a situation of abundance, or at least sufficiency of resources. On the other, and above all, there is *glory*, the 'internal gloriation or triumph of the mind': the passion 'which proceedeth from the imagination or conception of our own power, above the power of him that contendeth whith us'.[148] Without relationships, desire is not satisfied. Alienated from any connection, desire cannot quenched. Enclosed in itself, with its complex ramifications pruned and its multiform expansions simplified, the *conatus* finds substance in the 'pravity of human disposition', in the 'natural proclivity of men, to hurt each other'.[149] The individualistic deduction of *conservatio* exhausts itself into a reified quality (negative and passional – the opposite of the positive and rational one of Locke) which, in the long run, benefits from the 'inertial' dynamics

---

[145] Despite all the simplifications that follow from a very clear and cut interpretative framework, Macpherson's (1962) reading maintains, in this regard, an effective hermeneutic grip.

[146] *Lev*, I, 13; *EW* III, 111–13.

[147] *Lev*, I, 13; *EW* III, 111. On the criticism of the 'appetitus societatis' and the existence of a goal, or a good, objectively inscribed in social life, see *Lev*, XI and *De Cive* I, 2.

[148] *Elements*, I, 9; ed. Tönnies, 36–7.

[149] *De Cive*, VI, 4 and I, 12; *EW* II, 75 and 11.

with which it starts: aseptical, mechanical, and quantitative.[150] Even in this extreme point of commonality with Spinoza there still remains a fundamental asymmetry: in the Hobbesian state of nature, destruction (which tends to be unlimited, total, and general) implies self-destruction; the continual intent to harm others necessarily leads to self-harm. In Hobbes, however, this link remains external to the intimate nature of the *conatus*, and it simply traverses the tormented fluctuations of 'insecurity' and fear: the desire to attack is always accompanied by the possibility (and the fear) of retaliation. For Spinoza, the bond is wholly intrinsic to the individual, because in the universe of modes the individual is never given without 'the other', without substance, nature, and other modes: neither *timor* and death, nor safety and life. The duplicity of the *conatus* preserves its priority, avoiding being anticipated by a new, more or less hidden essence, which would then be inevitable for its own conceivability. The ontological connection of the mode welcomes harmony and conflict without yielding anything, and with no totalising reversals. The relative nature of the *conatus* implies the existence of society but it also excludes any one-sided definition of it. There is never any pure negativity of the passions, because being is always a form of acting, and to fear death is also an expression, however exposed and weak, of *power* (*potentia*): as long as there is life there is power. But neither is there reason alone (the end of all conflicts), since the echo of the *pati* is always resounding, now stronger and now weaker, within the constitutive bond. At the pinnacle of force – and truly specular to the all-encompassing Hobbesian destructiveness – we find Spinoza's 'glory', which includes this duplicity: it recognises and thereby controls its irreducible givenness and its 'irremediable' (*un-mediated*) effectuality.

Is this a natural sociality (*appetitus societatis*)? The answer is clearly negative. For an *appetitus* still implies a cosmos, a universe teleologically ordered according to gradually progressive ends.[151] Humans *believe* and *prefer* 'that definition which makes man a social animal',[152] *opinio*, rather than *scientia*,

---

[150] This opposition of 'mechanism' to 'moralism', 'natural law' to 'empiricism', and 'anthropological pessimism' to 'rational structure' has been often highlighted in the secondary literature (see Strauss 1988, but in some ways also the 'ethical' interpretative strand: Taylor 1938, Warrender 1957), and it can be emblematically subsumed in the chronology of the Hobbesian works and their unsystematic succession, pushed by the urgent priorities of political reflection; see Matteucci 1989. Cerroni indicates the origin of the oscillation in the Hobbesian concept of law, which 'now alludes to *being*, now to *having to be*' (1998: 115. My translation).

[151] On natural sociality in Aristotle see *Pol*, 1253a.

[152] *Ethics* IV, 35 Schol.; CWS I, 564.

doxa rather then *episteme*. The human being is not made for society, indeed it is not 'made for' anything but itself: its own *conservatio*, the desire of each individual 'to seek his own advantage'.[153] The dynamic tension of the *conatus* allows the linguistic articulation of such a good, as well as its expression in the unavoidable and compositive character of being-among (*inter-esse*). This is a tension that is not born out of an harmonious progress of essences, but from the circulation of the cause-power (*potentia*). On this topic, neither Locke (*ratio*) nor Hobbes (*lupus*), and certainly not Aristotle (*appetitus*, from a pre-ordained order, from a universal and shared *ethos*), can be compared to Spinoza:[154] the double character of the *conatus* shifts the reflection on human nature from the search for a unilateral 'definition' (i.e. a substantial quality: good-bad, sociable-unsociable, rational-irrational) to an acknowledgement of the motility of the relationships that constitute it.[155] Here we have a shift from foundation/deduction to *function*: 'networking' becomes the horizon of the *vis*, leading to the unveiling of the fiction that constructs, from solitude and silence, the individual/subject and its mask, its *formal* consistency and its juridical status. As such it is a challenge issued from the grounds of modernity that targets modernity itself. This position represents an original third – asymmetrical, not at all equidistant – with respect to both the Greek-Christian paths and the hegemonic and prevailing paradigms of modernity. It offers an alternative to both the ethical-traditional deduction of human nature, and to its definition in atomistic and, for that very reason, essentialist and reifying terms. Laid between nature and *ars*, the tracks of this challenge traverse also another central station of political modernity.

The Artifice of Nature

> A person, is he, whose words or actions are considered, either as his own, or as representing the words or actions of another man, or of any other thing to whom they are attributed, whether truly or by fiction. When they are considered as his own, then is he called a natural person; and when they are considered as representing the words and actions of another, then is he a feigned or artificial person.[156]

---

[153] *Ethics* IV, 20; CWS I, 557.
[154] On *ethos* as a pre-condition for the notions of 'order' and 'justice' in Aristotle see Zanetti (1993).
[155] Incidentally, this is what also explains the different and sometimes opposite Spinozan 'definitions' of human nature.
[156] *Lev*, I, 16; *EW* III, 147.

Natura and *ars* in the modern age: starting with the *Leviathan* and Hobbes' work the relationship between nature and *ars* becomes an urgent theoretical problem, an impelling logical-historical question – as long as one avoids hastily reducing it to its much more linear (and simplified) liberal interpretations. This is accompanied by a crisis of the cosmos, when human actions managed to break out of their ancient paths and to disrupt the strict coordinates of the *ordo universalis*, upsetting the immediate hierarchies and the spontaneous differences established by the natural politics that, having monopolised the theory and the common sense of an entire epoch and embodied, for centuries, the shared values of the Christian republic, finally collapsed – between the fifteenth and seventeenth centuries – under the centripetal force of the great geographical and astronomical discoveries, of the Reformation, and of religiously motivated civil wars.[157] Once the *summum bonum* faded from the horizon of human action, and the reassuring paths that led to the indubitable authority of the *finis ultimus* crumbled, human nature irrevocably lost its reifying essence and its ontological consistency.[158] Man was no longer 'something' – positively oriented towards a purpose (enabled to achieve a goal) – but is rather identified with a confused, chaotic, and impulsive dynamism, who proves incapable of achieving any goal or pursuing any long-lasting objective. Left to the immediacy of his instinctual urges, the Hobbesian self-preserving (*sese conservandi*) *conatus* cannot reach its goal, and rather resolves itself into the generalised logic of a destructive conflict, of a universal competition that disintegrates and reduces to 'nothing' – that *an-nihilates*.[159] Nature does not generate order but chaos, absolute disorder, utter negativity.

This is precisely why the creation of the political order cannot be configured as a process *according to nature*. The Leviathan is a product that goes *against nature*, the result of an unnatural gesture: it is an artifice that arises from 'fear', the only drive capable of completely eliminating all drives, the only instinct capable of neutralising all instincts.[160] Hence the enigmatic and restless aura that hangs around the *pactum*: 'I authorize and give up my right of governing myself, to this man, or to this assembly of men, on this

---

[157] On these topics see also Koyré 1970 and Skalweit 1982.

[158] On the 'crisis of European conscience' see the well-known Hazard 2005, as well as Schnur 1962 and Castrucci 1981.

[159] See *Lev*, I, 13: *EW* III, 110–13; and *De Cive*, I: *EW* II, 1–13.

[160] In this section (and for the considerations that follow) I have in mind Galli (1996a) in particular. On the artificiality or naturalness of political obligation in Hobbes, one cannot fail to mention the two specular interpretations offered by Schmitt 1986 and Tönnies 1971. On the Schmittian reading of Hobbes see Galli 1996b, 733–7.

condition, that thou give up thy right to him, and authorize all his actions in like manner.'[161] The *pactum unionis* ushers in an unlimited subjection, unbound and independent from the pact itself.[162] On the one hand, the Hobbesian formula assumes the reassuring and rational semblance of a liberal approach, including the potentially *democratic* (yet not necessarily liberal) status of an agreement or a union, a tendentially *universal* consensus. But, on the other hand, behind this mask, behind this *superficial* dimension (a façade, displaying the way modernity likes to self-represent itself) such a formula conceals *the demonic face of power*:[163] the arbitrary, irreducible, and independent dimension of political decision. Given the irrationality of nature and the inevitable negativity of 'fear', what makes the rational choice of a political order possible? And does not the very definition of the *pactum*, the very possibility of *negotiation*, require a 'formality' and a 'regularity' that already imply the existence of an order? In reality, power is not deduced from the pact; rather, the latter becomes viable and admissible thanks to the existence of power. Both the givenness of the *imperium* and the actuality of the political decision are matters of fact. At least originally, seen from an origin/beginning that allows the natural state of things to emerge out of nowhere, power turns out to be transcendental with respect to the *pactum*. And it is only when the order works at full capacity (*a regime*) between one and the other – between the impulsive immediacy of the decision and the rational mediation of consensus – that a logic of mutual reference and a process of mutual sustenance are established. The more the *imperium* strengthens itself the more it becomes able to rationalise itself, to support *conservatio*; the more power functions as it should the more it proves itself capable of 'representing', able to posit the 'represented' into being, to give it a form, a regulated personality, and a publicly recognised consistency:

[t]his is the generation of that great Leviathan, or rather, to speak more reverently, of that *mortal god*, to which we owe under the *immortal God*, our peace and defence. For by this authority, given him by every particular man in the commonwealth, he hath the use of so much power and strength conferred on him, that by terror thereof, he is enabled to

---

[161] *Lev*, II, 17; *EW* III, 158.
[162] See *Lev*, II, 18: *EW* III, 159–70; *De Cive*, III, 21 and V, 9–12: *EW* II, 42 and 69–71. On the peculiar, double nature of the '*pactum*' in Hobbes, see Bobbio 1979.
[163] Of course, I am referring, albeit rather loosely, to Ritter 1948.

perform the wills of them all, to peace at home, and mutual aid against their enemies abroad.[164]

Aimed at the overcoming of the destructive immediacy of nature and of the *conatus*, the complete artificiality of the Hobbesian order is able to lead, better than any other contemporary paradigm, towards a clear separation of the sphere of politics (the public sphere of decision, which removes conflict by concentrating power and the law onto itself) and that of the social (the 'private' universe, the unstable dimension of the passions, of interests, and of 'value'). A *functional* separation, an articulation of strictly distinct but complementary functions in which the logic of the modern State is resolved in the vacuum of every positive foundation, in the absolute negativity of nature. The crisis of 'plenitude' and of 'purpose' is answered with the automatisms of the new, very powerful *art*, with the movements of the 'mortal God', the machine of all machines (*machina machinarum*).

Ultimately, Hobbes' merit is that of exposing the constitutive tension of modernity, bringing to the fore the structural opacity that is carefully avoided by those *moderate* reconstructions which unilaterally approach the modern via its safest and most accessible route, that of a quiet and regular contractualism. Positing nature as the indistinct magma of the negative, the two faces of the Leviathan impute the unutterable nature of the beginning directly to the political sphere, to the unresolved circularity between the open and recognisable *ratio* of the *pactum* and the absolute artifice, the illogical, hard, and irreducible act of the *imperium*.

What about Spinoza? Within this predicament, he outlines a possible alternative path. Spinoza singles out the issue of the beginning (the enigma of the 'origin', once the certainties of a cosmic order are destroyed) as the crucial question of modernity. Far from being a delayed revival of ancient supremacies, this is the true meaning of his choice of starting from God and from metaphysics. In fact, he assigns a different *metaphysical* grounding to this contradiction: he anticipates it on the metaphysical level, moving it from the political sphere to that of the sources of the cause, a theoretical move that introduces the irrepressible positivity of nature as 'power'. The unresolvable reciprocity, the unmodifiable identity/diversity of the cause (both *causa sui* and *causa rerum*), nourishes the universal chain (*concatenatio*) of modes and constitutes them by means of a relationship (*se-alium*), thus making the continuum of power unassailable. Foreign to the teleologi-

---

[164] *Lev*, II, 17; *EW* III, 158. On representation in Hobbes see Galli 1988: 53–78. More generally, on the structural tensions of this modern notion, see Duso 1988.

cal progression of forms, nature thus banishes the abyss of the negative – the black hole of emptiness – from its interiority. A horizon that radically shifts the terms of the relationship, one that is strategic due to the essence of the political, between natural givenness and the transformations of the doing (*facere*).[165]

The problem (*this* problem, the one pertaining to the connection between 'nature' and 'art') is approached, in some very clear passages, at the beginning of the fourth chapter of the *TTP*. Reasoning about divine law, Spinoza introduces, as a premise, a brief examination of the notions of *lex*, *jus*, and their intersections. In general (*absolute sumptum*), the term *lex* indicates 'that according to which each individual, or all or some members of the same species, act in one and the same fixed and determinate way'.[166] This depends 'either on a necessity of nature or on a human decision', depending on whether it stems from natural necessity (from nature *sive definitione*, from the thing itself) or pertains to what humans 'prescribe for themselves and others, for the sake of living more safely and conveniently, or for some other causes'.[167] Only this second type of law can be properly called *jus*. The fact that a body, when colliding with a smaller one, 'loses as much of its motion as it communicates to the other body' is an example of a law imposed by natural necessity. On the other hand, 'that men should yield, or be compelled to yield, the right they have from nature, and bind themselves to a fixed way of living' refers precisely to the *jus*, being a fruit of their decision, their *placitum*.[168] The distinction between *lex* and *jus* is therefore weak yet not arbitrary, because it is derived directly from the essence of the *conatus*, from its double character of power and of necessary determination. It is weak, because no action nor decision made 'against nature' would ever be able to modify (to destroy, to annihilate, or to upset) the chain of things (*rerum concatenatio*): 'that everything is determined by the universal laws of nature to exist and produce effects in a fixed and determinate way'.[169] It is not arbitrary because the human, as a part of nature, contributes, with its own power,

---

[165] The literature on Hobbes and Spinoza is enormous; in addition to the collective Bostrenghi 1992 – and just to mention some of the most recent and significant surveys – see Chaui 1980; Gallicet Calvetti 1981; Matheron 1985; Boss 1987; Schumann 1987; Den Uyl and Warner 1987; Di Vona 1980; Curley 1991; Giancotti 1995; Cascione 1999; Lazzeri 1999; Heerich 2000; Kreische 2000; Salazar 2002; Del Lucchese 2004; Visentin 2017.
[166] *TTP* IV, 1; *CWS* II, 125.
[167] Ibid.
[168] *TTP* IV, 2; *CWS* II, 126.
[169] Ibid.

to the universal power: that is, there are things that proceed (*sequuntur*) specifically from human nature, even if they still do so necessarily (*etiamsi necessario*) and if they still emerge from nature itself, a nature that, in this case, is expressing itself via the form – the mode – of human nature.[170] It is also the case that 'we are completely ignorant of the order and connection of things itself, i.e., of how things are really ordered and connected. So for practical purposes it is better, indeed necessary, to consider things as possible.'[171] Nature opens itself to *ars* (to the human work of action and transformation) through the imagination of the 'possible', a doubtlessly fictitious horizon, because derived from the inevitable ignorance of the universal chain of causes (*concatenatio causarum*), but nonetheless productive and indeed necessary for the accumulation and the perseverance of power. Even in its peculiar, confused dynamism, fiction – *imaginatio* – lies within the logic of the *conatus*: 'it is better, indeed necessary, to consider things as possible'.[172] Intertwined with necessity and possibility, and structured by the encounter of both active and passive affects, human activities must however serve a 'purpose'; they must produce power, due to natural urgency, on pain of their succumbing. If the artifice does not stand up to the level of the sole purpose, no positive *jus* can ever seriously persist against the '*law which depends on a necessity of nature*',[173] against the universal power of *conservatio*.

This double register – moving between the sphere of nature and that of human doing – is also an inevitable condition for political power. Due to its peculiar character of *fabrica*, of a power that governs other powers,[174] the *imperium* is an *ars*, in the sense that it does not arise directly and immediately from the *conatus* but rather presents itself as a complex construction – a more or less conscious product – of human interactions. Even though it is still the result of human doing, no matter how derivative and artificial its mechanisms might be, even the *imperium* still partakes of universal/natural reality. The *imperium* is a *jus*: it proceeds from its own – internal and 'constructed' – normativity, yet without ever being able to truly deviate from the law of

---

[170] And perhaps for this very reason it cannot properly be said that the Spinozan man is 'a natural being who produces anti-nature' (Preposiet 1967: 199. My translation). On the internal character of the natural necessity of the human decision, see Tosel 1984: 188–9.
[171] *TTP* IV, 4; *CWS* II, 126.
[172] Ibid.
[173] *TTP* IV, 1; *CWS* II, 125.
[174] Referring to the State, the expression '*fabrica*' appears in *TTP* XVI, 30: '*quod fundamentum si tollatur, tota fabrica ruet*'; *CWS* II, 288: 'If this foundation is removed, the whole structure will easily fall.'

the *conatus*. It can get away from it, it can compress it and mortify it, but it will not be able to destroy it, because there is no *ars* capable of anticipating the essence of the mode, there is no artifice that can reproduce its 'nature'.

The Spinozist political order does not take the shape of a direct purpose or an immediate and essential (i.e. dictated by its essence) end of the human-mode. The *imperium* is an 'art': a strategy, an articulated answer formulated in view of *conservatio*. But the *ordo* itself excludes any Hobbesian transcendental dimension: power (*potestas*) still emanates from the untameable positivity and the unbroken physicality of power (*potentia*) (and powers (*potentiae*)). The political decision does not stand on the void of the negative, but it is always wholly (and inevitably) built within the continuum of nature. Like in Hobbes' case, Spinoza's *imperium* must necessarily respond to the *conatus*, it must operate at full capacity. But for Spinoza this means responding to the irrepressible existence of a relationship, to the inalienability of the relative and to the impelling effectiveness of the connective: *inter-esse*, being-between as a constitutive horizon (which 'constitutes' and can neither be removed nor suppressed) of nature and of *conservatio*.[175] Such is the *natural artificiality* of the *imperium*.

By voiding the relational value of *vis*, Hobbes (not unlike the moderate liberal paradigm of modernity, which, in the long run, proved to be the prevailing one) denies the *co-essentiality* – the *essential* compossibility – of reason and passions. Deduced as a concrete act against nature (an act that 'creates' a positivity out of nothing, introducing it into the chaos of natural impulses), the political order will then inevitably follow the structure of such an impossible compossibility: in order to 'function' at all it will have to proceed on the basis of a rigid separation of the political and the social, of the public and the private, of the universal and of the individual. On the other hand, Spinoza's *conatus* – attuned to the structurally intersected registers of the cause – brings the fictitious nature of that separation, as well as its 'critical' character, into the open: it reveals its inevitable and permanent placement within a dimension of crisis. In Spinoza's construal, the *conatus* admits the *ommium commune utile* (mutual cooperation, the potentially universal compossibility of the drives, of individual 'interests'), and yet it denies that this could either be given through a natural and immediate act or through pure reason.[176] Dependent, like everything else, on the law of *conservatio*,

---

[175] Zac's 'vitalist' interpretation comes to somewhat similar conclusions: '[s]ociety is not only at the service of life, but it is itself alive' (1963: 237. My translation).

[176] On the other hand, and in Kantian manner, Solari (1927: 232–5) insists on the 'rational' discontinuity of civil life with respect to the natural condition.

the *imperium* too is subjected to the natural rule of power (*potentia*). The mechanism of power will neither be *legitimate* nor *good* (meaningless definitions, for there is no meaning in nature). Rather, it will be stronger, more capable of accumulating power, not to annihilate, but to release energy and to multiply 'actions'. This is imposed by the very complexity of force, the raw material whose essence no human *fabrica* could ever change.

3

A Militant Design: The *Theological-Political Treatise*

In a response to Oldenburg, who inquired about the 'plan and aim'[1] of the *TTP*, Spinoza puts forward three orders of reasons. Through an effective epistolary synthesis there emerges an intertwining of science and militancy, of theory and contingency, as the backbone of his entire project. On the one hand, these reasons lead him to compose a treatise about his own way of interpreting the sacred texts (*de meo circa scripturam sensu*). He singles out the prejudices of the theologians as the most cumbersome obstacle, the most serious barrier that is encountered along the way of philosophical research: it is necessary to 'expose' such 'prejudices' and remove them 'from the minds of the more prudent'. He then feels the need to 'rebut', as much as possible, the 'opinion' of the common people, the *plebs*, who keep portraying him as an atheist. Finally, he explains how his book aims to defend, in any way, 'the freedom of philosophizing and saying what we think', a faculty continually attacked and threatened by the petulance and the excessive authority of the 'preachers'.[2] The subtitle of the work, which announces 'discussions' meant to demonstrate how 'the republic can grant freedom of philosophizing without harming its peace or piety, and cannot deny it without destroying its peace and piety',[3] refers directly to the specifically political character of this freedom, i.e., that it is necessarily and directly involved with the nature of the *respublica*. The *TTP*'s Preface, which is emblematic in its contents, its tone, and in its lively expressive registers, makes immediately clear the fact that the contents of the work are not merely concerned with pure principles, or represent an exercise in sterile theorisation. In a passionate and polemical way, far from the detached style and the 'cold calmness of the mathematical

---

[1] *Ep.* XXIX (Henry Oldenburg to Spinoza); CWS II, 11.
[2] *Ep.* XXX (to Henry Oldenburg); CWS II, 15.
[3] *TTP* Praef., 1; CWS II, 65.

reasoning'[4] that characterises the *Ethics*, Spinoza denounces the civil failures of superstition and the perverse theological-political connection that feeds it for the sole purpose of inculcating passivity and subjection in the minds of the people, a passivity on which all authoritarian hierarchies ground their power. Such a connection fuels the annihilating hallucinations of the monarchical regime, draining the rational and propulsive force of the free republic.

If humans everywhere succeeded in conducting themselves according to a 'definite plan' (*certo consilio*), or if fate was to always be favourable to them, then 'no one would be in the grip of superstition'. Instead, cornered by numerous adversities that they are unable to overcome, and pushed by an unbridled desire for the uncertain gifts of fate, they 'usually vacillate wretchedly between hope and fear', revealing themselves, for the most part, as inclined to believe anything at all. In favourable moments, even those who 'are quite inexperienced' react with bold and presumptuous disdain if someone offers them advice; conversely, in hardships, everyone desperately asks for help, and there is no advice 'so foolish, so absurd or groundless, that they do not follow it'. Faced with an unusual event, they immediately think it to be a prodigy that manifests the wrath of the gods or of the 'supreme divinity' so that, '[s]ubject to superstition and contrary to religion', they consider it a duty to placate the ire of the gods with sacrifices and offerings, mistaking their delusions, their dreams, and every other childish trifle for divine responses, as if nature as a whole were as crazy as they are. Thus, they come to believe that God does not love the wise, and that his will, manifested in the entrails of animals and not in their own mind, can be predicted and communicated by fools, by the demented, and by birds: '[t]hat's how crazy fear makes men'.[5] Superstition is born, preserved, and nourished by fear (*timor*), the most effective of all passive affects, the worst of the 'social' passions.[6] The *vulgus* is the main victim of this uncertain and changeable state of mind. The *vulgus*, which always lives in a miserable condition, never finds lasting satisfaction (*acquiescentia*) and constantly seeks changes and upheavals, pursuing the mirage of a new, ephemeral stability. Dazzled by a superstitious piety, the plebs are easily induced to worship their kings as gods

---

[4] See Droetto and Giancotti 1972: 11, in which the hypothesis (supported, among others, by Couchoud 1902) that the preface should be attributed to Meyer and not to Spinoza is questioned, underlining how the whole treatise is actually traversed by a strong tone and combative expressions.

[5] *TTP* Praef., 1; CWS II, 65.

[6] On *superstitio* as a consequence of the *metus* see *Ethics* III, 50 Schol; CWS I, 521–2.

or, on the contrary, to execrate them as the worst plague of mankind: a facile swaying of opinions from which many tumults and atrocious conflicts can derive. In order to avoid these perils, every religion is covered by an exterior ritual and an apparatus capable of guaranteeing, as much as possible, both a tangible appearance of superiority and the folk's constant obedience. It is precisely these 'remedies' which, rather than fighting against superstition, cultivate and exploit it, and indeed pave the way for other, equally serious social degenerations. For example, that of 'regarding the ministries of the Church as positions conferring status, its offices as sources of income'; greed and ambition, and a 'great desire to administer the sacred offices'. So, the temple becomes a theatre, where orators take the place of the doctors of the Church, 'not to teach the people, but to carry them away with admiration for himself'.[7] Faith is thus reduced to credulity and preconceptions that 'turn men from rational beings into beasts, since they completely prevent everyone from freely using their judgment, distinguishing the true from the false, and seem deliberately designed to put out the light of the intellect entirely'.[8] It is difficult to doubt that this strident denunciation of the corrupted worldliness of various religious sects had something to do with the Dutch social environment, and with Spinoza's painful personal experiences. But the political tone that the *praefatio* immediately assumes is even clearer, and all the more explicit if compared to the time of its writing, a historical phase during which the Netherlands was preparing for the decisive battle between the monarchist-Orangist faction and the republican factions still in power. According to Spinoza the decadence of *pietas* is accompanied by the logic and the interests of the monarchical government, whose greatest secret has the purpose

> to keep men deceived, and to cloak in the specious name of Religion the fear by which they must be checked, so that they will fight for slavery as they would for their survival, and will think it not shameful, but a most honorable achievement, to give their life and blood that one man may have a ground for boasting.[9]

The nature of a democratic regime is very different, for it absolutely abhors 'to fill the free judgment of each man with prejudices, or to restrain it in any way'. Spinoza adds that:

---

[7] *TTP* Praef., 15; CWS II, 70.
[8] *TTP* Praef., 16; CWS II, 70.
[9] *TTP* Praef., 10; CWS II, 68–9.

> [s]ince, then, we happen to have that rare good fortune – that we live in a Republic in which everyone is granted complete freedom of judgment, and is permitted to worship God according to his mentality, and in which nothing is thought to be dearer or sweeter than freedom – I believed I would be doing something neither unwelcome, nor useless, if I showed not only that this freedom can be granted without harm to piety and the peace of the Republic, but also that it cannot be abolished unless piety and the Peace of the Republic are abolished with it. That's the main thing I resolved to demonstrate in this treatise.[10]

The rhetorical artifice of the celebration barely conceals an obvious logical inconsistency, as well as its purely political meaning: if the freedom of the republic really corresponded to what Spinoza so uncompromisingly exalts, 'nothing would have been as useless as the Treatise he was presenting'.[11] In reality the Dutch freedom of the seventeenth century suffered many limitations and, in the years in question, it held many dangers, above all the re-emergence of religious conflicts, destined to extend where laws 'about speculative matters' were applied, yielding to the pressures of official cults, with the aim of judging and publicly condemning not only actions, but ideas and words as well. It is therefore necessary to fight against the 'the main prejudices regarding religion', as well as against false opinions about the rights of civil institutions which 'many, with the most shameless license, are eager to take away the greater part of'[12] by diverting the *vulgus*, under the pretext of religion, from freedom to ancient servitude. Hence the motivation for the two parts of the treatise: the theological-exegetical one, which occupies the first fifteen chapters, and the philosophical-political one, developed in the last five. The goal is the same: to extend the boundaries of freedom to better repel the seditious attacks that it receives, avoiding the grave and impending threat of a return to the old, deleterious servitude. In short, it is difficult to avoid the very clear impression that, starting with its opening pages, Spinoza's book breaks out of the precincts of an abstract intellectual dissertation, to take on the ardent and participatory cadence of social commitment, the meaning of an indirect yet very steadfast 'militant' contribution to the social present.[13]

---

[10] *TTP* Praef., 12; CWS II, 69.
[11] Droetto and Giancotti 1972: 14. My translation.
[12] *TTP* Praef., 13; CWS II, 69–70.
[13] 'Spinoza's political thought, like his ethical work, is above all a struggle with its own (philosophical-political) strategy, corresponding to the situation of the time. It is the procedure outlined in the *TTP* which, in different forms, continues and accompanies

It is precisely the intersection of political urgencies and cultural assumptions, and the mediations between the 'timely project' and the speculative analysis, that give the work a powerful and oblique charm, making it most unique among all of Spinoza's works.

Philosophy and Theology

'[S]eparating Philosophy from Theology', or again 'to separate faith from Philosophy': this is the announced aim, the 'main purpose of this whole work [the *TTP*]'.[14] Actually, as it can be immediately seen, such a disjunction does not imply any absolute equidistance nor – and this is grasped in a more internal way – any authentic and reciprocal autonomy. The task of dividing philosophy from faith openly aims, first of all, at the theoretical and historical objective of achieving a definitive emancipation of *ratio* and *imperium* from any theological foundation, or at least from any religious patronage. The way in which the *TTP* actually pursues this aim delineates a twofold supremacy of reason: from the methodological side – that of a hermeneutical procedure that soon appears tuned to the frequency modulations of the natural light – and from the standpoint of its final outcome, by virtue of which the breakdown of the traditional authoritative link between theology and politics ends up settling into a new assemblage, this time with a reversed hegemony, predominantly philosophical. Here is a re-consolidation that seems to add little to 'theory', and rather targets the risks and possibilities of 'practice', the anxieties and the opportunities of its time.

There are some obligatory steps to be taken towards the pursuit of the announced purpose: a new doctrine of revelation (*de prophetia*) and an interpretation of Scripture (*de interpretatione Scripturae*), outlined in four chapters (the first two, the seventh, and the fifteenth), which appear as the true architraves of Spinoza's exegesis, and of the first part of the work as a whole – the other sections clearly taking a complementary and subordinate position, exemplifying and supporting the rest of the argumentation. The fact that the problem of revelation is dealt with before the description of the new cornerstones of the hermeneutical procedure is likely an external and final concession to tradition just as this is about to be demolished. Indeed, such a sequence makes sense only where the thesis of the divine inspiration of Scripture is taken for granted, thus reducing the act of interpretation to

---

the fight that takes place in the scholia, prefaces, and appendices of the *Ethics*' (Bove 1996: 241. My translation).

[14] *TTP* II and XIV; *CWS* II, 93–110 and 263–71.

an instrument for its most effective and adequate confirmation, as is still the case for Hobbes.[15] If, on the other hand (as indeed happens) such a thesis is radically called into question, i.e., if inspiration (*inspiratio*) is no longer an unquestionable presupposition but rather a result to be verified and a conclusion whose precise meaning and actual contours are to be reconstructed, then hermeneutics regains a dominant position, or at least a new and autonomous one. This is a position, in any case, from which it is easy to identify the hegemonic structures and the strategic settlements of reason.

Spinoza observes how '[e]veryone says that Sacred Scripture is the word of God, which teaches men true blessedness or the way to salvation. But their deeds reveal a completely different view':[16] the *vulgus* is not concerned with living according to the teachings of the Scripture, and the theologian does nothing but extract his own 'inventions and fancies' out of it, with the sole objective to 'compel others to think as he does, under the pretext of religion'. When superstition – which leads us 'to scorn reason and nature, and to admire and venerate only what is contrary to both of these' – is accompanied by 'ambition and wickedness', the spirit of religion no longer consists in charity 'but in spreading dissension among men, and in propagating the most bitter hatred, which they shield under the false name of religious zeal and passionate devotion'.[17] To get rid of 'these confusions' and free the mind from all prejudices, it is first of all necessary to define a new 'method of interpreting Scripture and discussing it', in order to know with certainty what the Scripture actually teaches: and then, '[t]o sum up briefly, I say that the method of interpreting Scripture does not differ at all from the method of interpreting nature, but agrees with it completely'.[18] If inspiration cannot be accepted as a starting point, and if it is impossible to establish its consistency and content *a priori* (if not to superimpose, boldly and authoritatively, one's own opinions and aspirations onto it), the Bible then presents itself as an open field of investigation, the domain of a critical research project free of pre-established boundaries, other than those of its own reliability. But the reliability of this research is no different than the reliability of reasoning: Scripture cannot be immediately accepted as a wholly 'legitimate' source because, in this way, divine authority would

---

[15] On the novelty of the Spinozan approach see Bonifas 1904; Lods 1982: 89–90; Moreau 1988 and 1991. On the legitimacy of 'reversing the order of the *Theological-Political Treatise*, beginning with the exposition of chapter 7, the true centre of the first part', see Breton 1979: 56ff. My translation.

[16] *TTP* VII, 1; CWS II, 169.

[17] *TTP* VII, 4; CWS II, 170.

[18] *TTP* VII, 6; CWS II, 171.

always and inevitably end up being split into far too many contrasting human authorities. It should then be taken as a 'text', a document to be studied, examined, and probed – just like 'nature', the domain of rational inquiry *par excellence*. From the methodological standpoint this is a peculiarity of reason, which invites us, first of all, to *focus on the object*, to hold steady one's 'field' of investigation. *Scriptura secundum Scripturam*: '[s]o the knowledge of all these things, i.e., of almost everything in Scripture, must be sought only from Scripture itself, just as the knowledge of nature must be sought from nature itself'.[19] And since Scripture, like nature, 'does not give definitions of the things of which it speaks', it will be necessary, in order to know it, to rewrite its history: '[t]herefore, the universal rule in interpreting Scripture is to attribute nothing to Scripture as its teaching which we have not understood as clearly as possible from its history'.[20] It will then be necessary to examine, to begin with, 'the nature and properties' of the Hebrew language in which the texts were written, and which their authors used to express themselves. Then, claims made in each book should be collected and rearranged, by linking them to the main claims (*summa capita*), paying particular attention to obscure or contradictory ones, of which we must grasp the meaning without dissolving them by means of external superpositions. Finally, it will be necessary to know the life, the customs, and the culture of the authors, as well as the 'fortune' of every single book, the different and sometimes contrasting lessons handed down by the tradition, and the epoch and the place of its admission among the 'sacred codes'.[21] Approaching the Bible as an *opus* essentially means to begin one's investigation by paying attention to its form, language, and literary genre, as well as considering the vicissitudes it experienced over its history.[22] This enterprise, however, seems impossible, since we actually do not possess a 'complete knowledge' of the Hebrew language (i.e. a true mastery of its 'complete history' and of its many structural 'ambiguities'), and because we mostly ignore the events and happenings narrated in the texts, or we still have a very rough understanding of them. Moreover, many

---

[19] *TTP* VII, 10; CWS II, 171.
[20] *TTP* VII, 14; CWS II, 172. On the meaning of 'history', which here is etymologically – and in Baconian manner – meant as a 'collection' of data and elements, see Zac 1965: 29, as well as the more recent Zaltieri and Marcucci 2019. On the 'method' of the *TTP*, between philosophy, philology, and history, see Aurélio Pires 2019: 82–92.
[21] See *TTP* VII, 15–21; CWS II, 173–5.
[22] On the anticipatory, if not downright foundational character of modern biblical exegesis assumed here by the Spinozan interpretation, see the already mentioned Zac 1965.

'sacred' books have not reached us in their original version, but rather as translations and products of a tradition which, sometimes very far from the time of their original composition, increased their confusion and obscurity. And yet, Spinoza insists that

> we should note again that all these difficulties can prevent us from grasping the intention of the Prophets only concerning things we can't perceive and can only imagine – not concerning things we can grasp with the intellect and easily form a clear concept of.[23]

This is another crucial feature of reason: 'to hold steady' the object essentially means 'to constitute' it, not unlike what happens when 'examining natural things'. In the case of Scripture too, one will have to proceed by deriving what is found to be 'most universal' and what represents its basis and foundation, and 'what all the Prophets commend' as an extremely useful doctrine for all human beings.[24] In other words, it will be necessary to focus on the true and fundamental laws of Scripture: those corresponding to the laws of motion and rest in the natural domain, imparted everywhere in the sacred texts in such a clear and explicit way that no one ever doubted their meaning. These are very simple and easily intelligible principles which, like the steps of Euclid's reasoning, can be understood even without fully understanding the language in which they were expressed, the author's life and studies, or 'to whom and when he wrote, or its various readings'.[25] From these very general premises it will be possible to derive more specific and determinate truths, related to uses, customs, historical contingencies, subjective opinions, and so on:

> [n]o doubt everyone now sees that this method requires no light beyond the natural light itself. For the nature and excellence of this light consists above all in this: that by legitimate principles of inference it deduces and infers things obscure from things known, or given as known.[26]

The proposed method requires nothing else, and if 'it doesn't suffice for tracking down, with certainty, everything in the Bible', this does not depend on a flaw in such a method. Rather the reason is that

---

[23] *TTP* VII, 66; *CWS* II, 185.
[24] *TTP* VII, 21; *CWS* II, 175.
[25] *TTP* VII, 67; *CWS* II, 185.
[26] *TTP* VII, 70; *CWS* II, 186.

the way it teaches to be true and right has never been practiced or commonly used by men. So with the passage of time this way has become very difficult, and almost impenetrable. I think the difficulties I've raised establish this very clearly.[27]

The separation of reason and faith actually implies a sort of double protection, both in terms of method and of merit, that the first operates for the second. Certainly, it is not a question of following Maimonides and the dogmatists' strategy of adapting every content of Scripture to a standardised *ratio*, twisting it to fit predetermined geometric proofs and thus distorting the thought of the prophets. Yet, it is even more necessary to avoid the approach of Alfakhar and the sceptics who, moving from the correct ideal of '*Scriptura per Scripturam*', go on to passively accept even the most confused and unlikely of its assertions, thus completely renouncing 'judgment and reason':

> [i]t's certainly true that Scripture ought to be explained by Scripture, so long as we're only working out the meaning of the statements and the Prophets' intention. But once we've unearthed the true meaning, we must, necessarily, use judgment and reason to give it our assent.[28]

Reason is the 'light of the mind' – without which only ghosts and dreams remain – the faculty that evaluates and judges, welcomes and rejects, the testimonies of Scripture. The autonomy of reason and faith does not indicate their independence of means in view of the same end, almost as if they were parallel paths which – as happens in the Galilean attempt of a 'diplomatic' reconciliation – aim at different aspects of a single objective, of the same *veritas*.[29] Philosophy and theology have different tools, objectives, and results. In the end, the specific function of faith will be compatible (yet not identical) with the truth, of which reason will remain the sole holder. But such an outcome will be possible only after the parts of the drama will have been assigned by reason itself, the sole *viaticum*, the authentic and 'original text' of the word of God: the 'greatest gift' which cannot be sacrificed to the 'dead letter' of any written page.[30]

---

[27] Ibid.
[28] *TTP* XV, 8; *CWS* II, 274. On Maimonides see also *TTP* VII, 75–87; *CWS* II, 187–90; on his 'speculative or philosophical' exegetical method and on the specular one – based on a 'cordial' system – exemplified by Spinoza in Alfakhar, see Breton 1979: 62ff.
[29] In this regard, GCL is emblematic.
[30] *TTP* XV, 10; *CWS* II, 275.

Obedience

'[T]he purpose of Scripture is only to teach obedience':[31] if the goal of reason is truth, the purpose of faith is obedience; not adequate knowledge – of the laws of nature and of knowledge – but the constraints and the subjection of a 'command', of a moral imperative:

> [n]ext, obedience to God consists only in the love of your neighbor [. . .] From this it follows that the only knowledge Scripture commends is that necessary for all men if they are to be able to obey God according to this prescription, and without which men would necessarily be stiff-necked, or at least lacking in the discipline of obedience.[32]

And so

> [i]t also follows that Scripture does not touch on speculations which do not tend directly to this end, whether they are concerned with the knowledge of God or the knowledge of natural things. So such speculations ought to be separated from revealed Religion.[33]

Rational-philosophical knowledge 'is concerned with the knowledge of God or the knowledge of natural things', it does not impose or propose any constraint, neither 'commands' nor 'obedience'. Unlike reason, to execute and to be subjected is not something wholly extraneous to a form of 'understanding': 'the only knowledge Scripture commends is that necessary for all men if they are to be able to obey God according to this prescription'.[34] A kind of knowledge is, however, also implicit in the 'execution' of an order. Obedience derives from revelation and not from reason: but revelation is, in turn, the fruit of imagination. Faith is thus at once distinguished from knowledge and resolved within the Spinozist theory of knowledge. This is because imagination is still a kind of knowledge, a mutilated and confused form of the understanding, but an understanding nonetheless. Marked by passion and confusion, the imaginative process of the mind is open to the twin and opposite perspectives of strengthening and weakening of the mind itself, of the accumulation or the disintegration of its 'energies', and of the

---

[31] *TTP* XIV, 6; CWS II, 264. See also *TTP* XIII, 8; CWS II, 258.
[32] *TTP* XIII, 8; CWS II, 258.
[33] Ibid.
[34] Ibid.

multiplication or the fragmentation of its 'forces'. An alternative where, once again, the possibility of affirming the hegemony of reason over passion will be decisive.[35]

In general, revelation is 'the certain knowledge of some matter which God has revealed to men'.[36] Strictly speaking, then, the first revelation will be a natural knowledge (*cognitio naturalis*) common to all and supported by equally common foundations: as expressions of the one substance, the things we understand by means of natural light (*lumen naturae*) depend on 'knowledge of God and of his eternal decrees'.[37] A knowledge we possess in virtue of our being *modes*, participating in 'God's nature, insofar as we participate in it', through the attributes of thought and extension.[38] However, more traditionally, and more precisely, by 'revelation' we mean a biblical 'prophecy', which requires a 'prophet' to be interpreted and communicated to most human beings, who, unable to obtain secure knowledge, welcome it as mere faith. This revelation does not proceed from reason but is a product of the imagination, since the prophets perceived it only 'with the aid of the imagination, i.e., by the mediation of words or of images'.[39] Like any other phenomenon, prophecy too has its natural causes to which it must be traced in order to be adequately interpreted. The first kind of knowledge from which it derives is the only form exposed, by its very nature, to passion. That particular relationship of motion and stillness that gives rise to an 'individual', to a particular human body, inevitably remains 'disposed' – i.e., involved in the double relationship of actions and passions underlying the dynamics of the *disponi* – towards all other aggregates that, together, form the whole material individual, the 'face of the whole Universe'.[40] The mind perceives its own body only through these affections, in which the body is intertwined, without distinguishing itself from other external bodies. As long as the mind knows exclusively through such an order and such a connection of affects, it is bound to produce confused and inadequate notions

---

[35] 'The tool of the theoretical analysis of scriptural narrative is provided to Spinoza by the doctrine of the imagination, elaborated already in the first draft of the *Ethics*. Scripture is actually presented as the fundamental historical document of the imagination of the West. In this sense, Spinoza's interest in the interpretation of Scripture does not precede the construction of philosophy, but rather derives from an ongoing philosophical elaboration' (Mignini 1995b: 73. My translation).
[36] *TTP* I, 1; *CWS* II, 76.
[37] *TTP* I, 2–3; *CWS* II, 76–7.
[38] Ibid.
[39] *TTP* I, 43; *CWS* II, 90.
[40] See *Ethics* II, Post. 4; *CWS* I, 462.

of external objects, of its own body, and of itself. Notions of external objects will be inadequate since the ideas pertaining to them, constructed in close relation with the body, depend more on the constitution of such a body than on the nature of external objects. And the same goes for notions about the body, whose knowledge will always be dependent on its bond with external things, implicit in perceived affection. And finally, for inadequate notions of itself, because the body is the first object of the mind's idea so that its confused understanding and differentiation from external objects will determine an equally confused (self-)understanding of the mind itself.[41] Imagination is limited to mere 'memory', to pure presentation, to the empty evocation of these passive bonds; 'passive' because they mistakenly resolve the essence of the 'self' in an empirical relationship with what is 'outside of oneself'. Thus imagination does not grasp true knowledge, either on the immediate level of perceptions (of 'vague experience'), or on the more complex and elaborate one of opinions: those prejudices, superstitions, and false beliefs that arise from the re-elaboration and the merging of inadequate ideas.[42] When introduced into the universe of affects and modes, even prophecy is subordinated to the metaphysics of the cause, and thus unable to place itself in a dimension of exceptionality, of extraterritoriality, or to be free from the determinative continuity of the *facere* and of the *conatus*. To conceive it as a consequence of the power of God would therefore be only a vacuous talk (*garrire*):

[a]ll things are made through the power of God. Indeed, because the power of Nature is just God's power itself, insofar as we're ignorant of natural causes, we certainly don't understand God's power. So it's foolish to fall back on that power of God when we don't know the natural cause of a thing, i.e., when we don't know God's power itself.[43]

---

[41] *Ethics* II, 29 Cor.; CWS I, 471.
[42] *Ethics* II, 18 Schol.; CWS II, 466. On the active function of *imaginatio*, when the mind, through reason, appears aware of its own imagining (that is, it appears endowed with 'an idea that excludes the existence of those things that it imagines to be present to it'), see instead *Ethics* II, 17 Schol.; CWS II, 464–5. Among the studies that, from sometimes very different perspectives, insist on this side of the imagination (a fundamental one in the passage from passive affects to active ones), see Gueroult 1974: 217–35; Mignini 1981a; Deugd 1968; Semerari 1970; Bertrand 1983 and 1984; Haddad-Chamakh 1980 and 1985. On imagination, body, and sign see the important Vinciguerra 2001.
[43] *TTP* I, 44; CWS II, 92.

In Spinoza's metaphysics of substance, the individual things' (*res singulares*) relation of belonging to their principle loses all arbitrary and personalistic connotations, in order to assume the necessary and impassive connotation of operative energy, of causal production. The powerful 'imagining', the 'spirit' within the prophets' minds, is therefore 'of God' only in the generic sense that everything derives from the one Nature-Substance. Through this authentic understanding of the relation of belonging we can then also decipher the ancient and primitive meaning of Scripture, according to which every particular and extraordinary event, the presuppositions of which are unknown, is imaginatively attributed to the subjective and voluntary action of a supernatural – yet anthropomorphic – entity. The *spiritus Dei* can thus poetically represent the human mind, life, benevolence, and divine mercy, or the virtues of wisdom, prudence, and fortitude, or again a 'very daring heart', 'deep melancholy', any force that is 'beyond common knowledge', and a 'wind which is very violent, very dry and destructive'.[44] In short, prophets do not appear to be endowed with the most perfect mind, but 'with a power of imagining unusually vividly'.[45] And besides, some 'very prudent' men were not prophets, while others, 'countryfolk, without any education' – or even 'simple women' – were. Indeed, experience and reason demonstrate that those who are more talented in the use of imagination are also less suitable 'to grasp things by pure intellect', while on the contrary, those who cultivate the intellect have 'a more moderate power of imagining'. It follows that 'those who eagerly search the Prophetic books for wisdom, and knowledge of both natural and spiritual matters, go completely astray'.[46] Prophecies vary with the variation of the imaginative powers and of the physical constitution of their authors, but also according to the beliefs and opinions of which they served as 'funnels'. For this reason, revelation never could enrich their doctrine. Revelation appears to be different from natural knowledge, and it is indeed clearly inferior, because it lacks the self-evident certainty of mathematical reasoning. Prophecy always needs a 'sign' (a word, a thing, an event), able to enhance its strength and authority: '[u]nlike a clear and distinct idea, a simple imagination does not, by its nature, involve certainty [. . .]. So the Prophets were not certain about God's revelation by the revelation itself, but by some sign.'[47] Prophetic certainty is not, in short, of a rational-deductive kind but rather exclusively of a 'moral' nature: the

---

[44] *TTP* I, 32; *CWS* II, 88.
[45] *TTP* II, 1; *CWS* II, 93.
[46] *TTP* II, 2; *CWS* II, 94.
[47] *TTP* II, 4; *CWS* II, 94–5.

prophets must be given credit only with regards to this specific purpose and to this particular content of 'revelation'. Reconciling the axiological substance of Scripture with the truth of science remains, in any case, a task that only reason can fulfil.

Having thus placed the essence of faith on the terrain of the *imagination* – in the first segment of knowledge – Spinoza proceeds to critically reread terms and expressions taken from the sacred texts (aimed at delineating the subjective, voluntary, and authoritarian nature of the divine substance) by re-positioning them within the metaphysics of the cause, and attempting wherever possible some sort of unification, even if only external and formal, between philosophy and textual narrative. Such a transposition is justified precisely by the assumption that Scripture does not aim at the 'truth' about God (because its assertions appear in this regard to be too different, contradictory, vulgar, and paradoxical), but only at practical obedience to some principles or values with respect to which demonstrative science still holds its role of analysis and 'assent'.

'God's guidance' is 'the fixed and immutable order of nature, or the connection of natural things', and the 'eternal decrees of God' are nothing but the 'universal laws of nature', which always imply 'truth and necessity'.[48] Therefore divine law does not indicate any fanciful 'command', but rather our 'highest good', that is 'the knowledge and love of God', through the strengthening of the intellect:

> since nothing can be or be conceived without God, it is certain that all things in nature involve and express the concept of God, in proportion to their essence and perfection. Hence the more we know natural things, the greater and more perfect is the knowledge of God we acquire.[49]

And since knowing an effect through its cause means coming to know a property of the cause, the

> more we know natural things, the more perfectly we know God's essence, which is the cause of all things. So all our knowledge, i.e., our supreme good, not only depends on the knowledge of God, but consists entirely in it.[50]

---

[48] *TTP* III, 7–8; CWS II, 112.
[49] *TTP* IV, 11; CWS II, 128.
[50] Ibid.

Being universal, i.e., deduced from human nature and therefore common to all, the 'universal divine law' does not depend on particular historical events, does not require rites, and has its reward in itself: 'to know God and to love him from true freedom and with a whole and constant heart'. The punishment it imposes consists in 'the privation of these things', and in the inconstancy and the 'vacillating heart' of human beings.[51] Such a 'universal law' – innate, and indeed almost written in the mind of humans[52] – is not the *imperium* of a prince-legislator, and it is therefore different from the law of the Old Testament, revealed (i.e., imagined, grasped by force of imagination as revealed) by Jehovah to the Jewish people, and endowed with a particular civil efficacy and a very important, albeit limited and contingent, political value.[53] Even the 'God's aid' mentioned by Scripture can be translated from imagination to science, from the authoritarian theology of a providential and paternal divinity to the metaphysics of cause and *conatus*: since the power of all natural things 'is nothing but the power itself of God, through which alone all things happen and are determined', it follows that the human, as a part of nature,

> provides for himself, as an aid to preserving his being, or whatever nature supplies him with, without his doing anything himself, it is the power of God alone which provides these things for him, inasmuch as it acts either through human nature or through things outside human nature.[54]

Likewise, *fortuna* indicates God's guidance, i.e., the laws of nature by virtue of which it happens that 'external' causes – causes not foreseen by humans – determine their events and behaviour.[55] Finally, God's choice simply means that 'no one does anything except according to the predetermined order of nature', unless pushed, called forth, by the concatenation of causes to the accomplishment of some work or to the realisation of a certain manner of living (*vivendi ratio*). The Jews, therefore, were 'chosen' exclusively in the sense that, at a certain point in their history, the 'fortune' and the extraordinary power of the most powerful of the prophets led them to create a stable and lasting political and social order. God does not reveal to Moses the natural law, but rather a body of positive laws that allowed the Jewish

---

[51] *TTP* IV, 21; *CWS* II, 130.
[52] *TTP* V, 1; *CWS* II, 138.
[53] *TTP* IV, 39ff.; *CWS* II, 135ff.
[54] *TTP* III, 9; *CWS* II, 113.
[55] *TTP* III, 11; *CWS* II, 113.

people to achieve 'prosperity of the body, and freedom' – material prosperity and political freedom.[56] Consumed by their painful slavery, and being of crude and primitive ingenuity, the children of Israel would not have been able, after the Exodus, to 'enact new laws or to establish new legislation', nor to create and, 'as a body (*collegialiter*)', to preserve the *imperium*. Since 'he excelled the others in divine power', Moses managed to convince them of his superiority through many signs and testimonies, and he was therefore accepted as an authoritative and undisputed 'legislator'. He 'introduced religion into the Republic, so that the people would do their duty not so much from fear as from devotion', regulating in great detail all aspects of social life, so that humans, used to slavery and unable to self-govern, could act according to their impulses and emotions: 'for the people could do nothing without being bound at the same time to remember the law, and to carry out commands which depended only on the will of the ruler'.[57] An essentially 'civil' event, the choice (*electio*) of the Jews is like that of many other groups of people throughout history.[58] God's 'covenant' with 'his' people, as well as the laws and rituals that follow from it, does not concern bliss, intellect, or virtue – which are equally available to all human-modes – but rather pertains to the solidity of a socio-political organism. Like other prophets, due to a lack of knowledge and thought, Moses imagined God as a father and rector: he saw him 'as a ruler, a lawgiver, a king, as compassionate, just, etc'. Yet, these are attributes proper 'only of human nature', since the true God (Substance) actually 'acts and guides all things', simply as a consequence of his own necessity and his own perfection.[59] That imagination, however, performed an extraordinary connective function for an entire community in a delicate and specific moment of its history. The problem of truth and of the authenticity of faith appears wholly superfluous in Machiavelli's Moses – as 'the most acute Florentine' describes him in the sixth chapter of the *Prince* – since the question is made completely irrelevant by the politically decisive fact that it is believed to be authentic (and welcomed as such) by the people. Conversely, for Spinoza's Moses the intensity and the sincerity of that belief is an essential component of his own political power. The passionate perturbations of a force of religious imagination never before deployed by any other prophet allowed the founder of the Jewish State to identify the most

---

[56] *TTP* III, 10ff; *CWS* II, 113ff.
[57] *TTP* V, 29–30; *CWS* II, 145–6.
[58] *TTP* III, 50; *CWS* II, 123: 'God did not choose the Hebrews to eternity, but only on the same condition on which he previously chose the Canaanites.'
[59] *TTP* IV, 30 and 37; *CWS* II, 133 and 134.

adequate solution to the political problem: the democratic solution.[60] What such an outcome will actually consist in is explained in the second part of the treatise (and it will be examined in greater detail below). It is precisely this precious civil conquest that Spinoza considers as the deepest core of the biblical narrative, which recounts how Moses could hear the 'true voice' of God, communicating with him 'face to face' and 'mouth to mouth': affirmations with a 'real' foundation only within an imaginative context (i.e. only insofar as the productivity of imagination is shown to be real and effective), while remaining absolutely mysterious and meaningless in terms of adequate knowledge.[61] Thus resolved in the first, passionate, segment of knowledge, the Mosaic theological-political prophecy opens up to the secularisation of the *imperium* that Hobbes had located at the time of Saul's election, when God would have withdrawn from the world, leaving humans at the mercy of themselves, awaiting his return.[62] The integral 'humanity' of political power, which in Hobbes is nothing but a 'parenthesis' within the direct exercise of divine authority onto human beings, becomes in Spinoza a permanent *datum*, a subject of scientific investigation.

Even a miracle can be reconciled with rational knowledge. The exceptional events recounted in the Scripture, such as extraordinary and voluntary interventions by God, are in fact nothing but *opus naturae*, natural facts that are either not adequately understood by humans or narrated in 'poetic' terms in order to arouse devotion and admiration in the soul of the people – and to terrorise the armies of the enemy.[63] So, for example, according to the Jew's vulgar geocentric notions, common at the time of Joshua, a longer day than usual becomes the arrest of the course of the sun and the moon by decree of a divine being, demonstrating his superior strength and power over of the gods of the enemy: '[s]o partly because of religion and partly because of preconceived opinions they conceived and recounted the affair far differently than it really could have happened'.[64] The erroneous conception of a miracle as an event that disrupts and contradicts the laws of nature arises from ignorance of the true causes of phenomena, and the consequent naive belief 'that God does nothing so long as nature acts according to its usual order. Conversely, they think the power of nature and natural causes are

---

[60] See Caporali 2014: 71–105. On religion in Machiavelli see Tenenti 1978.
[61] *TTP* I, 21; *CWS* II, 83.
[62] See *Lev*, III, 35 and 40, 332–9 and 382–92. For a general comparison between Spinozan and Hobbesian biblical hermeneutics, see Osier 1987 and Walther 1992.
[63] *TTP* VI, 29; *CWS* II, 159.
[64] *TTP* VI, 56; *CWS* II, 165.

inactive.'⁶⁵ But the power of nature (*naturae potentia*) is 'the divine power and virtue itself', which in turn coincides with its essence: an infinite power, such as to exclude any illusory possibility of 'derogation', and any inadmissible faculty of 'exception'. To accept that God works against the laws of nature would mean accepting that he acts against himself: 'nothing would be more absurd than that'.⁶⁶ If, moreover, a miracle could really be configured as an extraordinary event, inaccessible to knowing *per causas*, the paradoxical situation would arise whereby precisely what most intimately belongs to the divine would confuse us about its real consistency:

> [s]o it is far from true that miracles (understood as works contrary to the order of nature) show us the existence of God. On the contrary, they would make us doubt his existence, since without them we could be absolutely certain of his existence, i.e., when we know that all things in nature follow a fixed and immutable order.⁶⁷

Always fed by ignorance, the *superstitio* of the miracle refers to the anthropocentric illusion of a God endowed with a power similar to that of kings, a God who defeats and subjugates nature because of humans, in order either to help or to oppose them, to reward or to punish what is the sole aim of the universe, the only beings who are truly 'analogous' to him. But anyone who 'is even a little wiser than the common people are' knows full well that 'God has neither a right hand nor a left hand, that he neither moves nor is at rest, that he is not in a place, but is absolutely infinite, and that all the perfections are contained in him.'⁶⁸ A *Deus* conceived *sive Natura* (the only truly

---

⁶⁵ *TTP* VI, 2; *CWS* II, 152.
⁶⁶ *TTP* VI, 9; *CWS* II, 154.
⁶⁷ *TTP* VI, 19; *CWS* II, 156–7.
⁶⁸ *TTP* VI, 58; *CWS* II, 165. Something similar can be found in Galileo: '[f]rom this follows, that whenever anyone, in exposing it, always wanted to stop to its bare letter, could – erroneously – detect in the Scriptures not only contradictions and propositions remote from the truth, but serious heresies and even blasphemies: then it would also be necessary to give God feet and hands and eyes, and no less corporal and human affections like anger, repentance, hatred, and even sometimes the forgetfulness of past things and the ignorance of future ones. The propositions dictated by the Holy Spirit were thus proffered by the sacred writers so as to accommodate themselves to the capacity of the vulgar and uneducated commoners. So for the benefit of those who deserve to be separated from the plebs it is necessary for wise expositors to explain their true meanings, and indicate the particular reasons why they are set down under such words. And this doctrine is so common and widespread among all theologians, that it would be superfluous to produce any evidence of it' (*GCL*, 558. My translation).

'conceivable' *Deus*) excludes the existence of any phenomenon beyond the cause-power, which for this reason would not be subject to an 'explanation', to a determinative and rational reconstruction:

> [s]o we conclude here, without qualification, that everything Scripture truly relates as having happened must have happened, as all things do, according to the laws of nature. And if anything should be found which can be conclusively demonstrated to be contrary to the laws of nature, or to have been unable to follow from them, we must believe without reservation that it has been added to the Sacred Texts by sacrilegious men. For whatever is contrary to nature is contrary to reason; and what is contrary to reason is absurd, and therefore to be rejected.[69]

Universal Faith

On the grounds of the method and of the articulation of imagination and reason that underly Spinoza's readings (as they are outlined in the first seven chapters of the book) he goes on to provide some concrete examples, taken from the Old and New Testaments. Through a close historical-philological examination (often considered as the first modern example of biblical exegesis), Spinoza comes to the conclusion that the Pentateuch – usually attributed to Moses – the book of Joshua, and that of Samuel, are all apocryphal, probably having been composed by Ezra, who simply collected different materials and stories without examining them or ordering them adequately, perhaps due to his premature death. Hence the many obscurities and the many chronological discrepancies present in these texts, further complicated by gaps, interpolations, and overlaps that occurred over time.[70] The same goes for the book of Daniel, only a small part of which can be considered authentic, since the rest probably originated from the Chaldean chroniclers.[71] The doubts, the contradictions, and the textual uncertainties would not, however, concern the central and essential core of all Scripture: its moral teachings (*moralia documenta*), preserved intact in their transparent simplicity, unamenable to divergent interpretations due to their transparent and immediate comprehensibility.[72] The exegetical exemplifications of the Old Testament, in substance, remain firmly attached to the fundamental

[69] *TTP* VI, 51; *CWS* II, 163–4.
[70] See *TTP* VIII and IX.
[71] See *TTP* X.
[72] *TTP* IX, 32; *CWS* II, 217.

objective of this part of the treatise, which makes obedience the purpose of faith and captures its essential content in a few core principles, clear and universally acceptable, and not passed through the sieve of an interpretation that would simply decode their outer shell, i.e., the poetic-imaginative frame within which they are expressed. The New Testament marks the 'historic' passage to such a universalisation: a turning point propelled by a markedly 'philosophical' reading of the figure of Christ, well beyond the *Scriptura per scripturam* principle, which the author of the text often takes as an object of critique.

From 'prophet' to 'doctor', as we move from imagination to science, if Moses 'speaks' with God, still relating to Him in a bodily manner ('through voice', 'face to face', still by way of imagination, yet the most 'true' and authoritative of its prophetic forms), Christ is the wise man who communicates with the divine 'with his mind': '[a]nd in this sense we can also say that God's Wisdom, that is, a Wisdom surpassing human wisdom, assumed a human nature in Christ, and that Christ was the way to salvation'.[73] This is all that the Scriptures can teach, and every other element added by the Church is both incomprehensible and unjustified. The prudent and somewhat reticent expressions employed by Spinoza in the *TTP* become much clearer and more explicit in his epistolary exchange with Oldenburg, who presses him on the subject. Is Christ the '*Redemptor*' and the only '*hominum Mediator*'?[74] He is, but only in the sense that God's eternal wisdom (the knowledge of power (*potential*), of nature-substance) is manifested in all things, and in particular in the human mind and – 'most of all' – in Jesus Christ. Without wisdom, in fact, there is no full *beatitudo* nor any notion of good and evil, of the true and the false:

> [a]s for what certain Churches add to this – that God assumed a human nature – I warned expressly that I don't know what they mean. Indeed, to confess the truth, they seem to me to speak no less absurdly than if someone were to say to me that a circle has assumed the nature of a square.[75]

But doesn't the Gospel explicitly claim that Christ has risen, and that God became incarnate in him?[76] Spinoza argues that the resurrection only serves to represent metaphorically the singular example of holiness provided

---

[73] *TTP* I, 23; *CWS* II, 84.
[74] *Ep.* LXXI (Henry Oldenburg to Spinoza); *CWS* II, 464.
[75] *Ep.* LXXIII (to Henry Oldenburg); *CWS* II, 468.
[76] *Ep.* LXXIV (Henry Oldenburg to Spinoza); *CWS* II, 469–70.

by Jesus, in both life and in death. In fact, words and rhetorical figures of oriental languages cannot be mechanically transposed into European languages:

> [h]owever that may be, do you believe that when Scripture says that God manifested himself in a Cloud, or that he dwelt in the Tabernacle, and in the Temple, God himself took on the nature of a Cloud, or a Tabernacle, or a temple? But this is the most Christ said of himself: that he was the temple of God, because, as I said in my letter, God manifested himself most in Christ. To express this more powerfully, John said that the word became flesh.[77]

But how is it possible to accept Christ's passion – his death, burial, and resurrection – only in a symbolic and non-literal way, which was 'painted with such lively and genuine colors'? And how can this allegorical interpretation be reconciled with the principle that nothing should be said about Scripture if not what can be undoubtedly found in it?[78]

> [h]owever that may be, I accept Christ's passion, death, and burial literally, as you do, but his resurrection, allegorically. I grant, certainly, that the Evangelists relate the resurrection too in such detail that we can't deny that they themselves believed that the body of Christ was resurrected and ascended into heaven, where he sits on the right hand of God [. . .] Nevertheless, they could have been deceived about this.[79]

That Christian religion and its truth as a whole rests on the dogma (*articulum*) of the resurrection is a problem for Oldenburg the believer, not for Spinoza the philosopher, so that if you '[t]ake this away ... the mission of Christ Jesus and his heavenly Teaching both collapse'.[80] Christ, in his 'flesh' and in his 'person', is not a necessary mediator between man and God, because the paths to wisdom are infinite, as are the chains of things and the nature of substance. Jesus is the wise man who teaches by means of persuasion and who instructs all humanity, by means of reason, about the

---

[77] *Ep.* LXXV (to Henry Oldenburg); *CWS* II, 473.
[78] *Ep.* LXXVII (Henry Oldenburg to Spinoza); *CWS* II, 479. And see Zac 1965: 199. My translation: 'But it is also indisputable that this conception of Christ does not derive in any way from the Interpretation of Scripture by itself, but from an adaptation of the Gospel to Spinozism. Oldenburg was therefore right to warn him that he was unlikely to convince the Christian, even the most liberal.'
[79] *Ep.* LXXVIII (to Henry Oldenburg); *CWS* II, 481.
[80] *Ep.* LXXIX (Henry Oldenburg to Spinoza); *CWS* II, 483.

same, very simple moral principles that the prophets imposed on the Jewish people alone as commandments, strengthening their authority and their fear of external signs and hardships.[81] Between the Old and New Testament – between the 'prophet' and the 'apostle' – there is the same difference that distinguishes Moses from Christ: the apostles preach as 'doctors'; they do not command, but rather demonstrate, argue, and convince. They were certainly prophets too, in the sense that they also operated through the use of imagination (for example in the case of the resurrection). But, more generally, they resorted to reasoning, so much so that – although preached by means of images and parables, telling the 'history' of the sage-saviour in a way that does not fall within the sphere of influence of *ratio* – 'by the natural light everyone can easily appreciate' the most important themes of their religion 'which, like the whole of Christ's teaching, consist chiefly of moral lessons' like Matthew's summaries in the sermon of the mount.[82] External, and in many ways opposed, to the dogmatic cornerstones of the Christian tradition, the universalisation that Spinoza attributes to the New Testament (the ecumenical argumentation of a 'Catholic' morality, addressed to the whole of humanity), plays a strategic role within the *TTP*, a connecting function between the negative moment of the traditional and authoritarian theological-political paradigm and the positive construction – the definition of a new, possible convergence – characterised by the supremacy of reason over faith, whose essential message can now definitively be taken as an object of rational inquiry.

Spinoza explains that

> [w]hat is called sacred and divine is what is destined for the practice of piety and religion. It will be sacred only so long as men use it in a religious manner. If they cease to be pious, at the same time it too ceases to be sacred.[83]

Once the question of divine *inspiratio* is framed in the 'affective' terms of a prophetic imagination, the whole exegetical procedure then aims to show the 'instrumental' meaning – the exquisitely human and contingent sense

---

[81] On the figure of Christ in the *TTP* see Matheron 1971, Zac 1965: 190–9, and Breton 1979: 132–9.

[82] *TTP* XI, 15; *CWS* II, 245. And see *TTP* XVIII, 1: through the Apostles, God revealed that his covenant is no longer written in ink, 'but written on the heart, by the spirit of God'; *CWS* II, 322. On the figure of Jesus Christ in Spinoza see Bettini 2005.

[83] *TTP* XII, 9; *CWS* II, 250.

– of the 'sacredness' attributable to Scripture. Only human practice (*usum*) adjudicates what is *sacer*: '[i]f they should be so organised that, according to their usage, they move the people reading them to devotion, then those words will be sacred. So will a book written with the words organised that way.' When such a function is lost, the words (*verba*) lose their significance and the text is completely neglected, 'then neither the words nor the book will be of any use. They will lose their holiness', thus becoming nothing but 'paper and ink'.[84] The Bible is not a work of God (*opus Dei*) (in the sense of being the product of a precise and specific divine intention), as if a certain number of volumes had descended upon humans by an act of heavenly transmission: this an idea that, on the philosophical level, would promote a return to imaginary conceptions of a personal God and of humans being made in his image and likeness. Moreover, on the historical-philological level it would be unable to explain, among other things, the random and different periods in which the texts were written, the need for four evangelists, or the incontrovertible fact that the books were assigned a sacred status – one among many human disputes – by the authority of councils.[85] Scripture can be understood as the word of God only insofar as it contains, in the form of a moral precept, the universal divine law: 'to love God above all else, and to love your neighbour as yourself'.[86] This is the Bible's only certain and constant teaching, which always remained intact, not consumed by the wear and tear of the times and uncorrupted by human malice. The Scripture 'does not contain lofty speculations, or philosophical matters, but only the simplest things'[87] understandable even by dimmer minds; demanding of humans only obedience, they condemn transgression, not ignorance.[88] 'The intellectual, or, exact, knowledge of God', does not pertain to faith.[89] The evangelical doctrine commands us to believe in God and to adore him, that is, to obey him. His law is that of love, the one commandment of the only true catholic religion, the sole and simple *fundamentum* of universal faith: 'God exists, i.e., there is a supreme being, supremely just and merciful, or a model of true life. Anyone who doesn't know, or doesn't believe, that God exists cannot obey him or know him as a Judge.'[90] This general assumption, this sort of 'moral axiom', can be articulated in a few other universally understandable

---

[84] *TTP* XII, 11 and 13; *CWS* II, 250 and 251.
[85] *TTP* XII, 28; *CWS* II, 254.
[86] *TTP* XII, 34; *CWS* II, 255.
[87] *TTP* XIII, 4; *CWS* II, 257.
[88] *TTP* XIII, 6; *CWS* II, 258.
[89] *TTP* XIII, 9; *CWS* II, 259.
[90] *TTP* XIV, 25; *CWS* II, 268. See also *TTP* V, 38; *CWS* II, 148.

and acceptable *principia*: that God, a supreme and just merciful entity, exists; that he is unique; that he is present everywhere and manifests himself in all things; that he holds a supreme *jus* over everything; that his worship consists only in love of one's neighbour; that those who will follow him in observing this prescription will be saved while the others will be lost in the slavery of passions; and that he forgives the sins of those who repent.[91] That is all faith needs, nothing more: it is not necessary to establish 'what God is' and if He is a 'model' for human beings 'because he has a just and merciful heart, or because all things exist and act through him'; if he is 'everywhere according to his essence or according to his power'; if 'he directs things from freedom or by a necessity of nature'; if he 'prescribes laws as a prince or teaches them as eternal truths'; if human beings obey him 'from freedom of the will or from the necessity of the divine decree'; or finally if the reward for the good and the punishment for the wicked is 'natural or supernatural'. Reason can directly answer all these questions, being the only faculty that knows, in a true and adequate way, the essence of God, the causal nature of the God-Nature-Substance.[92] To the point that 'someone who is not familiar with them' but 'nevertheless knows', someone who is able to know by means of natural light, 'is completely blessed' even if ignoring the revelation. Indeed, he or she would be more blessed than the vulgus, since 'in addition to true opinions, he has a clear and distinct conception'.[93]

But if this is so: 'then do we believe it?'[94] That is to say, if theology aims to achieve obedience and only philosophy is concerned with science, what is the purpose of obeying and of believing? Or rather, how is it possible to be certain that faith too can lead to authentic *beatitudo*? As Spinoza asks:

> [i]f we embrace it without reason, like blind men, then we too act foolishly and without judgment. On the other hand, if we want to maintain that we can demonstrate this foundation rationally, then Theology will be a part of Philosophy, and ought not to be separated from it.[95]

---

[91] *TTP* XIV, 26–8; *CWS* II, 268–9. Concerning the influence that Spinozan 'universal faith' may have had on the deism of the Enlightenment tradition (especially when it comes to extracting from faith a core that is not automatically rational but in any case compatible with rationality), see Vernière 1954, who considers Spinoza a common and 'contemporary' source of both French and English deism (indeed he is often considered as the only and fundamental source of the former).

[92] *TTP* XIV, 31; *CWS* II, 269–70.

[93] *TTP* V, 40; *CWS* II, 149. See also *TTP* VII, 67ff.; *CWS* II, 185–6.

[94] *TTP* XV, 26; *CWS* II, 278.

[95] *TTP* XV, 26–7; *CWS* II, 278.

The 'dogma' of obedience cannot be directly based on reason, which is foreign to the logic of obedience. And yet the natural light can highlight the *moral* utility and the *social* convenience of that dogma:

> [e]veryone, without exception, can obey. But only a very few (compared with the whole human race) acquire a habit of virtue from the guidance of reason alone. So, if we didn't have this testimony of Scripture, we would doubt nearly everyone's salvation.[96]

Adequate knowledge can explain the passions, it can moderate and control them – but it can never have complete 'reason' over them: no one, in fact, is bound by nature to acquire a philosophical knowledge of God (of the substance and the mechanisms that regulate his eternal, self-necessitating power), so that '[m]en, women, children, everyone in fact, is equally able to obey on command. But not everyone is equally able to be wise.'[97] Moreover, even where *ratio* prevails, the fire of the *pati* can never be completely extinguished, neither in the individual nor in the social body. The answer to the 'why believe?' (*cur credere*) question is actually implicit in the effort to lead theology back to the imagination. Unlike science, however, faith does not exclude any form of knowledge: faith is 'thinking such things about God that if you had no knowledge of them, obedience to God would be destroyed, whereas if you are obedient to God, you necessarily have these thoughts'.[98] Some kind of knowledge is also implicit in the act of obeying, just as not every passion increases *pati*. Once revelation is understood as imagination-passion, its (at least partial) irreducibility is posited, as well as its inevitable subordination to adequate knowledge. From here, in fact, the whole Spinozist interpretative parabola is meant to address the 'critical' definition (critical to selection and to rational argumentation) of an essentially 'positive' nucleus of faith, of its fundamental and universal content, different in status and purpose from the truths of science and yet in some way comparable and reconcilable to them through 'practice'. The result is a catholic religion which accepts, through the spontaneous immediacy of obedience, compatible moral principles and those 'operative' consequences that cannot be recomposed with the principles and the consequences of true wisdom, reached by means of long and complex mathematical concatenations of

---

[96] *TTP* XV, 45; *CWS* II, 282.
[97] *TTP* XIII, 16; *CWS* II, 260.
[98] *TTP* XIV, 13; *CWS* II, 266.

truth.[99] Indeed, 'universal faith' presents itself as an active 'passion' that guides individuals towards beatitude, as well as helping the form of society whose extraordinary power is well known by reason: the *imperium* that is most capable of unleashing *energeia*, of multiplying power. If obedience is a 'practical' matter, one concerning actions (*opera*) rather than opinions, the true Antichrists will be those 'who persecute honest men who love Justice, because they disagree with them'.[100] As for the followers of the various Christian denominations:

> we don't want to accuse [them] of impiety just because they accommodate the words of Scripture to their own opinions. For as Scripture was accommodated to the grasp of the common people, so everyone is permitted to accommodate it to his own opinions, if he sees that in that way he can obey God more wholeheartedly in matters of justice and loving-kindness.

Rather, they must be condemned when they do not want 'to grant this same freedom to others', and rather they want to persecute 'as God's enemies, everyone who does not think as they do'.[101] The articles of universal faith, being the true soul of Scripture, in their extreme extension unify all religious confessions and should therefore allow the coexistence of all the different sects, everything else being inessential and secondary. As a point of greater contiguity within the virtue of love (and this is no coincidence, since it is the affect in which activity and passivity are at their most overlapping,

---

[99] Mignini 1995b: 77. My translation: '[b]etween revealed religion, purified by its superstitious forms, and rational religion there is therefore no difference in content (it is the same precepts of reason), but rather an essential or formal difference, deriving from the different kind of knowledge on which they are based and concerning the perfection to which they lead. The first [...] is based on imaginative knowledge, and the perfection to which it leads is that of a heteronomous individual, obedient to others. The second, on the other hand, is founded on reason and intellect, and the perfection it expresses is that of an autonomous individual obedient to himself, that is to the laws of universal Nature, expressed by his own nature.' On the 'double' language of the *TTP* and on the two levels of reading (passional-theological – albeit rationalising – and philosophical) see Strauss 1947, as well as Tosel 1984: 116ff. Strauss's methodological lesson is one of the most relevant contributions to Spinozan studies of the last decades, far more extensive also than the pre-modern theological-political framework to which it is formally and polemically opposed. On this topic see Caporali 2016.

[100] *TTP* XIV, 18; *CWS* II, 268.

[101] *TTP* XIV, 3–4; *CWS* II, 264.

and indeed interchangeable), the effective convergence of reason and faith finally leads to politics, acting as the premise for a precise political solution. The emancipated classes and the more 'reasonable' believers – those belonging to the intellectual aristocracy and to less intransigent confessions – are pitted against those religious hierarchies and those civil institutions that, supported by the *vulgus*, continually threaten freedom. From the initial decomposition of theology and wisdom to their 'functional' aggregation, we have never lost sight of the contemporary relevance and the substantial 'political character' of the *Treatise*, its belonging and taking part in the dramatic challenges of history.

The Absolute of the *Respublica*

Spinoza writes:

> [s]o far we've taken care to separate Philosophy from Theology and to show the freedom of philosophizing which [Theology] grants to everyone. Now it's time for us to ask how far this freedom of thought, and of saying what you think, extends in the best Republic.[102]

The connection between the theological and the political parts of the *Treatise* is made explicit by seizing the opportunity for a more precise configuration of freedom with respect to authority, by the need for a more precise definition of the statute, and by the contribution of freedom and its actual consistency – its real boundaries – towards determining a republic as being *optima*. Such an investigation requires a preliminary (or at least contextual) exploration of the *imperium* and of its foundations, beginning with the natural right of everyone. The equation 'right = power' – realised out of the two constants of connectivity on the one hand, and the preponderance of passions on the other – implies the undeniable necessity of political power: '[n]ow if nature had so constituted men that they desired nothing except what true reason teaches them to desire, then of course a society could exist without laws'. It would be enough to teach the authentic 'moral teachings', and to make sure that everyone sought his or her own advantage 'voluntarily, wholeheartedly, and in a manner worthy of a free man'. Instead, human nature is very different, because everyone's actions derive 'from immoderate desire': '[t]hat's why no society can continue in existence without authority and force, and hence, laws which moderate and restrain men's immoderate

[102] *TTP* XVI, 1; *CWS* II, 282.

desires and unchecked impulses'.[103] If *societas* is implicit in the 'relativity' of right/*conatus*, then the political order is inherent in the fundamentally 'passional' structure of that very relativity. A 'powerful' authority is inscribed in the constitution of the *jus*, starting from the tension between 'in itself' and '*in alio*', and in the expression of this mutual determination under the incoherent and chaotic pressure of the passions/affects – *plerumque* – far more, and more often, than under the clear and constant 'guidance of reason'.[104] There can be '[n]o society . . . without authority and force':[105] the duplicity of right/power (*potentia*) implies the absolute simultaneity of society and power, which excludes any deductive sequence and any logical-historical priority. There is no priority of the 'social' over the 'political': neither in the Aristotelian-medieval sense of harmonious and spontaneous spheres of coexistence (from the family nucleus to the universal Christian republic), nor in the modern/liberal conception, which rigidly patrols the origin and the boundaries of the *imperium* according to the pre-defined needs of civil society. But neither is there a priority of power (*potestas*) over *civitas*, be it the theological *remedium iniquitatis* of Augustinian-Lutheran descent, or one deriving from the more 'decisionist' side of Hobbes. The interactive and the passional nature of the *conatus* constantly recall political subjection and its irreducible determination, its irrepressible 'physicality':

> [b]ecause we've already shown that [each person's] natural right is determined only by his power, it follows that as much of his power as he transfers to another, whether because he's forced to, or voluntarily, so much of his right does he also necessarily give up to the other person. It follows also that if a person has the supreme power, which enables him to compel everyone by force, and restrain them by fear of the supreme punishment (which everyone, without exception, fears), then that person has the supreme right over everyone.[106]

The relationship of domination is not independent from the *jus*, as something other than the natural intersection of powers (*potentiae*). Given the predominance of the affective-passional dimension, between the relations of the *conatus* there is always a decisive imbalance, a fundamental gap, in virtue

---

[103] *TTP* V, 20–2; *CWS* II, 144. See also *Ethics* IV, 37 Schol. 2; *CWS* I, 566–7, and *TP* VI, 3; *CWS* II, 532.
[104] *TTP* XVI, 21; *CWS* II, 286.
[105] *TTP* V, 22; *CWS* II, 159.
[106] *TTP* XVI, 24; *CWS* II, 287.

of which an individual or a collective subject concentrates on itself the power, the *surplus* of energy suitable for the 'government' of human beings and for the determination and 'normalisation' (regulation, normative management) of the domains of their *co-existence*. Far from the total negativity of pure Hobbesian powerlessness, this actuality of power (*potestas*) – its emanating from the interweaving of the *conatus* and from the living intersection of 'efforts' – explains both its absolute logic and its effective limits, its virtual insuperability and its practical determination:

> [f]or whoever has the supreme power, whether it's one person, or a few, or everyone, it's certain that he possesses the supreme right to command whatever he wishes. Moreover, it's certain that whoever has transferred his power to defend himself to another, whether voluntarily or because compelled by force, has completely yielded him his natural right, and consequently has decided to obey him in absolutely everything.[107]

Political power, grounded on the triumph of a power (*potentia*) aimed at directing another force, i.e., on the affirmation of a force that controls and directs other forces, is presented as the source of every other positive connotation of *societas*. A *jus civile privatum* can only emerge from *imperium* – 'the freedom each person has to preserve himself in his state, which is determined by the edicts of the supreme 'power, and is defended only by its authority' – and only by means of such a standard it is possible to evaluate the *iniuria* (the injuries that a citizen or a subject suffers from another 'contrary to the civil law, or to an edict of the supreme power'), to ascertain justice and injustice, which are realised in the correct or perverted and instrumental application of what belongs to each person on the basis of the *jus civile*, to judge a public crime (a *crimen laesae majestatis*), or to recognise the face of the enemy, or those who live outside the State 'without recognizing the state's sovereignty either as an ally or as a subject. For it is not hatred which makes an enemy of the state, but right.'[108] Here we clearly discern the modern supremacy of the political, in close proximity with the Machiavellian and above all Hobbesian ontological primacy which the public *potestas* assumes with respect to any other civil or moral imperative: '[f]or if the state is destroyed, nothing good can remain, but everything is at risk'.[109] The act of *pietas* which, aimed at the individual, causes damage to

---

[107] *TTP* XVI, 38; *CWS* II, 290.
[108] *TTP* XVI, 40ff.; *CWS* II, 290–1.
[109] *TTP* XIX, 22; *CWS* II, 336.

the State, represents the utmost impiety. On the contrary, nothing can be said to be 'impious to anyone' when it is done in view of public '*conservatio*'.[110] It is from this vantage point, that of the 'foundational' nature of the political order, that Spinoza takes a stance within the great European debate around the *jus circa sacra*, a controversy which articulates the emergence and the troubled historical-theoretical emancipation of the 'sovereignty' of a modern State from religious patronage or sectarian dependence: 'external religious worship and every exercise of piety must be accommodated to the peace and preservation of the republic'.[111] Even the *jus divinum* has no consistency outside the republic. God, in fact, does not exercise any direct authority, nor does he have any 'special kingdom', save 'through those who have sovereignty'. This 'imposition' is of a determinative-modal nature, since the sovereign, like everything else, is nothing but a *res*, an actual and necessary explication of the one substance-cause-power.[112] Besides, since 'in matters of religion' humans are more than ever exposed to error, to opinion, and to conflict:

> It is certain that if no one were bound by law to obey the supreme power in the things he thought pertained to religion, then the right of the state would depend on the varying judgment and affect of each person.[113]

Nor can there be a real contrast, as if between two homogeneous and independent entities: the *jus civile* of supreme power (*summa potestas*) and the 'revealed law' of Scripture. The latter, as we have seen, has no force before its Mosaic political realisation, i.e., before the 'pact' stipulated between God and the Jewish nation, so that outside of that particular historical situation it is no more binding than any other behavioural/prudential[114] norm. But also,

---

[110] *TTP* XIX, 22; *CWS* II, 337.
[111] *TTP* XIX, 21; *CWS* II, 336.
[112] *TTP* XIX, 6; *CWS* II, 333.
[113] *TTP* XVI, 63; *CWS* II, 295.
[114] *TTP* XVI, 58: '[s]omeone may still insist that the supreme powers are bound by this divine law just as much as subjects are. We've said, on the contrary, that they retain their natural right, and that by right everything is permitted to them. This whole difficulty arises not so much because of the state of nature as because of the right of nature. To remove it I say that in the state of nature each person is bound by revealed law in the same way he's bound to live according to the dictates of sound reason: it's more advantageous to him and necessary for his salvation. If he doesn't want to do this, he's permitted to act at his own risk'; *CWS* II, 293–4.

because the universal content of this *jus* – its message of love and charity – must primarily be in service of the republic, without which no relationship between human beings is possible:

> [f]or since we are bound by God's command to cherish everyone, without exception, in accordance with piety, and to harm no one, it follows that no one is permitted to aid one person at the expense of another, much less at the expense of the whole state.

But no private citizen can know what is best for the State 'except by the decrees of the supreme powers, who are the only ones whose job it is to treat public business'. Therefore, 'no one can practice piety rightly, nor obey God, unless he obeys all the decrees of the supreme power'.[115] It is necessary to doggedly defend the *imperium* and its primacy, and to feel obliged to execute its *mandata* without hesitation, even if they appear *absurdissima*: in fact, in human reality, nothing is more absurd than the absence of political power, and between two evils the lesser one must always be chosen.[116] Spinoza notes that

> [p]erhaps someone will think that in this way we make subjects slaves, because he thinks someone who acts according to a command is a slave, whereas someone who governs his conduct according to his own heart is a free man.[117]

This is actually not 'absolutely' true, since those who are 'drawn by [their] own pleasure' are maximally enslaved, and unable to discern what is truly beneficial to them. If obedience then doubtlessly (*aliquo modo*) deprives us of all freedom, it does not make us slaves either: the *utilitas* of obedience is the '*actionis ratio*', the genuine distinction between subjection and servitude. When the aim of the action is not 'the advantage of the agent himself, but of the person who issues the command, then the agent is a slave, useless to himself'.[118] This universal well-being, however, cannot distinguish (as Aristotle would) one regime from another, almost functioning as a sort of extrinsic criterion, drawn from 'outside' the political order. The preliminary

---

[115] *TTP* XIX, 26; *CWS* II, 337.
[116] *TTP* XVI, 24ff; *CWS* II, 287–8.
[117] *TTP* XVI, 32; *CWS* II, 288.
[118] *TTP* XVI, 32–3; *CWS* II, 288.

and incontrovertible *datum* remains: only the supreme power[119] can ultimately be the positive interpreter of the common good.

Spinoza then proceeds to explain that

> [i]n the last Chapter we considered the right the supreme powers have to do everything, and the natural right each person has transferred to them. Though the view expressed therein agrees in no small measure with practice, and a practice could be established which approached more and more closely to the condition we described, still, it will never happen that this view does not remain, in many respects, merely theoretical.[120]

Propelled by a relationship of force-power (*potentia*), political power appears to be constantly aimed towards self-affirmation, towards attesting itself (*testatum*) *in omnia* according to the law of the *conatus* without ever succeeding in truly unfolding itself *in omnia*. For that would entail the loss of itself and of its very source of energy: otherness and resistance will always remain implicit – albeit in a thinned and minimised form – in its 'relational' nature. From the standpoint of the 'subjects' of a power, then, '[n]o one will ever be able to transfer to another his power, or consequently, his right, in such a way that he ceases to be a man', up to the annihilation of that unity of mind and body which represents his or her being a 'human-mode', as well as that of power (*potestas*): 'there will never be a supreme power who can get everything to happen just as he wishes'.[121] Supported by the intersections of force, the *jus* of political power is preserved as long as its *pre-dominance* is effectively preserved: 'no one stronger will be bound to obey him unless he wishes to'.[122] This is precisely why it is impossible to govern only by means of violence and fear:

> [s]o only very rarely can it happen that the supreme powers command great absurdities. To look out for their own interests and retain their sovereignty, it is incumbent on them most of all to consult the common good, and to direct everything according to the dictate.[123]

---

[119] TTP XIX, 24; CWS II, 337. For a comparison with Hobbes' strategy, so far wholly analogous, see the third part of the *Leviathan*. On Spinoza's position in the debate around the *jus circa sacra*, see Solari 1930.
[120] TTP XVII, 1; CWS II, 296.
[121] TTP XVII, 2; CWS II, 296.
[122] TTP XVI, 24; CWS II, 287.
[123] TTP XVI, 29; CWS II, 288.

Once again, nothing overlaps with – nothing precedes – the *vis* and the *conatus* (the essence of the human); there is no anticipation (religious, moral, cultural) of political action in its naked essence. It is the logic of *conservatio* that pushes power in the direction of stability and productivity towards the common good. As a relationship of power, the political order is always direct, 'face to face': it is a relationship between subjects and *imperium* which leaves no space for 'strangers' and unconstrained and undetermined constituents. In the Spinozist context, Hobbes' 'third' (the sovereign to whom everyone willingly relinquishes their *jus* without conditions and without return) appears as an *escamotage*, a metaphysical proliferation unrealistically positioned to guard the confines of 'physical' intersections, a juridical cover fabricated as a fictitious safeguard for fictitious boundaries: 'In a situation of force against force, it will not necessarily be the Sovereign who will prevail.'[124] The sovereign always returns to his subjects. He is always forced to do so, since he fears them: '[b]ut if those who were most feared had the greatest authority, then the subjects of Tyrants would surely have it. For they are most feared by their Tyrants'.[125] The heart of the reciprocal relationship between *imperium* and *societas* beats the rhythm of a double circulation of fear. On the one hand, the subject's fear of power and of the arbitrariness of *auctoritas* (fear of the public *vis*, which remains the fundamental vehicle for the realisation of their own forces/powers (*potentiae*)). On the other, power's fear of its subjects, in the awareness, or instinctive premonition, that its own permanence, its own unlimited consisting and persisting always depends on the threshold of the subject's fear.[126] Nor is it enough to govern 'well'. The predominantly passional, protean, and inconstant nature of human beings makes it insufficient to look at the common good in order to obtain external obedience and, above all, to shape an inner disposition of the soul towards obedience. The *reges*, then, try to construe themselves as 'substantially' different, thus erecting a sacred barrier between them and their subjects, now presenting themselves as descendants of the gods, now as direct interpreters and vicars of divine will on earth. And yet: 'we've never reached the point where a state is not in more danger from its own citizens than from its enemies, and where the rulers don't fear their citizens more than their enemies.'[127] The recurrent discovery of 'equality', the reciprocal referring and

---

[124] Moreau 2021: 385.
[125] *TTP* XVII, 8; *CWS* II, 298.
[126] On the double track of the 'fear of the masses' (the fear both felt and aroused by the multitude of subjects), see Balibar 1985: 354ff. and 1990: 51.
[127] *TTP* XVII, 17; *CWS* II, 299.

intertwining within the *continuum* of *jus/potentia*, maintains a perpetually open double tension, both constitutive and oppositional, between the sovereign and the 'subjects', between commands and obedience, conservation and change. The variables introduced by the forms of the *imperium* play a decisive role within this tension.

The Free Republic

If one conceives the political order as a relationship of strength/power (*potentia*), it becomes impractical to approach it in terms of 'justification' or 'condemnation'. The moment the *summa potestas* is wholly assimilated by the dynamics of the *conatus* and of *conservatio*, any possibility of a classification and arrangement of its variants becomes impossible, starting from an archetypal order, a founding value, an immediately and spontaneously shared 'ethics' which would allow, as happens in the classical model, an evaluation according to the pre-established criteria of goodness and degeneration, of integrity and corruption. An evaluation cannot be grounded on power's greater or lesser closeness to the perfection of a 'foundation' that no longer exists, but only on its actual 'functionality'. Supported by power, the outcomes of the modern political order will not be 'better' or more 'just', but they will be 'better/stronger/more efficient' when they grant greater operativity and productivity to that force/power (*potentia*).

This inessential essence, this 'relative' nature, keeps the *imperium* on the hot coals of an unavoidable bipolarity. The political order is absolutely oriented towards its own *conservatio* (the imperative of maintaining and persevering itself as a form of supremacy and command); but, in order to achieve such *conservation*, it is also absolutely projected out of itself (since there is no command without obedience, and no supremacy without subjugation). The political order thus experiences in full the duplicity of the mode, which makes it both the same and different – under the same conditions – to all other singular determinations. Power (*potestas*) – the 'public' – concentrates upon itself the extraordinary surplus necessary to support the 'weapons' and the 'laws': a neutralised force, stolen from other individuals (or from a domain, a sphere of human activity), which are therefore 'de-prived' (*privati*) of it. And yet power is still a *res*, either individual or collective. There is still something or someone, a modal reality, which by its very nature is interdependent and interacting with all other realities. The separation between *imperium* and *societas* has no fundamental value (that is, it does not arise from a presupposed principle, one able to characterise them), but only a functional one, since the concentration of 'public' power has to support and to allow the diffusion and the expansion of 'private' power, of that 'energy' that the politician is called upon to guarantee at the very moment in which he or she undermines its authority. Hence the necessity of mutual fear with respect to which the peculiarity and the originality of the Spinozist position within the modern political spectrum is better understood.

Compare Hobbes' position:

> [n]either do the conveniences or inconveniences which are found to be more in one kind of government than another, arise from hence, namely, because the government itself, or the administration of its affairs, are better committed to one than many; or on the other side, to many than to some few. For government is the *power*, the administration of it is the *act*. Now the *power* in all kinds of government is equal; the *acts* only differ, that is to say, the *actions* and *motions* of a commonweal, as they flow from the deliberations of many or few, of skilful or impertinent men.[128]

Hobbes was perhaps the first theorist who knew how to look at the non-substantial nature of the diversity of *imperium* and *societas* and, consequently, at the exquisitely operational-preferential character of every analysis of forms of government. His explicit preference for the monarchy indeed originates – as a reaction to such an awareness – from the assumption that the more a State is able to exorcise its lack of grounding, the more it can manage to reify and to crystallise the relativity of difference, the more solid it will be. Hence the particular aspect of the Hobbesian *pactum* which, being binding for the contracting parties and not for the sovereign, aims to create a point of legal non-return from power (*potestas*):

> [a]nd consequently they that have already instituted a commonwealth, being thereby bound by covenant, to own the actions, and judgments of one, cannot lawfully make a new covenant, amongst themselves, to be obedient to any other, in any thing whatsoever, without his permission.[129]

For this reason, the 'contract' is a formal guarantee against the collapse of the political order. In any case, the awareness of the exceptional origin of the norm remains well-established. That is to say, it is obvious that, ultimately, it will always be impossible to protect oneself from the 'exception'

---

[128] *De Cive*, X, 16; *EW* II, 140.
[129] *Lev*, II, 17; *EW* III, 160.

by means of the 'rule', and that in any case the 'good weapons' will arbitrate both the bad and the good laws.

Spinoza overturns the Hobbesian equation: the more the separation between State and civil society (or between public and private) is sustained, the easier it will be to regulate its secret (*arcanum*), its *unmotivated* character and its functional (and non-substantial) constitution. It will be easier to amplify its resonant circularity in the void, bringing into the open the abyss of absence and of *non-origin*. Every rigid barrier between the political and the social produces a dangerous increase in the threshold of fear. It is therefore necessary, to the extent that it is possible, to keep the communication open and the borders permeable, up to the – virtual, tendential – limit of the annihilation of the difference itself:

> [f]rom these [foundations] it follows, first, that either the whole society should hold sovereignty as a body (if this can be done), so that everyone is bound to be subject to himself, and no one is bound to be subject to his equal – or else, if a few men have sovereignty, or one man alone, he ought to have something above ordinary human nature. If he does not surpass ordinary human nature, he at least must strive with all his might to persuade the common people of this.[130]

Modernity *sive democratia*. Once the groundlessness of political power is posited (its 'modality', its relational character), the mechanism of accumulation and centralisation of power which it represents (the automatism of concentration and thinning of power, in which it resolves itself), inevitably produces the detritus of 'fear', whose emissions will be directly proportional to the level of corruption of power (*potestas*), and inversely proportional to the solidity and the productivity of the *imperium*. On this level, the Spinozan approach introduces a frontal caesura between the forms of 'government'. This is not a 'natural' variant, but rather a vertical alternative of efficiency, where, once again, the *facere* presents itself as the only essence, and the *operari* as the sole substance.

Conducted on the ground of freedom, the opposition of monarchy and democracy – which, in the first treatise, replaces a more articulated analysis of the forms of power – is therefore motivated by both theoretical and polemical-militant reasons. The monarchic solution appears to be the one with the highest internal tensions, because it is built on the most rigid and inflexible separation of natural power into the authority of one individual,

---

[130] *TTP* V, 23; *CWS* II, 144.

on the one hand, and the bond of obedience of all the 'others' – the total submission of the 'many' – on the other. As we have seen, the monarchical system attempts to tame this inequality by adopting, more or less consciously, the strategy of an *ideological* response, so that whoever exercises the supreme power must succeed in making the subjects believe that he or she has 'something above ordinary human nature'.[131] An ever formidable *instrumentum regni*, religion provides the monarchical regime with its supreme secret, which actually consists in disguising a state of slavery as a source of salvation in the collective sacrifice for the honour and glory of a single individual.[132] The separation between divine sovereignty and the equality of the rights of all (*hominum suffragium*), as well as the conviction that the *imperium* plays God's role on earth – and is thus preserved and defended by a singular act of divine will – represents the most secure justification for this form of government. This represents the rigidity of an act of imagination, of *pati*, through which the political-theological order of the royal republic aims to cut all those (inescapable) ties of reciprocity that bind it to society, aiming at its subject's 'addiction', i.e., the consolidation of a spontaneous, unreflective, and unquestioned subjugation. As the only form of governance in which, at least potentially, human opinions can be completely influenced, the monarchical *regime*, however, runs the very serious risk of falling into the ruinous circle of death that leads from one tyrant to another. The subjects' fear would remain high and most volatile, and yet they would still be unable, even when revolting, to think of themselves as an order without a positive reference to a *rex*:

> [f]or a people accustomed to royal authority, and held in check only by that authority, will disdain a lesser authority and mock it. So if the people removes one monarch from their midst, they will have to choose another in his place (as long ago the Prophets had to). And this new monarch will be a tyrant, not because he wants to, but because he must. [. . .] If he wants to be a King, and does not want to acknowledge the people as the judge of Kings, and his master, or to rule at their pleasure, he must avenge the death of his predecessor and set a contrary example for his own benefit, so that the people will not dare to commit such a crime again.[133]

A limpid conjoining of democracy and freedom is opposed to the murky and authoritarian monarchical order, which Spinoza 'preferred to treat . . .

---

[131] Ibid.
[132] *TTP* Praef., 10; *CWS* II, 68.
[133] *TTP* XVIII, 30–1; *CWS* II, 329.

before all others, because it seemed the most natural state, and the one which approached most nearly the freedom nature concedes to everyone'.[134] The democratic solution is then presented as the only one that allows the relativity of the *imperium* to be accepted and turned into a productive force, as well as the only political form based on the substantial equality – the identity of nature (that of a power-*conatus*) – of both commanding and obeying:

> since obedience consists in someone's carrying out a command solely on the authority of the person who commands it, it follows that obedience has no place in a social order where sovereignty is in the hands of everyone and laws are enacted by common consent, and that whether the laws in such a social order are increased or diminished, the people nevertheless remains equally free, because it does not act from the authority of someone else, but by its own consent. But the opposite happens where one person alone holds sovereignty absolutely. For everyone carries out the commands of the state solely because of the authority of one person.[135]

Unlike the monarchical order, the democratic *imperium* keeps the channels of power open, because here power is exercised collegially by all, or by the great majority of citizens, up to an almost perfect continuity between the political and the civil, between 'nature' and 'art': '[i]n this way everyone remains equal, as they were before, in the state of nature'.[136] The truth is that not even democracy can disregard the need for a (functional) separation of political power from civil power, with the risk of voiding its *imperium* into a sort of complete overlap or identity with society. Rather, the democratic form succeeds in asserting the maximum circularity of the 'natural' towards the power (*potestas*), the broadest 'participation' of the civil particular (of *every* civil particular) in the political universal. Indeed, in a democratic government, 'no one so transfers his natural right to another that in the future there is no consultation with him'.[137] When all the forces that circulate within the social sphere gain access to the sphere of politics, the state secret (*arcanum imperii*) is brought to light, and the repressed power, the common ground, and the reciprocity that underlies the separation between power (*potestas*) and *societas* (and its purely operational value) is unleashed. In the monarchical and in the aristocratic order, that artic-

---

[134] *TTP* XVI, 36; *CWS* II, 239.
[135] *TTP* V, 25; *CWS* II, 144–5.
[136] *TTP* XVI, 36; *CWS* II, 289.
[137] Ibid.

ulation remains blocked, reified through simplified and fulfilled subjects, either barricaded in the fortress of their unassailable 'superiority', or caged within the iron prison of mere *pati*: a gap that hides but cannot suppress their mutual dependence, since even the mere fact of being submitted still implies – in the act of enduring such submission – a minimal degree of activity and presence. On the contrary, the free republic emanates from everyone, and its acts are guided by the majority, pushing interdependence to the highest level and, inversely, reducing fear to the lowest. In this way decisions are always taken by a large part of the republic, from which no one is ever preventively and permanently excluded. Democracy thus transforms the irrepressible connective multiplicity of that 'natural' force that can be repressed and compressed but never eliminated (for otherwise power itself would be suppressed) into a positive energy, a political fuel. And '[t]o this we may add that in a democratic state, absurdities are less to be feared. If the assembly is large, it's almost impossible that the majority of its members should agree on one absurd action'.[138] When this form of power (*potestas*) functions properly it becomes 'virtue', and it assigns a positive value to the motility and passional nature of human beings, something that a long tradition of thought (at least from Plato onwards) had considered to be the most serious threat to political order, and that for Spinoza himself, as we have already seen, represents a permanent threat to the monarch, even if he or she operates in the general interest of the State. The *cives*, adaptable and thus able to face the inevitable variations of events, are more capable of correcting public errors, thus safeguarding the stability of the *imperium* by means of their very dynamism and multiplicity – which, for the other *species* of political organisation, is considered as a subversive trait. It is likely that this idea has a Machiavellian origin: the untamed pride of the people of the republican State and the Prince's objective psychological impossibility of withstanding the inexorable variability of circumstances.[139] But this is a theme that – beyond some often-highlighted Rousseauvian assonances – does not actually permit the association of this Spinozist solution with any holistic kind of transcendent unanimous will, or any metaphysics of the

---

[138] *TTP* XVI, 30; *CWS* II, 288.
[139] See *Dis.* I, 4 and *FH* III, 1; ed. Martelli: 82–3 and 690–1. On the peculiarity of the conflict in the 'mixed' Machiavellian state see Esposito 1984: 111–78 and 179–220; Matteucci 1970; Sasso 1966: 223ff. and 1980: 455–65. The more recent Del Lucchese 2004 is very important in the context of a wide flowering of studies on Machiavelli and Spinoza. On the relationship between philosophical anthropology and political conflict in Machiavelli see Vincieri 1984: 13–46 and Zeppi 1976.

'*volonté general*'.[140] Spinoza's democracy brings the protean nature of the *populus* with all their diverse and infinite resonances, judgments, moods, interests, and passions into the field of political decision-making, thus giving it full political dignity. Qualitatively different from the substantial political unification promoted by Rousseau, Spinoza's stance is equally distinguished from the purely 'negative' dimension of the Hobbesian (but also liberal) paradigm, which is grounded on the elimination of every conflict *within* the political domain, and on the rigid separation of *imperium* and *societas*. This is a paradigm assumed, in both the *De Cive* and the *Leviathan*, as an immutable presupposition for the dynamics of the forms of government. These become dependent variables, distinct and hierarchically organised on the grounds of the internal efficacy of this liberal paradigm. While Hobbes tends to remove the insubstantial nature of the difference, Spinoza instead accepts it as a challenge, taking the impervious road of plurality, a delicate but powerful path aimed at turning conflict and diversity into a resource. Hence, from this system – which encapsulates the most profound theoretical-political layer of the treatise – comes the actualising epilogue that celebrates the value of freedom of thought and speech in a State that will prove to be all the stronger the more it limits fear, finding its ultimate and authentic *ratio* in the preservation, rather than the subjugation, of humans in perseverance, and not in the annihilation of their bodies and their minds:

> [t]he end of the Republic, I say, is not to change men from rational beings into beasts or automata, but to enable their minds and bodies to perform their functions safely, to enable them to use their reason freely, and not to clash with one another in hatred, anger or deception, or deal inequitably with one another. So the end of the Republic is really freedom.[141]

---

[140] Substantial discontinuity between Spinoza and Rousseau is addressed, among others, by Negri 1981: 97ff, on the irreducibility of *potentia* to the 'general will'; Bodei 1991: 139–40, on the relationship between authority and freedom; and Geismann 1989, on the philosophy of law. Francès 1951, Vernière 1954, and De Lachelière 1963, on the other hand, explore a fundamental equivalence between Spinozan and Rousseauvian democratic theory. Derathé 1950 and Eckstein 1944 must be remembered as historical reconstructions regarding the influence that Spinoza's thought undoubtedly exerts on that of Rousseau.

[141] *TTP* XX, 12; *CWS* II, 346.

The *Pactum*

If the *imperium* is a 'mode', no exorcism and no repression can simplify its identity or stabilise its nature. And yet, even adopting a political form that best seems to support the inessentiality of domination gives rise to troubles. What guarantees – for example – that freedom of thought and speech will not ultimately be turned against the authority of the republic, perhaps against the very freedom that the State fosters and practices as its fundamental principle? Of course, the first and most solid distinction is that between ideas and actions, for only the latter can be publicly prosecuted. But there are no doubts that in the world of the *conatus* and of power (*potentia*) there is also a practical dimension of opinions, a subversive charge of thoughts. Spinoza paraphrases Hobbes, while inverting his meaning: 'I confess, of course, that sometimes such freedom has its disadvantages. But what was ever so wisely instituted that nothing inconvenient could come from it?'[142] The non-substantial condition of the *imperium* presupposes its own *relativity* and its constitutive *precariousness*. Precisely for this reason, in the case of democracy, the problem remains: how can the mechanism that keeps its non-fundamental nature continuously revealed – institutionally kept in the open – work efficiently, until the introduction of difference and competition in its political heart? In other words: how is it possible that motility, passion, and a vast multiplicity of reasons and passions could converge to give strength to the *dominium* instead of undermining it? Whence that *reductio ad unum*, in which the republic still consists, and within which the contrasts and the conflict engendered by the '*plural*' not only do not break the pillars of the State, but indeed reinforce its 'orders'? In sum: which democracy?

> [t]he Hebrews didn't transfer their right to anyone else, but everyone surrendered his right equally, as in a Democracy, and they cried out in one voice 'whatever God says' (without any explicit mediator) 'we will do.' It follows that everyone remained completely equal by this covenant, that the right to consult God, and to receive and interpret his laws, was equal for everyone. Everyone held the whole administration of the state equally, without qualification.[143]

In the Spinozan reconstruction, the first 'historical' form of democratic *imperium* is paradoxically grounded on a 'fundamental' presupposition, starting

---

[142] *TTP* XX, 24; *CWS* II, 348.
[143] *TTP* XVII, 33; *CWS* II, 303.

from a theological-imaginative principle. After their slavery in Egypt, the Jews, following Moses' advice, decided to confer the public *dominium* not to a man but to God, thus committing to the absolute obedience of his commandments: a '*Regnum Dei*' or a '*Theocratia*'[144] in appearance; but actually a democracy *in re*: '[b]ut all these things consisted more in opinion than in fact; really the Hebrews retained the right of the state absolutely'.[145] This was a very short-lived experience, whose decisive influence, however, reverberates also in the political phase that followed. Terrified and bewildered upon hearing the voice of God (under the veneer of myth: unable to govern themselves and thus in need of a legislator, due to their long habit of servitude and the coarseness of their conditions), the Jews entrusted themselves to Moses as the sole and universally accepted interpreter of the will of God. And the 'constituent' work of the greatest of all prophets was aimed at the creation of structures, mechanisms, and institutions that would facilitate a freedom, guaranteed and protected by God's sovereign influence. After Moses' death, the Jewish State presented an architecture that, due to its theocratic origins, cannot be equated with any of the three classical forms but – in this Spinozistic reconstruction – highlights a number of elements typical of a democratic-republican order, for example, one where tribes belong to a 'city' and are 'federated' (politically united and equal because equally subject to the one God), and in which a preliminary separation between religious functions and political prerogatives as well as a certain division/articulation of powers, especially of the legislative and the judiciary, is predetermined. In this kind of political order there is a sort of popular ratification, occurring every seven years, of all normative activities, where the ruling elite and the judiciary are chosen by age and merit, rather than by birth or wealth, and where the love of citizens for their country is promoted: a sense of belonging produced by civil religiosity (which keeps all individuals absolutely free while absolutely submitting them to the divinity), and that increases with education, with the development of city militias and material utility, and with the spread of wealth, partly redistributed during the jubilee through the remission of debts. So, accustomed to pride and flexibility, the Jewish people

> easily corrected itself in disasters, turned to God, and revived the laws. In this way it extricated itself from every danger. The kings, on the other hand, whose spirit was always equally elevated and could not be altered

---

[144] *TTP* XVII, 30 and 32; CWS II, 303.
[145] *TTP* XVII, 32; CWS II, 302–3.

without disgrace, clung stubbornly to their vices right up to the final destruction of the city.[146]

The plural and the manifold of the State appears to be supported by organisms built by the powerful theological/prophetic imagination of its legislator. The republic releases energies from the cement of a boundless passion, from the irresistible centripetal force of an omnipotent and omnipresent sovereign God. Animated and unified by its religious 'virtue', the tendentially 'democratic' theocracy of the children of Israel began to decay after the decadence – equally 'affective' and passion-driven – of its first principle.[147] It is useful to evaluate institutions and customs, but this 'ancient' example, taken from the biblical world, cannot be employed to answer the basic theoretical question about the modern democratic *imperium*. Realised as a result of theological imagination, such an example demonstrates how the dominion operates, starting from a still substantial principle not involved in the dominion itself. It is therefore unable to indicate a truly 'internal' place, within the dynamics of the State, by virtue of which the multiple and the plural converge towards political unity, strengthening instead of attempting to undermine it:

> if we consider that without mutual aid men must live most wretchedly and without any cultivation of reason, we shall see very clearly that to live, not only securely, but very well, men had to agree in having one purpose. So they brought it about that they would have collectively the natural right each one had to all things.[148]

Emancipated from religious imagination, the other political form – the modern and authentic form of democracy – emerges here as a mature and conscious choice, a universal, collective act of *ratio*: 'no one can doubt how much more advantageous it is to man to live according to the laws and certain dictates of our reason. As we've said, these laws and dictates aim only at the true advantage of men.'[149] Everyone desires security and wants to avoid fear, but

> this simply can't happen so long as everyone is permitted to do whatever he likes, and reason is granted no more right than hatred and anger.

---

[146] *TTP* XVIII, 21; *CWS* II, 327.
[147] *TTP* XVII, 93ff.; *CWS* II, 317ff.
[148] *TTP* XVI, 12; *CWS* II, 284.
[149] Ibid.

> There is no one who lives among hostilities, hatreds, anger and deceptions, who does not live anxiously, and who does not strive to avoid these things, as far as he can.[150]

And so:

> they had to make a very firm resolution and contract to direct everything only according to the dictate of reason. No one dares to be openly contrary to that, for fear of seeming mindless. They had to agree to rein in their appetites, insofar as those appetites urge something harmful to someone else, to do nothing to anyone which they would not want done to themselves, and finally, to defend another person's right as if it were their own.[151]

From theological origin to rational decision, the democratic *imperium*, the unity of a power capable of funnelling and accepting within itself the dynamic energy of difference, is constituted through an ecumenical gesture of reason, emerging from the crucible of senses and passions as an awareness of the maximal 'utility' of democracy, of its greater adequacy for the commonality of human-modes, their interdependence, and their always being related. This idea of a *pactum* is present throughout the whole political section of the *Treatise*, and yet – as demonstrated by the many, varied historiographical approaches through which this idea has been recurrently interpreted – it also introduces a number of questions, revealing itself in an uncertain and problematic light.[152]

---

[150] *TTP* XVI, 12–13; *CWS* II, 284.
[151] *TTP* XVI, 14; *CWS* II, 285.
[152] On the sources of the Spinozan notion of *pactum* see Eckstein 1971. Its central and positive function is recognised by the 'juridical-rationalistic' readings of Spinoza's political thought: see, among many, Gierke 1880; Solari 1927; and many subsequent 'liberal' reinterpretations (about which see Feuer 1958). On the other hand, naturalistic approaches (Fischer 1909; Worm 1897; Carp 1921; Del Vecchio 1922) and utilitarian ones (Pollock 1880 and 1921; Vaughan 1925) tend to devalue the *pactum* to a mere rhetorical superfetation. Among the most recent scholars, Negri (1981 and 1992) excludes that this concept has a real depth in Spinoza's political philosophy, centred on the physical-metaphysical irreducibility of power (*potentia*), while Balibar (1990) highlights its vicious circularity and its logical inconsistency. Finally, an intermediate position, so to speak, is defended by those interpreters who grant coherence and importance to this idea, while weakening its 'artificial' potential, in order to re-read it as a spontaneous and necessary outcome of natural drives: see Preposiet 1967; Matheron 1969; Tosel 1984; Giancotti 1990.

If, in social life, passions prevail, it is not clear how it would be possible to infer that 'no one can doubt' the superiority of a life conducted 'according to the laws and certain dictates of our reason'; nor will a presumed and psychologistic 'moral' value of *ratio* (the fear of appearing to be 'mindless') suffice to hold back everyone's instincts. More generally, since it is precisely the spread of passive affects that suggests the givenness and the untameable nature of the *imperium* (a *conatus* among others, and as such subjected to the urgency of the *pati*) as well as its contextuality with respect to society (the same that also makes it different from the others, a force aimed at supporting and governing/managing other forces), there follows the impossibility of singling out reason as a source and a guarantee – a point of coagulation, a unifying centre – for the State. This is especially true for a democratic state, politically open to the many, and often contradictory, demands of the universality of its 'citizens-subjects'. If power is summoned by a lack of a reason, then it will not be possible for power to come from reason. Even when starting from Spinoza's philosophical-political presuppositions, as long as we limit ourselves to the *pactum* (an act of pure reason), we cannot get out of the theoretical short circuit – substantially re-proposed in every modern variant of contractualism – which consists in a rational agreement between mostly irrational subjects, apodictically postulating, within the unbroken fullness of forces and the bubbling of instincts and drives, a kind of *epoché*, a suspension during which the large fish would stop and, instead of eating them, argue with the small ones. The relative and inter-connected nature of the modes implies the connaturality of *imperium* and human life, thus excluding the possibility of an origin or a contingent genesis of dominion. Although difficult to place within the general structure of Spinoza's political philosophy, the *pactum* remains however central to the definition of the primacy of democracy, which is the aim of both his political philosophy as a whole and of the *TTP* in particular. Unmanageable from within a merely 'theoretical' structure, the idea of a contract probably refers to the objectives of 'practice': to a particular and actualising function, to an outcome that is no longer just conceptual, and where the intersection of cultural prerequisites and militant demands begins to assume a precise and substantial historical physiognomy.

Perhaps, then, the *pactum* represents, from this point of view, the terminal point, the last resort of a reconversion of theology and politics in liberal and rationalistic terms, the aim towards which the whole essay proceeds, in contrast (and as an alternative) to the authoritarian configuration, which sees both the supporters of the monarchy and the official cults engaged in an act of absolutist normalisation of the Dutch experience. Spinoza probably starts from the conviction that, in the predicament of the Netherlands, it would be possible to achieve an articulation and a development of the 'powers' – a deployment of reasons and affections, of ideas and interests – such as to make possible the regulation and the restraint of *passio*, now placed under the control and the hegemony of reason. The 'current' conditions of the country, in essence, would allow an alliance between the newest and most active part of Dutch society under the banner of strengthening democracy, of freedom, and of tolerance. In this context, the passion of *imperium* implies the need for a confessional component, a renewed theological contribution towards political unification. This invitation is addressed, as privileged interlocutors, to those denominations which, due to their communal and 'informal' (anti-authoritarian and anti-hierarchical) nature, could be more receptive to a new libertarian merging of theology and politics. More than a theoretical architrave, more than a logical principle capable of supporting and explaining the essence and the nature of the *imperium*, the idea of a contract seems to assume the situated (i.e. limited, temporary) value of a metaphor/project, of a political-cultural keyword. The objective is to reach a great (conscious and desirable) agreement between the economic/intellectual aristocracy – bearer of an emancipated reason – and the less dogmatic and 'more reasonable' among the religious sects, which by their nature are more prone, in political practice, towards republican rationality. It follows that the philosophical reader to which the *Treatise* is addressed (deliberately and preliminarily excluding the *vulgus*) is not the scholar strictly conceived: a specialist to whom, if anything, the *Ethics* is more suited. Rather – much like Dante's *Convivio* (*The Banquet*) – the *TTP* is meant for a medium/high social class and for a certain kind of cultured and 'disenchanted' man of faith. The ideal of the pact, in this case, does not entail the transparency (as perfect as it is unjustified) of the *imperium*, since religion remains a fundamental vehicle of political composition.[153] Nevertheless it is a solution with a strong rational justification, suitable for an evolved and developed society, capable of demystifying ancient power relations and ready to replace them with newer and more 'universal' ones.

However, even retracing the evolution of its form and consistency from pure theory to political design, this perspective still presents problems and

---

[153] This is why readings with a strong 'Enlightenment bias' lose sight of some of the multiple registers of the *TTP*: see, for example, Tosel 1984, who, however, deserves credit for giving this work the contours of a precise political project. More generally, for an interpretation of Spinozan political thought in a markedly pre-Enlightenment sense, see Schäfer 1989.

gaps. First of all, it proceeds from the non-trivial assumption that the more tolerant sects will prove to be willing to accept the universal faith reconstructed by reason: that is, that they would be ready for a drastic rationalisation according to which the only possible point of institutional convergence between reason and religion (a one-way convergence, pre-defined and pre-constituted by reason) is to be found in 'catholic' precepts. But above all, the democratic design of the *Treatise* excludes the 'people', and avoids coming to terms with the *vulgus*. The republican 'bloc' is still explicitly conceived as minoritarian, perhaps by means of the unexpressed Enlightenment (but hardly Spinozan) belief that the force of its 'truth' can, as such, prevail over the superstition and the impulsive resistances of the *multitudo*. There no longer is a point of external coagulation for democracy (Mosaic theology), but only an internal theological-political segment operating within society and whose rationalising drives should, in virtue of their intrinsic power, prevail over the other affects: a stance from which it follows that the 'optimism of the will' – creative political planning – tries to avoid the inflexible and disenchanted demonstrations of 'doctrine'.

The historical failure of the republican faction also determines the fall and the abandonment of a political-cultural project. The assassination of the De Witt brothers marks the decline of a design aimed at the 'political reasonableness' of theology. A design – it should be reiterated – that while demonstrating the impossibility of the *imperium* as pure reason, still proceeded from its trust in reason's autonomous power of progression and conquest. The compatibility of passions (of interests) does not traverse pure reason nor a new compromise of theology and politics. Both on a philosophical and on a practical-political level, the *Treatise* does not resolve the issue of a higher productivity and greater power of democratic unification. In the painful and secluded retreat that inevitably follows defeat, the (meta) physics of power pushes Spinoza's theoretical research elsewhere.

4

Between Realism and Project: The *Political Treatise*

'The rest is lacking' (*Reliqua desiderantur*): the very final line of the *Tractatus Politicus* expresses the romantic charm of an unfinished work, especially when such a fate befalls the *last* work of an author, and when the darkness of a premature death casts its irrevocable shadows on every further development and on every explicitly ascertained outcome. More generally, there exists a certain fascination for the unsaid, for the fragmented and the sketchy. In the episodic or in the contingent (see Plato's *Letter VII* or Marx's 'Marginal Notes on Wagner'), a greater interpretive freedom is always possible, so that one can outline the 'true' face of the author, a physiognomy whose 'reliability' is accompanied by its unusual nature, and whose 'authenticity' is confirmed by its unexpectedness.

The rest is lacking: a posthumous voice, external and off-stage, which abruptly declares the end of Spinoza's philosophy, and of his life. Much was left out of the *TP*, which was interrupted at the beginning of the chapter (or chapters?) on democracy, after the five chapters dedicated to a general theoretical set-up, two on monarchy, and three on the aristocratic form of *imperium*.[1] What was left out is the soul of Spinoza's previous theoretical work on the political: a new *logos tripolitikós* – a return to the classical system, the analytical examination of the three fundamental variants of power and

---

[1] As is known, a presentation of the topics relating to the first seven chapters can be found in *Ep.* LXXXIV; *CWS* II, 488, addressed to a friend who remained unknown (perhaps Jelles): 'The first contains, as it were, an Introduction to the Work itself; the second treats of natural Right; the third, of the Right of the Supreme 'Powers; the fourth, what matters of State depend only on the governance of the Supreme 'Powers; fifth, what is the ultimate thing a State can aim at; and sixth, how a Monarchic Government must be set up, so as not to fall into Tyranny. Now I am busy with the seventh chapter, where I demonstrate Methodically all the main points of the preceding sixth chapter, concerning the organisation of a well-ordered Monarchy.'

the State – seems to replace completely the polemical contrasts and the passionate theoretical caesuras examined in his previous work.

It is in this forced absence that we must identify the main source of the broad spectrum of hermeneutical reconstructions, which have unravelled an infinite series of possible intermediate arrangements between the extremes of a perfect coherence between the previous philosophical stance and the new ones on the one hand, and of their complete overturning on the other (a substantial linearity versus a real reversal of the already consolidated conceptual acquisitions).

All the readings that consider the *TP* to be simply a shift of perspective, a mere change of viewpoint in the analysis – from the 'individuals' to the *imperium*, from subjective rights to the dynamics of the State, while preserving the modern complementarity and the mutual functionality of freedom and authority, of the particular and the universal[2] – tend to highlight continuity and coherence. On the other hand, those reinterpretations that want to detect in Spinoza's last work a clear historical-political reversal, a decisive transition from democracy to absolutism, in harmony with the new historical predicament,[3] insist on discontinuity, a clean break with the past. More often it is the categories of 'the scientific' and of 'realism' that make a difference, variously applied to the new architecture of the *TP*. The *TP* has a structure that, moving away from the frontal and participated conflict between democracy and monarchy (a conflict that can involve, as we have seen, not only the organisation of the dominion but entire systems of 'civilisation', the quality of knowledge, social cohesion, and the level of religiosity), adopts a more detached argumentative trend according to which all forms of power acquire, under particular conditions, a positive and propulsive dimension.[4] Some of the most stimulating interpretations offered in recent years outline a hypothesis of a significant discontinuity marked by the *TP*, both with respect to the *TTP* and *vis-à-vis* the whole Spinozist project broadly conceived, with regards to which it should be seen as a sort of extreme upheaval, of a final and enlightening mooring; this is a novel proposal which, based on the centrality of the notion of *multitudo*, ends up foreshadowing a new and indirect emergence of the democratic *imperium*.[5]

---

[2] See, for example, Adelphe 1914; Solari 1927; Francès 1954; Giancotti 1990.
[3] Menzel 1898; Meinecke 1957. Against this thesis see Mcshea 1968: 123ff.
[4] See, among others, Droetto 1958; Corsi 1978; Pezzillo 1991.
[5] In particular, the latter is Negri's position, who sees in the *TP* a reversal of the *Ethics* with regards to the relations between '*potestas*' and '*potentia*' (1992: 27); in general, a perspective of difference and change is welcomed by Balibar 1990; Matheron 1969; Mugnier-Pollet 1976; and Wernham 1978.

Compared to these readings, the interpretive path taken by this book adopts, first of all, the assumption of 'scientific realism', without however accepting, as its direct consequence, the ideal of disengagement, of 'indifference' and of lack of valuation. Distancing Spinoza from the urgencies of his time, and towards a more mediated reflection on the nature of the political order, the political defeat of 1672 plays for the Dutch philosopher the role that the fall of the Republic of Florence played for Machiavelli. Spinoza's last *Treatise*, then, abandons the more straightforwardly militant aspects of his previous work, while further developing its most fertile and fruitful theoretical ingredients. Indeed, the idea of *multitudo* appears to be the backbone of the new work, a concept able to enclose all the reciprocal interactions and the relational functions of the subject and the State, the *civitas* and the *populus*. Indeed this idea – and this is another guiding hypothesis of my work – seems to be better understood as not breaking with the metaphysical project of the *Ethics* but, on the contrary, running in strong contiguity with the more capacious (and more complex) of its principles, that of *causa sui*. In the *TP* we find a civil revisiting, a social adaptation of that principle and of the tensions pertaining to its realisability. Finally, and in accord with the most recent readings, by means of the concept of *multitudo* the *TP* seems to be built around the constitutive primacy of democracy which, in its extraordinary power and in its organic instability – together and under the same conditions – far from presenting itself as a simple variant of political organisation, equal among others, is rather characterised as the only pivot and as the preliminary condition of every relation of *imperium*. Such a privileged placement cannot be derived, of course, from a direct analysis (which does *not* exist, since – precisely – it is lacking (*desideratur*)), but can rather be barely discerned in outline, through the new general arrangement of the 'principles' and the analytical trend of the other two forms. Nor will it be a matter of pure speculation: the determination of the 'type' of government – moving from the uncertain and not entirely consolidated institutional structures of the Netherlands – could and should begin anew, starting from the frank recognition of the primacy of democracy. This new methodological perspective – the 'political science' tone employed by the *TP* – produces a final and more coherent fusion between 'theory' and 'actuality', between the cold deductive rigour of thought and the hot stimulations of the political 'project'.

Realism

However one may wish to resolve the internal relationship between Spinoza's works, it is difficult to escape the impression that the first steps of the political elaboration that followed his *TTP* mark a distancing and a definite departure from the militant outcome, the ideological-rationalising approach that, superimposed onto more solid and coherent theoretical registers that operate even in that context, characterised the basic coordinates of the *TTP*'s project.

Emblematic, in the first place, is the argumentative structure that supports the well-known Scholium of the fourth part of the *Ethics*, in which Spinoza introduces the positivistic nature of the concepts of merit and sin and briefly returns to argue about 'man's natural state and his civil state'. This formula undoubtedly refers to his previous claims:

> [i]n order, therefore, that men may be able to live harmoniously and be of assistance to one another, it is necessary for them to give up their natural right and to make one another confident that they will do nothing which could harm others.[6]

What remains is a need for the transfer of the natural right of every individual to political power although the *pactum*'s reason is now gone and supplanted by the more compelling urgencies of the passions. Every individual refrains from causing harm to others just because – and this is a crucial point, repeated through the *Ethics* – '[n]o affect can be restrained except by an affect stronger than and contrary', due to the fear that a transgression might produce 'a greater harm' than a possible immediate advantage. The *status civilis* is fuelled by a harsh mechanism of repression, a pure automatism of subjection:

> [b]y this law, therefore, Society can be maintained, provided it appropriates to itself the right everyone has of avenging himself, and of judging concerning good and evil. In this way Society has the power to prescribe a common rule of life, to make laws, and to maintain them – not by reason, which cannot restrain the affects [. . .], but by threats.[7]

---

[6] *Ethics* IV, 37 Schol. 2; CWS II, 586.
[7] Ibid.

Obviously, this new topology of relations, or at least this clearer repositioning of the links that hold between reason and affects in the determination of the *imperium*, still cannot, by itself, completely obscure the contractual perspective (nor is it enough, for this purpose, to point out that in the *Ethics* neither a *pactum* nor a *contractus* are ever mentioned). And besides, didn't the Hobbesian way of the pact – leading towards a mortal God (*deus mortalis*) – also seem to traverse an intricate forest of reasons and passions, of calculations and fears?

> [Dear Friend], as far as Politics is concerned, the difference you ask about, between Hobbes and me, is this: I always preserve natural Right unimpaired, and I maintain that in each State the Supreme Magistrate has no more right over its subjects than it has greater power over them. This is always the case in the state of Nature.[8]

In a letter from 1674 Spinoza uses enigmatic words and concepts in this answer to Jelles. The first move would seem to be aimed at *providing protection*: 'I always preserve natural Right unimpaired'. Conversely, the second move overturns the rules of the political relationship *qua* exchange, turning the table of the rational/liberal game: the '*Supremus Magistratus*' is everywhere (*in qualibet Urbe*) endowed with an authority/supremacy, dominion (*potestas*) itself that he or she actually manages to exert on the subjects. These two phases give rise to an apparently paradoxical juxtaposition: if the inviolability of natural law is a valid principle, then a *de facto* subjection to dominion should not hold true, and vice versa. The logic of the *pactum* – both in its 'soft' version of partial alienation, and in the 'hard' and absolute version (of Hobbesian inspiration) of non-return from alienation – is not compatible with subordination as a *fact*, and with the relationship of domination as a *given*. In reality, the nature of the *imperium* is here developed in another direction: '[t]his is always the case in the state of Nature'. Right remains intact for the simple reason that power (*potestas*) springs out of it. Sovereign power does not derive from an exchange but from *jus naturalis*, that is, in Spinozan terms, *by means of force*: not from a transfer, but from violent coercion; not from rational alienation, but from subjection. Far from any clear subordination of thought, a relationship of pure power is established, in the factory of the *imperium*, between the subjects and the political authority.

---

[8] *Ep*. L (to Jarig Jelles); CWS II, 406.

Spinoza writes:

[p]hilosophers conceive the affects by which we're torn as vices, which men fall into by their own fault. That's why they usually laugh at them, weep over them, censure them, or (if they want to seem particularly holy) curse them.[9]

How often has the fifteenth chapter of Machiavelli's *Prince* been referred to as an inspiration for the realist doctrine, so austere and indeed Machiavellian, which opens the *TP*? We have the immediate feeling that this passage indicates, albeit indirectly, a path of re-reading and of self-critical revision. Spinoza very explicitly turns against the 'philosophers' and the 'politicians': against the abstract reason of the former, who strive 'to praise in many ways a human nature which doesn't exist anywhere' in order 'to bewail the way men really are', incapable of constructing a viable ethics and politics, and at best giving rise to a 'satire instead of Ethics' and producing a theory 'which would be thought a Fantasy, possible only in Utopia, or in the golden age of the Poets, where there'd be absolutely no need for it'.[10] Spinoza then turns to the pragmatism of the latter, more realist than the philosophers because trained by the experience that 'as long as there are men, there will be vices', and yet better described as 'shrewd' rather than 'wise'; locked up in their narrow horizon of a small, static, and conservative empiricism aimed at the simple repression of instincts and affects.[11] Compared to this double approach – not exactly symmetric, because if nobody is less suitable than the philosophers to take care of public affairs (*regendae rei publicae*), the 'politicians' way to deal with them has been much better (*multo Melius*)[12] but still unsatisfactory – the *TP* tries to take a direction that holds firm both, from the theoretical point of view, the doctrine of the *Ethics* on the irrepressibility of passions (on the need 'not to laugh at human actions, or mourn them, or curse them, but only to understand them') and – from the political point of view – the impossibility of any strategy based on the absolute, foundational primacy of reason:

[m]oreover, though we've shown that reason can do much to restrain and moderate the affects, we've also seen that the path reason teaches us to

---

[9] *TP* I, 1; *CWS* II, 503.
[10] *TP* I, 1; *CWS* II, 503.
[11] *TP* I, 2; *CWS* II, 504.
[12] Ibid.

follow is very difficult. So people who persuade themselves that a multitude, which may be divided over public affairs, can be induced to live only according to the prescription of reason, those people are dreaming of the golden age of the Poets.[13]

The rational impossibility of politics seems to put a definitive end to the two actualising assumptions that guided the *TTP*: that of a theological-political compromise under the strong hegemony of reason, and that – wholly complementary – of the possible prevailing of an enlightened minority over the passions and the superstitions of the majority thanks to a dissemination of knowledge deriving from their conquest of the truth. Indeed, this insistence on both passions and power for the constitution of the *imperium* is a distancing move aimed at the overcoming of the 'ideology' of the *TTP*. It does not, however, affect its 'philosophy', its deeper theoretical strata. Indeed, the *TP* – and this is what is generally ignored by interpretations based on an alleged 'naturalistic' caesura to be placed precisely at the moment of its composition[14] – proposes those same ideas time and again in its first five chapters, through an argumentative progression that is wholly similar to that of the *TTP*.

It is neither because of 'sin' nor 'vice' that passions prevail in humanity: precisely because everything strives to preserve its own being (and its very essence resolves around this effort), it is unquestionable that, if human nature was constituted in such a way that it could always be regulated 'only according to the prescription of reason', the *jus naturae* proper to humankind would be determined only by the sole power of reason.[15] But, in reality, humans are driven by '*blind desire*',[16] due to their original, anthropological, make-up. There is no 'fall' from an imaginary, pristine, and primitive virginity of 'thought': not even in Adam's case, who – had he really been 'of sound mind' and 'the master of his will' – could have avoided the devil's deception (and perhaps could have deceived the devil himself?). Therefore, 'it must be acknowledged that it wasn't in the first man's power to use reason correctly. Like us, he was subject to affects.'[17] Tormented by anger, envy, and other affects deriving from hatred, humans generally end up being in mutual conflict and 'by nature enemies':

---

[13] *TP* I, 5; *CWS* II, 506.
[14] See, for example, Mugnier-Pollet 1976: 120ff.
[15] *TP* II, 5; *CWS* II, 508.
[16] *TP* II, 6; *CWS* II, 509.
[17] *TP* II, 6; *CWS* II, 510.

[f]or these things are certain (and we've demonstrated them in our *Ethics*): men are necessarily subject to affects; they're so constituted that they pity those whose affairs are going badly, and envy those who are prospering; they're more inclined to vengeance than to mercy; moreover, everyone wants others to live according to his mentality, so that they approve what he approves, and reject what he rejects. Since everyone wants to be first, they fall into quarrels and try as hard as they can to crush each other. Whoever turns out to be the winner prides himself more on harming the loser than on doing good for himself.[18]

The impossibility, for reason, to hold a strong grip on *imperium* is not a late Spinozan doctrine. The *TTP*, as we have seen, had already proposed a very similar idea, although it was – in the final analysis – somewhat derailed (if not downright contradicted) by its contractualist outcome. Nor are the more than evident Hobbesian resonances enough to make a difference here, since here too Spinoza's thought remains clearly distinct from that of Hobbes.[19] In this respect, in short, there is a substantial continuity between the two works, indeed exemplified by a significant and literal paraphrasis of Hobbes:

[f]rom these considerations, it follows that the Right and established practice of nature, under which all men are born and for the most part live, prohibits nothing except what no one desires and no one can do; it does not prohibit disputes, or hatreds, or anger, or deceptions, and it is absolutely not averse to anything appetite urges.[20]

Wholly analogous to Spinoza's previous tenets, such a primacy of the passions in the constitution of natural law expresses both the 'givenness' and the inescapable 'generality' of the *imperium*, as well as its perpetual determination within the dynamics of *conservatio*, within the limit of a power relationship:

[t]herefore, when disagreements and rebellions are stirred up in a Commonwealth – as they often are – the result is never that the citizens dissolve the Commonwealth – though this often happens in other kinds of society. Instead, if they can't settle their disagreements while preserving

---

[18] *TP* I, 5; *CWS* II, 505–6.
[19] Including the image of men by nature 'contrary to one another': *TP* II, 14; *CWS* II, 513.
[20] *TP* II, 8; *CWS* II, 511. This passage is an exact paraphrase of *TTP* XVI, 9; *CWS* II, 284.

the form of the Commonwealth, they change its form to another.²¹
[...]
[f]inally, because all men everywhere, whether Barbarians or civilised, combine their practices and form some sort of civil order, we must seek the causes and natural foundations of the state, not from the teachings of reason, but from the common nature, or condition, of men.²²

When reason's procedures leave the field open to the 'the common nature, or condition, of men' the accent always falls on the logical/historical primacy of power. Since, in the state of nature, 'it's futile for one person alone to try to protect himself from all others', it follows that as long as natural right is determined by the power of the singular, it will be always be destined to resolve in nothingness. Without an *imperium*, without a shared *jus* that allows the existence of 'lands they can inhabit and cultivate, are able to protect themselves, fend off any force, and live according to the common opinion of all (*ex communi sententia*)',²³ the right of every single individual remains a mere opinion. Only when starting from the inevitable being-an-effect of dominion can a positive value be assigned to sin, to justice, and to the laws.²⁴ Natural law does not seem to apply to the individual except *after* (a purely *methodological* coordinate, useful for theoretical and critical/reflective decompositions) the creation of an *imperium*. Similar to the arguments of the *TTP*, these passages also seem to be oriented towards the clear ontological priority of *potestas* on *societas* and on the *potentia* (the right) of human beings. And yet, just as happened in the *TTP*, Spinoza's position does not converge towards a Hobbesian political theology and its *representative* outcome, imposed, so to speak, *from above*. The *imperium* is not an instantaneous act that brings non-being into being, a 'magic wand' capable of giving form to what could not exist before:

> when we say each person can decide whatever he wishes concerning a thing of which he is the master, this power must be defined not only by the power of the agent, but also by the property of what, or indeed who, he's acting upon (*aptitudo patientis*).²⁵

---

²¹ *TP* VI, 2; CWS II, 532.
²² *TP* I, 7; CWS II, 506.
²³ *TP* II, 15; CWS II, 513–14.
²⁴ See *TP* II, 18 (CWS II, 514–15); II, 23 (CWS II, 516); III, 15 (CWS II, 524).
²⁵ *TP* IV, 4; CWS II, 526. Translation modified.

Even mere opinion is a form of power (*potentia*), and no *ars* can distort the profound nature and the univocal essence of the *conatus*, expressed both in the power of the agent and in the *aptitudo patientis*. The *jus* of supreme power is 'nothing more than the Right of nature' and therefore

> as each person in the natural state has as much right as he has power, so also the body and mind of the whole state have as much right as they have power. So each citizen, or subject, has less right in proportion as the Commonwealth itself is more powerful than he is.[26]

Although inversely proportional, the power relationship is still a 'relationship' such as to exclude any possibility of an authentic annihilation of 'each person's Right of nature'. Indeed, '[b]oth in the natural state and in the civil order, man acts according to the laws of his own nature and looks out for his own advantage'.[27] *Nature*, in Spinoza, is a power (*potentia*) that is always necessarily unfolded and determined: the *conatus* can be thinned, it can be compressed down to an 'attitude towards patience', but it cannot be, in Hobbesian fashion, reduced to the metaphorical/paradoxical condition of a 'non-state', of pure negativity. The *imperium* remains anchored in the inextricable intertwining of nature and art. The *dominium* is actually a *natural-artificial* power relationship: '[f]or the right of the state is defined only by power'.[28] *Potestas* is always anticipated by *potentia*, which 'de-fines' it and circumscribes it, in the dual sense implied by the *conatus*. Like every single individual and every living being, *potestas* also proceeds both 'by itself' and 'in something else' (*in alio*): it is a tendentially unlimited self-expansion, but it exists 'for itself' only in connection with something other than itself. As a particularly special kind of *fabrica* – as an *ars* of relationships between men – this is a relationship of force destined to unleash energies, to multiply powers [*potentiae*] while, at the same time, feeding itself. The *imperium* is a relationship of production of force. The essence, the *recta ratio*, of the State machine, lies entirely in its capacity to feed power (*potentia*), for otherwise its own persistence would be threatened. The continuity of the *conatus* turns the *ars* of power into a mechanism of mutual determination (by either a process of strengthening or of implosion): of both itself and of human beings.

The insistence on the importance of force and passions found in the *TP*, while sufficient to mark its distance from the ideological-militant register of

---

[26] TP III, 2; CWS II, 517.
[27] TP III, 3; CWS II, 518.
[28] TP VII, 25; CWS II, 555.

the *TTP* – up to the explicit adoption, at times, of Hobbesian language – is not enough to demonstrate a real mutation of the most important theoretical achievements of the earlier work. The *ratio* of the *imperium*, distilled in the crucible of the senses, and laboriously abstracted from the turmoil of the impulses and instincts through which the *conatus* is mostly expressed, assumes now (as it did before) its function of *ordo*, its nature of 'relationship', all the more capable of self-preservation the more it guarantees the *preservatio* and *conservatio* of individuals. This is not where the true discontinuity lies. The authentic turning point of Spinoza's last work begins here and then proceeds towards the energetic focus, the centre of irradiation of the relative of the *dominium* and of the connective of the political.

In his 1670 work the contrast between the two fundamental alternatives of the *imperium* pivoted around a different balance of reason and faith: in a monarchy, a dogmatic and authoritarian theology spreads fear and awe, trampling reason and freedom; in a democracy there is a 'liberal' compromise between rational knowledge and Catholic religion: a compromise, as I have attempted to demonstrate, synthetically represented with the *ideological* formula of the *pactum*, an actualising shortcut, a militant simplification, difficult to reconnect with more authentic and solid theoretical premises. The *TP* bypasses this approach by simply ignoring it, to the point of divesting the theological (and contractual) dimension of any strategic role.[29] Having taken some distance from the immediate urgency of political commitment (which is, however, never extraneous to the pressures and lessons of the present time), Spinoza can now turn to the remote sources and the most uncertain and protean origins of political modernity.

Multitudo

> After the tragic event of 1672 [the Orange Revolution], which 'verifies' his prediction while contradicting his efforts, Spinoza [...] will try to tackle again the whole problem of the 'foundations' of the State in a way that is both more radical (by making the *multitudo* the very concept of the

---

[29] As all Spinoza scholars know, his late work contains a single reference to the *contractus*, aiming to outline – not without uncertainties – the double direction of political order between the substantial absoluteness of the *multitudo* and the formal absoluteness of the *potestas*: '[t]here's no doubt that the contract, or the laws by which a multitude transfers its right to a Council or a man, ought to be violated when it's in the interest of the general welfare to violate them. But no private person is entitled to make the judgment about whether it's in the interest of the general welfare to violate them or not. Only the sovereign can rightly do this'; *TP* IV, 6; CWS II, 528.

people that is to be governed, and within which the rulers are chosen) and less 'savage' (by shifting the analysis of imaginary processes to legal institutions and administrative statistics).[30]

Thanks to a contemporary current of secondary literature of Italian-French origin, the novelty of the *multitudo* – the frequency and the new specific weight that this term acquires in the *TP* (as compared to its sporadic previous appearances) – has finally been brought to light.[31]

When reading the two political works of Spinoza, and making use of the numerous and precious lexical analyses available today,[32] it is indeed easy to identify a bond of substantial mutual exclusion between the use the term '*multitudo*' and how other words with a comparable semantic extension[33] (like '*vulgus*', '*plebs*', and '*populus*') are employed. In the *TTP* the word '*multitudo*' appears very rarely (only six times) and when it does its meaning almost always coincides with those of the other terms I just mentioned. In the *TP* the relationship is reversed through a logic that goes well beyond its 'quantity' or pure lexical 'absorption', for it broadens the semantic range of the term to reach the conceptually dominant nodes of the work as a whole. In sum, the other terms always refer to a 'determined partiality', a molecular entity, a segment of the entire community, secondary and subordinate to the *imperium* – even if a numerically large segment, or indeed a majority, because condensable and recognisable by their already-established identifying structure. Conversely, in Spinoza's last work '*multitudo*' is extended far beyond its initial characterisation in order to assume a dimension of global and universal interrelatedness (yet without losing its previous and more limited connotation) capable of entering into a much more complex relationship

---

[30] Balibar 1985: 369. My translation.
[31] Two authors in particular: Negri (1981 and 1992) and the already mentioned Balibar (1985 and 1990); but see also Matheron 1969 and 1971; Tosel 1984; Garulli 1982; Yovel 1985. In the wake of these surveys, more explorations and variations have proliferated; see, among others: Zourabichvili 1992; Bove 1996: 259–321; Visentin 2001: 261–327; Del Lucchese 2003; Ciccarelli 2003, 169ff.; Morfino 2005; Chaui 2007; Santos Campos 2010.
[32] Giancotti 1970 and the digitised indexes by Moreau and Bouveresse 1979 (for the *TP*), Guéret, Robinet and Tombeur 1977 (for *Ethics*), Totaro and Canone 1991 (for *TdIE*), and Totaro and Veneziani 1993 (for the *TTP*).
[33] Have inevitably and dutifully kept in mind the careful semantic exploration performed by Saccaro Battisti (1984), even in the context of a hermeneutic perspective different from the one she proposed, since she attributes to the *multitudo* – even in the context of the *TP* – a conceptual function substantially analogous to those recognisable in other terms. See also Saccaro Battisti 1977a and 1977b.

with power (*potestas*), inserting itself in a dynamic and decisive way between 'origin' and 'function', being both a 'constituent of' and 'constituted by' political power.

Up to the *TP* (where it appears only twice), '*vulgus*' is the most recurrent word among those I have mentioned. It does not indicate an economic condition (a modern 'class') or a legal status (a pre-modern 'social group'), but rather a 'cultural' and 'sociological' area, generally (but not necessarily) corresponding to the lower strata of society. In any case the term always bears a strong negative connotation: it indexes a category of people that can be united on the basis of 'two main characters: an inadequate or false form of knowledge, and a behaviour guided by the passions that lead to social conflict'.[34] The *vulgus* is *rudis*, uncultured: it disdains natural knowledge because it is common to everyone, and it always craves rare and different things, it feeds on prejudices and preconceptions, expressing itself only by means of 'opinions' and 'modes of imagining'.[35] Spinoza's derogatory tone – which finds its closest example in libertinism,[36] although it can be placed in the context of a long tradition which traverses most of western culture (starting, at least, from the recurrent Platonic polemic against the ignorance and incompleteness of the *plethos*) – becomes even more strident and evident when it comes to the topic of *faith*. This is the domain that is still presented as the most important from the *social* point of view, the fundamental ground for collective interactions: that of a religion produced from fear and superstition, the only effective vehicle of submission to political power. The naive and primitive belief in a personal, corporeal, and masculine God, sitting on his throne in the vault of heaven, exercising his free will in the extraordinary and super-natural act of the miracle, and creator of man in his image and likeness, makes possible the observance of the norms that govern society, whether the widespread and participated rules of Mosaic democracy (theologically supported by the biblical message, composed and revealed in conformity with the convictions of the *vulgus* and the prophets),[37] or – indeed more often – the purely repressive and authoritarian laws of an autocratic power, for which the image of a divine being represents

---

[34] Saccaro Battisti 1984: 460. My translation.
[35] See *TTP*: XIII, 29 (*CWS* II, 263); I, 2 (*CWS*, 76–7); XV, 3 (*CWS* II, 272); *Ep*. XXX (to Henry Oldenburg) (*CWS* II, 14–15); *Ethics* I, App. (*CWS* I, 443–4).
[36] See Saccaro Battisti 1984: 61ff, and the extensive bibliographic indications contained therein.
[37] See *TTP* VI, 57 (*CWS* II, 165) and *Ep*. LIV (to Hugo Boxel) (*CWS* II, 414); *Ethics* II, 3 Schol. (*CWS* I, 449); *TTP* VI, 1, 14, 69 (*CWS* II, 152, 155, 168), *TTP* XIV, 1 and 33 (*CWS* II, 263 and 270).

the most effective tool to achieve the subjection and acquiescence of its subjects. Indeed this is the character of the *vulgus* (at best characterised by a confused and chaotic reactivity) through which it enters into a relationship with the *imperium*: fickle (*varius et incostans*), incapable of moderation, and always '*wretched*', the *vulgus* is never at peace and desires above all what is new and has not yet been a source of disappointment: an instability which has often been the cause of tumults and heinous wars.[38] Vulnerable to the ideological incursions of demagogues and schismatics,[39] 'the mob is terrifying, if unafraid'.[40] It must be kept at bay, as far as possible – as a horse with a rein – by promising what is dearest to it in exchange for the respect of the law, and threatening it with what it most fears for its violation.[41] Always negatively characterised by knowledge, sociality, and politics, it is only in Spinoza's early works that a single, indirect (and extremely important) positive function is acknowledged to the *vulgus*: that of first producing the *verba*, of creating – although as the result of an error, a whim of the imagination – those same words that will then be used to articulate the truths of philosophers.[42] After the *De emendatione* and the *Cogitata Metaphysica*, however, every trace of this extraordinary inventive ability disappears.

The relations between the political order and the *vulgus* always seem to be characterised by consequentiality and determination. The *vulgus* is given only within an *already* constituted power: its jumble of instincts and drives can represent for the *imperium* both a threat and a source of consensus, a danger and a support. Either way, it comes 'after' the *imperium*, and it is always 'within' an established and (more or less) functioning order. An entity *in* power: the *vulgus* is a reality that weaves with power a complex and ambivalent dynamic of either conflict or favour, of strengthening or weakening – but always 'after', *starting from* power.

This condition – a combination of subordination and interaction with respect to power (*potestas*) – is even more evident in the case of the *populus* (a term which can only be found in the *TTP*) aimed at indicating the larger part of a whole that also includes both the king and the nobles,[43] a plurality

---

[38] *Ethics* IV, 58 Schol. (*CWS* I, 578), and *TTP* XIV, 1 (*CWS* II, 263), *TP* VII, 27 (*CWS* II, 558–9), *TTP* Praef., 5–6 (*CWS* II, 67).
[39] *Ethics* III, 29 (*CWS* I, 510); *TTP* XX, 31 and 41 (*CWS* II, 350 and 352).
[40] *Ethics* IV, 54 Schol. (*CWS* I, 576); *TP* VII, 27 (*CWS* II, 558–9). On classical (Xenophon, Laberium) and modern (Campanella) antecedents of this double fear, see Bodei 1991: 129n
[41] *TTP* IV, 5; *CWS* II, 126–7.
[42] *TdIE* 88 (*CWS* I, 38); *CM*, I, 6 (*CWS* I, 312).
[43] See for example, *TTP* XVI, 38; *CWS* II, 290.

that is politically structured by the two alternative poles of the positive of freedom and the negative of submission,[44] but which, on closer inspection, is still realised as a consequence, the acquired result of the *imperium*. Even when (as in a democracy) the power belongs to the people, it does not come from the people, but from the pact of each with everyone; it is not the people who produce democracy but democracy that produces the people (who, in turn, are also democracy's subject). The status of society (*societas*) is similar. This term is undoubtedly the most 'universal' among those under consideration: on the one hand it indicates an entire community, and in this it is distinguished from the more restricted meaning of the other terms;[45] on the other it remains an effect of political power, sometimes designating what will later be called 'civil society' (the 'private' moment: that of the useful, of economics, of opinion),[46] and sometimes indicating the *imperium* itself 'in action', the very operativity of the *civitas*,[47] without dissolving the preliminary and constituent knot of the 'principle', of the formation and origin.

Unlike '*vulgus*' and '*populus*' – terms that are substantially absent in Spinoza's last work – '*plebs*' (or '*communis plebs*') is instead widely used in both the *TTP* and the *TP*. In his 1670 work the *plebs* is not distinguished from the 'common people' by means of negative features and functions. The *plebs* is the majority of the human race and – incapable of understanding high matters – is fragile on the mental/intellectual level, hinders the probes and the virtuous, and does not know how to be silent or refrain from judging (something that, at least, it shares with 'the wisest').[48] Political power exploits the *vulgus*' superstition and fear, and when it favours it (when it listens to its insane wrath, fighting opinions and persecuting free spirits), devastating social lacerations and conflicts ensue.[49] Religion remains the most effective means of governing and controlling the *vulgus*' superstition: in a positive manner, as happens with Scripture, when it stimulates its devotion and manages to contain it, by means of faith and within the limits of

---

[44] *TTP*: V, 23 (*CWS* II, 144); XVI, 30 (*CWS* II, 288); XVII, 63ff. (*CWS* II, 310ff); XVIII, 1ff. (*CWS* II, 336ff); XIX, 22ff. (*CWS* II, 336ff); XX, 1ff. (*CWS* II, 344–5).
[45] *TdIE* 14 (*CWS* I, 10; 563–4); *Ethics*: IV, 35 Schol. (*CWS* I, 563–4); IV, 40 (*CWS* I, 569); IV, App. 14 (*CWS* I, 589); IV, App. 17 (*CWS* I, 590); V, 10 Schol. (*CWS* I, 601–3); *TTP* V, 23 and XVII, 29 (*CWS* I, 144 and 302).
[46] *Ethics* II, 49 Schol. (*CWS* I, 491); *TTP* V, 20 and XVI, 36 (*CWS* II, 143–4 and 289).
[47] *Ethics* IV, 37 Schol. 2 (*CWS* I, 567); *TTP* III, 13–14 (*CWS* I, 114).
[48] *TTP* V, 35ff. (*CWS* II, 147ff); *Ep*. XIX (to Willem van Blijenbergh) (*CWS* I, 360); *TTP* IX, 45 (*CWS* I, 220); *TTP* XVIII, 23 and XX, 21 (*CWS* II, 327 and 348).
[49] *TTP* XVIII, 22ff. and XX, 8–10 and 29; *CWS* II, 327–8, 345–6 and 349.

virtue;[50] negatively, when the priests supplant the kings, and religious power dissolves the political one. This is a nefarious function, in which the Church of Rome has always excelled, second only to the Islamic clergy in deceiving the plebs.[51]

The class condition of the *plebs*, its formal and effective exclusion from the *imperium*, is not modified in the *TP*, at least where it appears to define, in a complementary fashion, the best functionality of the aristocratic State. Appearing mostly in the eighth chapter, it is assigned some guarantees and it is admitted to bureaucratic-administrative functions, but it remains strictly excluded from the fundamental organisms and mechanisms of power, from the army, from the councils, and it has no right to vote.[52] And yet this is not the only way in which the *vulgus* is presented in Spinoza's last work:

> [w]hat we've written may be ridiculed by those who think the vices common to all mortals belong only to the plebeians – those who think that there's no moderation in the common people [*vulgus*]; that they're terrifying, unless they themselves are cowed by fear; or that the plebeians either serve humbly or rule proudly, like despots, and that there's neither truth nor judgment, etc. But everyone shares a common nature.[53]

It is in the context of this open palinode, on this explicit self-critical conversion, that this term makes its appearance in the *TP*. Now the *plebs* lacks knowledge of truth and governmental ability solely due to its inexperience; since it is excluded from the managing of 'the chief business of the state' it will be capable of formulating conjectures only with regard to those few issues that cannot be kept hidden from it.[54] Since human nature is the same for everyone, pride and vice will not be the prerogative of anyone in particular, but will affect all those who are in command; nobles are no less arrogant than the masses, even if they dissimulate their vices with luxury and lavishness. And so 'it's sheer stupidity to want to do everything in secrecy', for the citizens will pass negative judgments, or they will interpret everything in a negative way: '[i]f the plebeians could restrain themselves, and suspend

---

[50] *Ep.* XIX (to Willem van Blijenbergh) (*CWS* I, 360); *TTP*: V, 37–8, VI, 49, XIII, 4 and 27 (*CWS* II, 148, 163, 257, 262).
[51] *TTP* Praef, 9 (*CWS* I, 68); *Ep.* LXXVI (to Albert Burgh) (*CWS* II, 477).
[52] See *TP* VIII, 6, 28, 41, 44, 45, 46; *CWS* II, 567, 575–6, 583–4, 585ff.
[53] *TP* VII, 27; *CWS* II, 558. I will return to this aspect later in this chapter.
[54] *TP* VII, 27; *CWS* II, 559.

judgment on matters they know little about, or judge things correctly from scanty information, they would be more worthy to rule than to be ruled'.[55] It is no coincidence that this 'revision', which recalls an analogous comment made by Machiavelli,[56] is formulated just when the term '*plebs*' is presented as interchangeable and equivalent with '*multitudo*'.

The first occurrences of the term '*multitudo*' appear in a theological or mathematical context: either to demonstrate the unity of God, beginning from the assumption that his essence must involve its existence, and bearing in mind that the definition of a thing must necessarily concern the nature of the thing itself and not 'any multiplicity or any definite number of individuals';[57] or to support, against the critics, the irreducibility of the concept of infinity to the sum of its parts, to a vast yet measurable, assessable, and ponderable multiplicity.[58] In these contexts, *multitudo* is 'nothing but Modes of thinking', an artifice of thought, an 'aid of the imagination', like 'measure', 'time' and 'number', concepts that cannot tap into the infinite and that, although applicable to finite *res*, are unable to add anything to their reality.[59]

In the *TTP* the word '*multitudo*' plays a wholly secondary role: it is infrequently used, as we have said, and with a meaning altogether similar to those of '*plebs*' and '*vulgus*' to which it is sometimes placed side by side as an hendiadys, or used as a synonym, always emphasising its negative characteristics of superstition, instability, and vice.[60] Before the *TP*, in sum, the concept of '*multitudo*' has little depth and appears only with sporadic frequency: it occurs about fifteen times, in ten contexts of various nature, distributed through three letters, the *Cogitata Metaphysica*, and the *TTP* (not in the *Ethics*, from which it is completely missing). Conversely, in Spinoza's last work the word can be found about sixty-nine times, employed in forty different argumentations. This very clear difference and obvious disproportion should be enough, on its own, to undermine the plausibility of interpretations stressing continuity and minimalism, those suggesting that the new

---

[55] Ibid.
[56] See *Dis*. (I, 58; I, 47; III, 29: ed. Martelli, 140–2, 129–30, 235–6), where the usual passive image of the multitude is preserved (I, 44; I, 53; I, 57: ed. Martelli, 126–7, 134–6, 139–40). On the overcoming of the *arcana juris* and on the peculiar position of Spinoza with respect to the Reason of State, see Pacchiani 1979: 79ff.
[57] *Ep*. XXXIV (to Johannes Hudde); CWS II, 25.
[58] *Ep*. XII (to Lodewijk Meyer); CWS I, 222–3. And see also *Ep*. LXXXI (to Ehrenfried Walther von Tschirnhaus); CWS II, 485.
[59] *Ep*. XII (to Lodewijk Meyer); CWS I, 222–3.
[60] TTP Praef., 8 and 13, XVII, 13 and XVIII, 23; CWS I, 68, 69, 298, 327.

occurrences of this term would only be a coincidence, or that their number means nothing beyond sheer repetition.[61]

As an aggregate of human beings, whose nature of modifications of substance makes them both unique and interdependent (both 'absolute' and 'relative'), the *multitudo* in the *TP* realises the novelty of a relationship with the *imperium* characterised by a three-faced conceptual function. As the global expression of the intersections between various *conatus*, it contains, in the first place, power (the State), both in the sense that the right/power of the *potestas* is not distinguished – by 'nature', by its origin-essence – from any other form of right/power (the political order having to subsume itself, like all modes, in the effort-tension to subsist, to persevere into existence) and, above all,

[61] The global calculations are approximate, but still sufficient to detect an obvious and clear discrepancy. Paolo Cristofolini hypothesises that *multitudo*, far from being an authentic theoretical novelty, should be understood essentially as a synonym of *populus*, an interchangeability that Spinoza would have obtained from Machiavelli, having once again read the latter's *Discorsi* in view of the composition of the *TP*. This thesis is argued with the usual expertise by a master of Spinoza studies, to whom everyone owes something, but the evidence is only mildly circumstantial, unable to explain (indeed not even in terms of likelihood, or probability) the alleged slippage semantic of the *TP*. Again on a circumstantial basis, the Machiavellian *populus* = *multitudo* equivalence should have pushed Spinoza to persist in the use of *populus*, or at the most to alternate this lemma indifferently with *multitudo*, as happens in the *Discourses*. And yet in the *TP populus* 'is eclipsed', and *multitudo* 'spreads itself' (these are Cristofolini's own words), while maintaining, in some cases, the negative connotation (opposite to that of *populus*) it has in the *TTP*, where, for example, it is emphasised that experience has shown how the 'multitude ought to be directed, *or* restrained within definite limits' (*TP* I, 3). Moreover, it is worth noting – if only incidentally – that although the Machiavelli of the *Discorsi* undoubtedly assumes a fundamental importance in Spinoza's second treatise (as an eminent, austere lesson of both realism and political admonition to popular freedom), the influence of his thought appears to be far from absent in the *TTP* in its own dilemmatic and combative tone, which recalls the *Prince*'s style, in the typically republican assumption according to which 'in a democratic state, absurdities are less to be feared' (XVI); in its reference to *fortuna*, obviously repositioned within the Spinozan ontology of Nature-Substance, and in the admonition to the difficulty – almost the impossibility – of changing the form of *imperium*, both for the people accustomed to freedom, and for those accustomed to awe. A warning that is repeated in the *TP*, and that seems to count not – as Cristofolini reads it – as a conviction of principle against 'parricide' (against the killing of the king, against the Monarchomachs), but as a warning, more limited and common to both treaties, against the removal of 'a Tyrant from their midst, when they can't remove' the causes that determined it in the first place (*TP* V, 7). Although he does not have the 'dominant' position he holds in the *TP*, Machiavelli is, in short, also very much present in the *TTP* where, as we have seen, *multitudo* has no particular importance. See Cristofolini 2007.

because the *imperium* is constituted by the *multitudo*: 'the Commonwealth's Right is defined by the common power of a multitude'.[62] The classic natural hierarchies have been demolished; the *Christian republic* – and its theological foundation – has tragically sunk into the catastrophe of the civil war of religion; the rationalistic-juridical path of the alienation of the *pactum*, somehow still present in the *TTP*, becomes impossible, because the existence of humans capable of following the dictates of reason – all together, in the same place and at the same time – appears now only as a novelist's fantasy, a dream from the 'golden age of the Poets'; and, finally, the complete identity, without residues, of *jus* and power (*potentia*) is posited. The *imperium* refers to *multitudo* as its origin and source. Political power is not a transcendental entity (let alone transcendent) with respect to the multitude; on the contrary, it is the multitude that also contains political power. The force and the power of the State (its 'right') always refer, in the last instance, to the power/force of the *multitudo*: that of the whole, of the '*communis multitudo*'. The '*multitudinis potentia*' does not define a single form of the *imperium*: '[t]his right, which is defined by the power of a multitude, is usually called Sovereignty [*imperium*]'.[63] All species of common- or state- law derive, directly or indirectly, from a greater or lesser power (*potentia*) (from a strength or from a weakness, from a condensation or from a rarefaction) of the multitude. Consistently with Spinoza's philosophical anthropology, this general principle (stronger or weaker, more direct or more mediated) of *constitutive democracy* underpins every particular configuration of the political order. Besides, only that specific *genus* – that particular political codification in which the *imperium* will be the direct expression of the *multitudo* – can be called ideal (*optimum*). This is the only truly Spinozan 'absolute' form, when the multitude not only appears less terrifying for the *civitas* (a greater or lesser amount of 'fear' is always organic to the ruler-ruled relationship), but indeed represents an inexhaustible source of propulsion, of multiplication of its strength.[64] Democracy *ex communi multitudine*: coming from a whole multitude, capable of self-government and of civil and political autonomy. This eventually leads to the celebration of multiplicity, of the plurality of vectors of participation to political power: an explicitly Machiavellian reassessment of the presence of the 'many' at the heart of the *imperium*, against the insistence on the inevitable and presumed necessity of a secret (*arcanum*), in the management of power.[65]

---

[62] *TP* III, 9; *CWS* II, 521.
[63] *TP* II, 17; *CWS* II, 514.
[64] See *supra*, Chapter 3.
[65] According to the main references, see *TP* II, 17 (*CWS* II, 514) and *TP* III, 2, 7 and

The *imperium* is always anticipated by the power of the multitude (*multitudinis potentia*), which defines and limits it. And yet – and this is the second pillar on which the political-philosophical architecture of the *TP* rests – that very power will still be deployed, it will still be oriented by the *imperium*: 'the Right of a state, or of the supreme powers, is nothing more than the Right of nature, determined not by the power of each person, but by the power of a multitude, led as if by one mind (*una veluti mente*)'.[66] Given that the ontology of cause-power implies both the absoluteness and the relativity of the *res singulares*, the notion of *multitudo* in the *TP* encapsulates the 'common space' of human determinations, the place of equal intersection of all human-modes. Essential for the *res* – and yet a mode and not substance (not *causa sui*) – this global domain of relationships assumes constancy and stability only insofar as there continuously emerges – from the mobile and relative 'potential' which it represents – a force in action, an unfolded *vis* that still allows its effective *operari*, its authentic positivity and its productive *facere*.[67] Identical to any other *res*, from the standpoint of its 'principle' (its nature as a 'mode'), the *imperium* is however distinct by means of its 'function': as a very special *fabrica*, an *ars* of relations between men, power exists for itself (*in se*) just as it sustains (governs, ensures, feeds) the power (*potentia*) of the modes (*in alio*). The *jus* of supreme power (*summa potestas*) proceeds from the power of the multitude (*multitudinis potentia*); but the latter, in turn, emanates from unity, from the unifying vector of supreme power: as if by one mind. The multitude is then configured as the place of constitution of the political which, in turn, is presented as the domain of determination and expansion of the multitude. It is precisely this reciprocity, which in some way translates the metaphysical link between substance and the *res singulares* exposed in the first part of *Ethics* into politics, that nourishes the surplus in which the third moment of the relationship can be found:

> [t]herefore, when disagreements and rebellions are stirred up in a Commonwealth – as they often are – the result is never that the citizens dissolve the Commonwealth – though this often happens in other kinds

---

9 (*CWS* II, 517, 520, 521: on *multitudo*, *imperium* and democracy); *TP* VIII, 3 and 4 (*CWS* II, 566 and 567: on democracy); *TP* V, 5–7, and *TP* VII, 27 and 29 (*CWS* II, 558–60: on the plural power – *potential* – of the *multitudo* in a democracy and against state secrets). As for Machiavelli see, for example, *Dis.* I, 58.

[66] *TP* III, 2; *CWS* II, 517.

[67] Albeit from a different perspective, similar considerations can be found in Bonicalzi 1999: 114ff.

of society. Instead, if they can't settle their disagreements while preserving the form of the Commonwealth, they change its form to another.[68]

The inescapability of political power does not void the primacy of the multitude, not even in its 'outgoing' movement with respect to any codified form of the *imperium*. This is a natural priority that, conversely, Hobbesian rationalist artificialism (but ultimately also the ambiguity of the *TTP* with regard to a 'pact') tends to elide, making the *Leviathan* a point of non-return, a definitive separation from the common impulses and from the structural intersections of the natural. Multitudinous relationships do not erase individuals but rather constitute them in their inescapably flexible, stratified, and pluralised character. The condition of the human-mode presents itself with the traits of a singularity that is quite foreign to a self-fulfilled, solipsistic Hobbesian (and Cartesian, and Lockean-liberal) individualism.[69] As a mere moment, a segment of the overall process of constant composition and decomposition of power (*potentia*), the structure of each individual human being is not defined by the meta-temporal fixity of its essence, the completeness of an autonomous and unchangeable identity. Rather, it remains inextricably involved in the dynamism of its own *strength*: in the mobility of a *conatus*, the instability of a desire (*cupiditas*) which is, by its very nature, devoted to action and the construction of relationships. Spinoza's modal anthropology introduces a *multiversal* human being, irreducible to the compact rigidity of the modern 'subject'. Here the true dimension of individual unfolding appears to be precisely that of the 'multitude', at the antipodes of 'solitude'. The latter is the worst evil, the condition in which, in the absence of others, one inevitably cannot even be oneself: *solitudinis metus* (where *metus* is more than 'fear' and should properly be translated as 'terror').[70] The wholly isolated individual (capable of wanting, of knowing, and of living in full autonomy) is only an illusion, the fruit of a proud ignorance. It is the *multitudo* – the opposite of *solitudo* – that determines the human condition: the complex intertwining of cause and being caused, of doing and suffering, of acting and enduring, which entirely resolves its existence. Extraneous

---

[68] TP VI, 2; CWS II, 532.

[69] The modal nature of the individual clarifies both its indispensability and its relational constitution: this is why *multitudo* does not produce 'an almost total eclipse of the Spinozan notion of individuality' (this is Cristofolini's thesis) but, on the contrary, just as it gathers the active space of this complex articulation, it proposes itself as a peculiar variant, an alternative to the prevailing, and highly successful, 'individualistic' understanding of the modern individual; see Cristofolini 2002: 29–50.

[70] TP VI, 1; CWS II, 532. And see Cristofolini 2002: 17–23; Bostrenghi 2003.

to any metaphysical reification (that is alien to both the organicism of the ancient tradition and to the Rousseauvian transubstantiation of the *volonté générale*), the 'multitude' amounts to a reciprocity, an interdependence between humans that does not exclude either collaboration or conflict. The isolation of humans appears, in the Spinozan perspective, as an extreme and sterile case, a useless conceptual abstraction. In both agreement and struggle, humans *naturally* remain equal and sociable: not for holistic-teleological reasons, but due to necessary mechanisms of life, for mandatory operations of power (*potentia*).

On the one hand, then, the interrelations of *multitudo* cannot but place themselves within the political nexus, within the need for a positive, institutionalised restriction, such as to contain and manage (as far as possible) the structural instability of relationships. And it is on this level that *legal* distinctions emerge: temporary, codified expressions of the continuous blending, production, and reproduction of political and civil intersections. From those distinctions that police the border of *civitas* – as between friend and enemy – to the internal ones that establish bonds of subjection (*commander/ commanded*) or of public equality: among tribes in a monarchy, among the nobles in an aristocracy, among citizens in a democracy, all the way to those fault lines that run along social or gender divisions (servant/master, man/ woman, and cultured/uncultured) they lose the centrality they enjoy in the *TTP*, and are demoted to just one of the many factors of collective relationality. But, on the other hand, on these more or less legally acknowledged and established equalities and inequalities, the *communis natura* of the *multitudo* always comes into play: the intertwining of the natural, which takes away any substantiality from the restrictions of political order by continuously practising and undermining its *modal-functional* nature.

In the *TTP* the complex dynamics of the *conatus* are supplemented by a streamlining of the rational-liberal couplet 'individual-State'. On the other hand, the circular link that the *TP* introduces between the *imperium* and the *multitude* refers, from the social standpoint (that of human determinations) to the metaphysical heart of Spinoza's *Ethics*. In the world of human determinations, the *multitudo* acts towards the *imperium* as substance does with respect to the *res singulares*. Substance is the cause of itself in the same sense in which it is the cause of things, it is *causa sui* just as it is *causa rerum*: this makes it both incommensurable with regards to the modes and yet always and totally 'unfolded' in and 'expressed' through them. In quite a parallel and consequential way, *multitudo* is constituted through the constitution of power: a condition that makes it 'superabundant', irreducible to power, but always and completely 'explicated' and necessarily 'self-determined' within power. In the universe of the chain of causes, *potentia* is a constitutive and subversive condition of *potestas*, in the strictest sense: it determines it just as it consumes it. *Potentia* opens up to a particular form of *potestas* just as it makes another particular form of *potestas* crumble. *Potentia* cannot avoid (producing) *potestas*, it cannot exempt itself from *potestas*. But, by causing it, it necessarily causes itself.[71]

Drastically reconfigured and rigorously adapted to the structure of metaphysics (and the anthropology of the *conatus*), the political philosophy of the *TP* definitively brings into focus the peculiarity of the Spinozan stance with respect to the prevailing perspectives of modernity: both the one that can be attributed, with a rough approximation, to the line of thought that goes from Locke to Kant – and based on the primacy of the individual and of 'civil society' in the construction of the political order – and to that going from Hobbes to Hegel, oriented instead towards the 'formative' priority of the State. With regard to these different political stances Spinoza holds firm the idea of the dissolution of all natural hierarchies (the natural equality of men) and the consequent character of absolute 'inevitability' and 'humanity' of the political domain. But, being a *radically* modern thinker, he also keeps firm – and indeed puts at the centre of his reflection – the collective constitution of modernity: its continuous, chaotic, and impulsive dynamism, made of tensions and 'mass' relations. This is a decisive determination of modernity, introduced (as it is bound to be) by hegemonic vectors, only to be immediately removed – a cumbersome and dangerous presence.

The Kinds of State

In the *TP* the forms of power (*potestas*) are distributed between the opposite extremes of, on the one hand, absolute *imperium* (diffused power, held by an *integra multitudo*) and, on the other, the disposition of those who are acted upon (*aptitudo patientis*): that condition which – the least active one, proper of the more concentrated variables of the *imperium* – still implies a decisive role for the multitude, the conclusive task of its 'bearing'. The 'realistic' and

---

[71] The 'retroactive' function of the *imperium* on the *multitudo* is underexamined by Negri 1981, for whom it presents itself as a pure and vertical alternative to *potestas*, the subversive and 'Dionysian' side of the political order, a position only partially revised in Negri 1992. On these aspects – and on the importance of Negri's innovative reading – see Caporali 1993. '*Potentia* is an important concept, but it remains always within the legal frameworks of *potestas* and *sub alterius potestate*': a sort of reversal of the primacy of *potentia* over *potestas* is hypothesised – through a close engagement with Negri's theses – by Terpstra 1994.

'strategizing' tone of the treatise – connected to this philosophical-political approach – is explicitly intertwined, in several parts, with direct and indirect references to Machiavelli (through an anti-historical, 'oblique' interpretation of the *Prince* as a text aimed at educating people towards freedom).[72] There is realism: for the concrete arrangement, the empirical articulation of forces does not always make it possible or opportune to adopt the perspective of the *imperium absolutum*, which, by way of hypothesis, is the strongest and most rational form, because aimed at actively involving everyone in the management of power (*potestas*). In certain particular circumstances, generally determined by habit and experience, such a solution could indeed prove to be the least indicated and most dangerous one: '[o]ne [multitude] which has become accustomed to another form of state won't be able to uproot the foundations they've received without a great danger of overthrowing the whole state and changing its structure'.[73] There is also strategizing: given the inevitable plurality of solutions, it will always be possible to identify strategies to 'optimise' the forms of government, preserving *multitudo* as the determining principle of the *imperium*. It is through this 'binary' trend that Spinoza articulates the 'political science' tone of the *Treatise*, by means of the assumption – now definitively accepted and put into practice – that no theory directly governs the dynamics of power by virtue of its supposedly intrinsic and autonomous force of truth. The *vis* of the 'doctrine' is, if anything, itself a particular and interacting factor, a composite and constitutive element of power (*potentia*). In order to challenge reality with the hope of being effective, science – which as such analyses and constructs, 'describes' and 'prescribes' – must first take into account its own inevitable *relativity* (the relativity of its placement in positive contexts of relationships and determinations). The new role of the *multitudo* opens the space for political science as a middle term, as a border region, a strategic area of communication between the 'principles' (the metaphysics of the *imperium*) and actual militancy and contingent political commitment. The unfinished transition

---

[72] TP V, 7; CWS II, 530. This reading of *The Prince* – later adopted, among others, by Boccalini and Rousseau, Alfieri and Foscolo – dates back, as is well-known, to Alberico Gentili. On the diffusion of Machiavelli's 'republican' interpretation in Anglo-Saxon and Dutch political thought see respectively Pocock 1975 and Van Gelderen 1990; more generally, on Machiavelli's *fortuna* in modern European culture, see Procacci 1995. Without forgetting older surveys (Ravà 1958; Gallicet Calvetti 1972), on the meaning and presence, in Spinoza, of the 'ever shrewd' Machiavelli (*TP* V, 7), important recent studies are Morfino 2002; Cristofolini 2002; Del Lucchese 2004; Visentin 2004; Torres 2007; Tatian 2014.
[73] TP VII, 26; CWS II, 558.

of the United Provinces thus remains the concrete background of the connections and interactions with which the 'doctrine' intends to measure itself. If the first five chapters of the *TP* aim at the theoretical constitution of *multitudo*, reorganising the previous theoretical tenets around this objective, the second (interrupted) part of the work turns to a more focused investigation of the contextualised and realisable variants of power, and to the deduction – situated and axiological – of its practicable experiences. As Spinoza writes:

> I am fully persuaded that experience has shown all the kinds of State which might conceivably enable men to live in harmony, as well as the means by which a multitude ought to be directed, or restrained within definite limits. So I don't believe reflection on this subject can come up with anything not completely at variance with experience, or practice, which hasn't yet been learned and tested by experience.[74]

No science can 'bring into being', invent, or contradict reality. A *good* science, however, knows how to judge, ponder, and select reality; moreover, it knows how to become an integral and active part of it. The analysis of the various kinds of state does not therefore concern 'all' the *thinkable* forms of political power, all the variants liable to elaboration and reflection. A critical inquiry will not be pure deductivism, nor generic sociology, nor – even less so – abstruse and fanciful arbitrariness, a mere whimsy of the mind. Political science selects and discriminates by looking at its own 'applicability', at its active and 'evaluative' scope, in the context of the finite plurality and the limited multiplicity of the variables indicated by experience. Spinoza recalls that

> when I applied my mind to Politics, I didn't intend to advance anything new or unheard of, but only to demonstrate the things which agree best with practice, in a certain and indubitable way, and to deduce them from the condition of human nature.[75]

The centrality of *multitudo* and its 'double' relationship with the *imperium* – the bivalent connection by virtue of which the multitude is never completely resolved in power but is always deployed and wholly 'expressed' in power – invalidates a simple alternative between two possible absolutising

[74] *TP* I, 3; *CWS* II, 504–5.
[75] *TP* I, 4; *CWS* II, 505.

(and simplifying) perspectives: the utopian and unrealistic perspectives of the 'philosophers', aimed at the deduction of an abstractly 'better' power (*potestas*) excluded from such centrality and obtained regardless of this reciprocity, and that of mere empiricism, of an indifferent assumption, the narrow road, the small-minded commerce of the 'politicians'. There is no 'legitimising' foundation (both 'legitimacy' and 'justification' are criteria internal to political power and to its necessity/unavoidability), nor a valuation: it is rather a distinction between the data of a particular experience, of the elements that are *optime*. Advantageous in their real determination, with respect to the 'principle' of the political, with the (imperfect) reversibility of *multitudo* and *imperium*, they allow for a more intense productivity and a wider 'functionality':[76]

> [t]his right, which is defined by the power of a multitude, is usually called Sovereignty. Whoever, by common agreement, has responsibility for public Affairs – that is, the rights of making, interpreting, and repealing laws, fortifying cities, and making decisions about war and peace, etc. – has this right absolutely. If this responsibility is the business of a Council made up of the common multitude, then the State is called a Democracy; if the council is made up only of certain select people, it's called an Aristocracy; and finally, if the responsibility for Public Affairs, and hence sovereignty, is vested in one person, it's called a Monarchy.[77]

Where the *TTP* had exhausted the typologies of the *imperium* by means of a frontal opposition between a widespread and dynamic government of all on the one hand, and the static and punctual power (*potestas*) of the king on the other, the new theory presented in the *TP* takes up the challenge of

---

[76] Paolo Cristofolini observes how 'political science' in the *TP* presents itself as 'intuitive science', articulated on the double register of 'science of institutional mechanisms' and 'production of balances modulated on concrete circumstances'. Political analysis thus proceeds from the third kind of knowledge, a deduction of the particular from the two constitutive attributes of human nature: 'utopia is not so much a paradise of the imagination, but a paradise of reason (the paradises of the imagination are the ultramundane ones promised by the prophets; utopia is instead a secular and earthly form). It is an abstract model of social perfection, deduced from a common notion of man (goodness of the original impulses and desires, uniformity and immutability of the human constitutive structure). Resorting – unlike utopians – to the deduction of the third kind of knowledge means moving towards the *inventio* of those modalities of the arrangement of the mechanism of the state which correspond to the historical-cultural determinations of man (*res singulares*)' (1987: 129. My translation).

[77] *TP* II, 17; *CWS* II, 514.

a wider givenness, of a more complex actuality, as was clearly made explicit by contemporary socio-political events. And if no 'engineering' and no 'institutional modelling' as such can arbitrate the real (by overlapping with that entanglement of powers that alone can produce the 'form'), a political theory will nevertheless be able to measure every single concentration of the *imperium* according to the common meter of its exclusive *ratio*, of its unique constitutive paradigm. Unable to direct experience *tout court*, a critical analysis will however be able to select the fields of investigation, to privilege segments of 'practice' that leave it a space and a *chance* – i.e. that allow it to condense itself into 'strength', a vehicle of acceleration for actions and interactions between forces.

On Monarchy

Monarchy, that form of government where 'all power is conferred on one man',[78] is wholly secondary in the *TP*. Sifted through the *imperium-multitudo* circularity, this particular power certainly falls within the range of possible variations, but it still appears as its most negative and least functional form, being stuck on the minimum threshold of power (*potentia*) and paralysed by the mutual fear that runs between the king and his subjects. This solution is also the most science-proof, because it is the most difficult to modify (being always precariously balanced between enormous risks and minor advantages), and obsessed, unlike the mobile and tumultuous nature of the popular republic (*respublica popularia*), with the arid stability and the sterile continuity guaranteed by the subjugation of the people.[79] The evaluative-prescriptive inquiry looks elsewhere: at least for the monarchical form of *imperium* (but the problem, albeit in other terms, also pertains to aristocracy), for it analyses that 'intermediate' situation in which a *multitudo* results, incapable of self-government while still appearing to be able to exercise some function, some (direct or indirect) form of verification and control of the 'civitas'. This 'doctrine', in essence, assumes the characteristics of a strategy aimed at the partial recovery of a role for *multitudo* in a moment of crisis; or rather, in those transitional phases in which the displacement of forces still makes it possible to avoid the extreme and negative outcomes of renunciation: a fruitless passivity, an infertile dependence, a mere loss of authority. Such a dislocation, as it looks at the practical possibilities of

[78] *TP* VI, 4; *CWS* II, 533.
[79] *TP* V, 7; *CWS* II, 531.

thought, also deals with 'the best condition of each state'.[80] Indeed, once certain conditions are given and the inevitability and the opportunity of other forms of power (*potestas*) than those of democracy – the only form of government that proceeds by absolute reciprocity with the multitude – is posited, the best 'disposition' and the best 'constitution' of such forms will necessarily be sought in the space of greater proximity (as allowed by their own nature) to that reciprocity. That is to say, it will be sought in the borderland that runs between the peculiarities of each single determination of the *imperium* and, in what remains – albeit compressed, restricted, and concealed – the only origin/beginning of the *imperium*. If the realisation of the political order at the intersection with the *multitudo* is implicit in its essence, the political forms that find their *raison d'être* precisely in the exclusion of the *multitudo* will be evaluated according to the degree and the relativity of such an exclusion. Those that are better suited to multiply energies – to produce power – will be deemed better: they will be situations which, even after the *summa potestas* is concentrated in the hands of one or of a few, still allow the existence of channels of dialogue with the multitude. Those are conditions, in sum, in which the direct or indirect weight of the multitude will still appear such as to prevent a (tendentially) crystallised self-referentiality of political power.

Since humans 'are guided more by affect than by reason', a *multitudo* will spontaneously coalesce and will want to be guided 'as if by one mind': not on the basis of rational decisions but 'because of some common affect. . . . [T]hey have a common hope, or fear, or a common desire to avenge some harm.'[81] Moreover, it is precisely the prevailing passive affects that prevent us from wishing for what is 'most useful' to everyone, and what requires the *ars* of the *imperium*, a power established in such a way that both those who govern and those who are governed – 'whether they want to or not', 'whether of his own accord, or by force, or by necessity' – are forced to live according to the dictates of reason: '[t]his happens if the affairs of the state are so arranged that nothing which concerns the common well-being is committed absolutely to the good faith of any one person'. No one, in fact, is ever 'so alert' as to never doze off, from time to time, and no one has ever been so strong and adamant as not to falter just when his or her virtue would have been the most necessary. After all, one cannot expect from others what one cannot obtain from oneself: 'that he not be greedy, or envious, or ambitious, etc., especially when every day he has the strongest incentives to

---

[80] *TP* V, 1; *CWS* II, 528–9.
[81] *TP* VI, 1; *CWS* II, 532.

all the affects'.[82] Experience, however, would seem to teach us that, in order to reach 'peace and concord', it is preferable to entrust all power (*potestas*) to a single person. Absolute monarchy ('absolute' not in the Spinozan sense, but in the traditional one, as for example the *imperium* of the Turks), in fact, appears to be much more stable and solid than democracy, with respect to which 'none have been less lasting'. And yet, in reality, this political regime feeds on a feigned peace and guarantees very poor living conditions to its subjects:

> [s]till, if slavery, barbarism, and being without protection are to be called peace, nothing is more wretched for men than peace. No doubt . . . [t]o transfer all power to one man makes for bondage, not peace. As we've said, peace does not consist in the privation of war, but in a union or harmony of minds.[83]

However, no situation will be worse, for a *civitas*, than the gradual decay of a previously 'excellent' state. Not so much collapsing – as it is certainly impossible – 'at a single stroke', but rather showing advanced and progressive signs of disintegration, plagued by incurable divisions and seditious tendencies. It would be much better, in this case, to hand over all power to a single individual rather 'than to agree to uncertain and empty or ineffective conditions for liberty, and thus to make the way ready for future generations to descend into the cruelest slavery'.[84] Focusing on its own diagnostic-therapeutic capabilities, political science favours, among the infinite variants of the monarchical order, one that is by no means 'scholastic' and indeed very real, very close to the contingency of a republican condition such as the Dutch one, a country still experiencing a phase of confused and indeterminate transformations.

Since everyone – paraphrasing the Sallustian tradition – 'prefers ruling to being ruled', in a context like the one outlined above the *multitudo* will transfer to the king as little power as possible, only as much as it cannot keep for itself, namely the right to settle disputes and to take timely decisions.[85] Wherever it will be possible to freely choose a king, such a choice will be taken without any explicit conditions. And the existence of 'laws to be so

---

[82] *TP* VI, 3; *CWS* II, 533.
[83] *TP* VI, 4; *CWS* II, 533.
[84] *TP* VII, 2; *CWS* II, 545.
[85] *TP* VII, 5; *CWS* II, 547.

firmly established that not even the King himself can repeal them'[86] does not contradict either reason or experience. Either by means of rational persuasion or passion, it is much better that humans institute 'valid and firmly established rights and laws'.[87] The 'fundamental principles of the state' will therefore be considered as 'eternal decrees of the King', to the point that the ministers of the monarch – like Ulysses' sailors upon hearing the siren song – will completely obey him even when opposing his particular decisions, such as to contradict those very foundations. As Spinoza puts it: '[i]f a Monarchic state is to be stable, it must be set up in such a way that . . . all law is the King's will, as it has been made known, but that not everything the King wills is law'.[88] This is the only way to avoid the most serious risks typical of this form of government. Since the *imperium* is always more threatened by its citizens than by its enemies, the (Hobbesian) absolute monarch would, first of all, think about his own interest, trying to undermine his subjects (especially the most influential ones, either because rich or because wise) instead of providing for them. His own children, especially if experts in the arts of war and peace, would be looked upon with distrust and fear,[89] also because the more power is deferred to a single individual, the more easily it will be transferable to another.[90] And in any case, in actual practice, it is virtually impossible for supreme power (*summa potestas*) to be truly held by a single individual: if right derives from *potentia*, the *potestas* of an individual will be absolutely inadequate 'to bearing such a burden';[91] the king that is elected by the multitude will look for 'commanders', 'counsellors', and 'friends', to whom to entrust 'his own well-being and that of everyone else'. However, in this way an absolute monarchy turns out to be a secret or disguised aristocracy, the worst of its kind. Since a single person cannot keep everything under control, nor can he always be ready to reflect and decide (without considering the possibility of illness, old age, and of so many other events) it is therefore necessary for the king to be explicitly and officially supported by advisers who can help him and can make up for his absences, so as to guarantee unity, stability, and continuity of direction to the *imperium*.[92] A solidly constituted government will then be one in which the 'Monarch will be secure, and the multitude will have peace', for the two will overlap, feeding

[86] *TP* VII, 1; *CWS* II, 544.
[87] *TP* VII, 2; *CWS* II, 545.
[88] *TP* VII, 1; *CWS* II, 544–5.
[89] *TP* VI, 6; *CWS* II, 534.
[90] *TP* VI, 7; *CWS* II, 534.
[91] *TP* VI, 5; *CWS* II, 533.
[92] *TP* VII, 3; *CWS* II, 546.

each other, even beyond the particular wills and the contingent intentions of their various actors. In other words, it is necessary to think of the 'fundamental principles of the state' such that the more a king appears *sui juris*, the more he (due to an institutionally codified relationship of power, rather than his subjective disposition) will take care of the well-being of the *multitudo*:[93]

> [w]e conclude, then, that a multitude can preserve a full enough freedom under a King, so long as it brings it about that the King's power is determined only by the power of the multitude, and is preserved by the multitude's support. And this was the only Rule I followed in laying the foundations of a Monarchic state.[94]

The first condition for such a form of *imperium* is juridical equality, whereby all citizens can enjoy 'the same rights'.[95] The inhabitants of the cities and of the countryside will be divided into 'clans',[96] and criminals, mutes, madmen, servants (*famuli*), and all those 'who make their living by performing some servile function'[97] will be deprived of any political right. The king will be elected for the first time by the *multitudo*, chosen among the members of one of these families. 'For the citizens to be as equal as possible' (which appears to be supremely necessary, for the sake of the republic), only the descendants of the monarch will be considered 'Nobles'. It will be forbidden to them – up to the third and fourth degree of kinship – to take a wife, and the path towards political and administrative positions will be

---

[93] *TP* VI, 8; *CWS* II, 534.
[94] *TP* VII, 31; *CWS* II, 563.
[95] *TP* VI, 9; *CWS* II, 534.
[96] For most commentators that of 'clan' is a rather confused and uncertain notion; to be compared to the Roman *gens* according to Appuhn (1928); to the 'tribes' of Israel, according to Zac (1968); and to the medieval consortiums and the mercantile aristocracies of Genoa and Venice – 'evanescent notion', probably deduced from Moro's Utopia – according to Droetto (*TP* 227n). While justifiable, any such comparison risks losing sight of the objective and the conceptually modern functionality of the Spinozist 'clan', aimed at affirming legal equality and the overcoming of social classes.
[97] *Restricted* discrimination, compared to Platonic discrimination (which also involves craftsmen and merchants, see Droetto (*TP* 228n). Pezzillo (*TP* 38n) does not eliminate the impression of an interference due to *age* – the historical-political conditions, the culture and the mentality of the *time* – in the most universal and rigorous conceptual consequences that follow from notion of *multitudo*. After all, something similar also happens in the last chapter of the *TP*, regarding the exclusion of women from democratic power and biological difference, but on this see below, the concluding paragraph of this chapter.

precluded to any illegitimate children they might have. In fact, were the king's relatives left free to multiply, they would soon become too numerous, thus compromising civil equality and representing a burden and a danger for all citizens, since '[m]en who have too much leisure often spend their time contemplating wicked actions'.[98] The same need for equality must also cover religious policy, which must forbid – as Spinoza's *TTP* had already indicated – the existence of an official cult and of a privileged priestly class: no temple will be built at public expense and every religious denomination will remain limited within the context of the choices and donations of private individuals or groups of citizens.[99]

The 'supreme council' presents itself as the fundamental institution for this kind of *imperium*.[100] The members of this institution should be numerous, and they must be chosen among the citizens who are at least fifty years of age, in groups of three, four, or five for each family. Every year some of them will have to be renewed: both because a life-long appointment would exclude the majority from the hope of being chosen (thus dampening that desire for glory by which we are all animated, and which can instead be transformed into the raw material of political energy); and because councillors elected for life would not be held back by the fear of the judgment of their successors, and would thus commit all sorts of abuse, without encountering obstacles from the king, to whom they would submit with flattery and servility; and finally because a partial and annual renewal avoids the risk of the Council being temporarily constituted by either all novices or all veterans. The king will be in charge of appointing them, but he will only be able to choose among the candidates nominated by each clan (among which, however, at least one legal expert must always be chosen).[101] Each family

---

[98] *TP* VI, 13 and VII, 20; *CWS* II, 535 and 554.
[99] *TP* VI, 40; *CWS* II, 543.
[100] *TP* VII, 15; *CWS* II, 552.
[101] See *TP*: VI, 21 (*CWS* II, 538); VI, 15 (*CWS* II, 536); VII, 6 (*CWS* II, 548); VII, 13 (*CWS* II, 550); VI, 16 (*CWS* II, 536–7); VII, 18 (*CWS* II, 553). The 'jurist' is a figure probably inspired by that of the 'Grand Pensionary', who leads his provincial delegation to the States General of the United Provinces. This whole elaboration, and even more that which relates to the aristocratic form, is woven of clear or implicit references to the concrete Dutch experience. This has been repeatedly underlined by the commentators, also in the technical-juridical details: see the *Kommentar* by Gebhardt (*Spinoza Opera*, V, 133–96); the French versions of the *TP* edited by Appuhn (1928), by Francès (1954) and by Moreau (1979), as well as the Italian one by Droetto (1958). Here we will only mention some of the most striking examples, in order not to lose sight of the need, constantly explored by political science, for effective intervention on the political and institutional problems of the Netherlands.

will be represented by the same number of councillors and will be entitled to a single vote, so that each city will be able to count on a number of representatives proportional to that of its citizens: the only criterion by which it is possible to evaluate the 'power of a state'.[102] In such a Council, many will be people 'whose mentality is quite uncultivated', devoid of culture and wisdom; but human nature, 'strongly disposed by his affects', pursues its own 'personal advantage', and everyone seems willing to defend the interests of others only when they can thereby obtain their own benefit. Those who will be elected, therefore, will have to be citizens for whom their private business depends on the health and peace of all. And since 'each of them will be shrewd and clever enough in matters he has long been passionately involved in', those who have dealt with their own affairs in an honourable manner up to the age of fifty will be preferred.[103] The main task of the Council is the defence of the 'fundamental rights of this state'. The discussion about the best measures to be adopted will end with a suggestion, to be submitted to the monarch for ratification. If a unanimous resolution is not reached, the king will be presented only those proposals that have obtained at least one hundred votes: he will then choose independently among them, but not outside of them, since he will be unable to take decisions that are contrary to board resolutions. Only in this way will it be possible to maintain the equilibrium that makes the 'people's well-being' coincide with the 'King's highest right'.[104] And besides, the monarch – driven by the fear of the multitude, or by the desire to tie the multitude to himself, or again due to a generosity of spirit that would make him prioritise public utility – will almost always adopt the opinion that was voted for by the majority, considering it to be the most useful to the greater number of citizens. Otherwise, he will try the way of mediation/conciliation, with the aim of reaching a general agreement.[105] The duties of the Council also include: the executive tasks of promulgating the monarch's decrees and provisions as well as providing for their practical implementation; the necessary and obligatory mediation between the *rex*, on the one hand, and either the citizens or other States, on the other; and finally the education of the king's children as well as their protection – Spinoza has at hand the example of William III of Orange, son of William II – in the case of the king's death.[106] Convened in plenary session at least

---

[102] *TP* VII, 18; CWS II, 553.
[103] *TP* VII, 4; CWS II, 546.
[104] *TP* VI, 25 (CWS II, 539–40); VI, 17 (CWS II, 537); VII, 5 (CWS II, 547–8).
[105] *TP* VII, 11; CWS II, 549.
[106] *TP* VI, 18–20; CWS II, 537–8.

four times a year, the supreme Council must register the presence of all its members when discussing problems, such as those relating to peace and war, that involve the life and interests of the whole *civitas*: absent councillors will send their substitutes (among the candidates of the same clan), and in case of non-compliance they will have to pay high fines. Regarding 'daily' governance, the Council appoints fifty of its members to represent the whole, who will meet every day in a room near the king's apartments, to take care (always within the framework of the deliberations of the supreme body) of the treasury, the defensive works, and the sons of the monarch.[107] Clearly, the designs and intentions of such an *imperium* cannot be kept hidden; but it is better to allow the enemies of the state to know the 'the state's proper and true plans', rather than hide the 'tyrant's wicked secrets' from the citizens.[108] Those who conduct the 'business of the state' in secret have absolute power and, just as in war they tend to ambush enemies, in peace they adopt the same strategy with their own the citizens. Once the *multitudo* is placed at the heart of power (*potestas*), every idea pertaining to the necessity and inevitability of state secrets – as well as of a *raison d'état* that would be better (even morally so) when subtracted from the confused and inexperienced whole of the *civitas* – is completely abandoned.[109] It is true, as Hobbes argued,[110] that silence is often useful to the rulers, but it is false that, without it, governing is impossible. Moreover, no king is safer than the one at the head of such a *civitas*: if the monarch's greatest dangers originate from those who are closest to him, the larger his entourage the stronger the king will be, since a large number of councillors (equal among themselves, and in office for a fixed time) will never succeed in agreeing to commit the same crime, thus representing, for the sovereign, not a danger but rather a solid, reliable, and trustworthy source of support.[111]

Grounded on the obligation to cover the expenses of its own defence, the legal equality between cities is a fundamental principle of this form of *imperium*, which Spinoza partly derives from similar provisions laid down in the constitution of the United Provinces. The citizens, in fact, are undoubtedly all the more powerful (and therefore all the more '*sui juris*') the larger and more heavily fortified their cities are. The more the place in which they live

---

[107] *TP* VI, 24; *CWS* II, 539.
[108] *TP* VII, 29; *CWS* II, 560.
[109] With these theses Spinoza could take a critical stance with regard to the two books of Clapmayer and Besold, *De arc*. Of course, the classic work by Meinecke (1957) should be the first reference when it comes to the idea of a 'reason of State'.
[110] *Lev*, XIX.
[111] *TP* VII, 29 (*CWS* II, 560) and VII, 14 (*CWS* II, 551–2).

is well-guarded, the more they can protect their freedom and their safety from both internal and external enemies. The cities that have to resort to 'another's power (*alterius potentia*)' to defend themselves do not, on the contrary, have an equal right, but will be considered subjects, in proportion to their dependence on the strength of others.[112] Precisely for this reason the army must be composed 'only of citizens, without exception': because the 'armed man' is master of himself more than the 'unarmed' one. In order to achieve this goal it is necessary to take advantage of human avarice, one of the most tenacious and influential of all the passions, which makes most people reluctant to incur the huge costs necessary to hire mercenary troops.[113] Since the king cannot hope to control everyone through fear, his power (*potentia*) will be proportional to the number of soldiers under his command and, above all, to their virtue and their loyalty, which will persist only as long as they are motivated by a need, either an honest or a dishonest one. For the monarch to favour his citizens (allowing them to remain 'free' within the limits allowed by the 'civil order' and 'equity'), the army will therefore have to be composed only by the citizens themselves, who also have access to the Supreme Council.[114] The army – divided, in each family in cohorts and legions (whose commanders will be in office for life) – will have a supreme commander only in case of war, and only for a year, without the possibility of re-election.[115] That is because both sacred and profane history teaches us that if a single individual is left in command for a time long enough to let him acquire sufficient military glory – so much to be acclaimed more than the king himself – he can become the true arbiter and depositary of power. The *duces* are then chosen among the advisors or ex-councillors of the sovereign at a rather advanced age, when prudence and a lack of interest for adventures and coups prevail in their character.[116] Instead, it would be 'sheer stupidity' for a monarch to elect himself out of a multitude in view of a war (as happened in Holland in 1672, when William III of Orange, in order to cope with the French invasion, was granted both the positions of captain general and *stadhouder*, something that had been forbidden by De Witt in 1670): '[t]o wage war more successfully, people are willing to be slaves in peace'.[117]

[112] TP VII, 16 (CWS II, 552) and VI, 9 (CWS II, 534).
[113] TP VI, 10 (CWS II, 552) and VII, 17 (CWS II, 552–3).
[114] TP VII, 12; CWS II, 549–50.
[115] TP VI, 10; CWS II, 535.
[116] TP VII, 17; CWS II, 552–3.
[117] TP VII, 5; CWS II, 547. On the Tacitean and Sallustian echoes found in these passages (and on their actualising political tendency) see Proietti 1985: 210–17, a very useful tool for surveying classical presences in Spinozan texts.

Furthermore, no pay should be granted to soldiers in times of peace, '[f]or the army's greatest reward is freedom'.[118] During a war, those who have a daily job are paid regularly, while the booty achieved with the final victory is reserved for commanders and officers; the prize of the citizen-soldier is the achievement of a *sui juris* condition, granting freedom and self-mastery.[119] In this way, the army's goal will always be peace. The 'professional soldiers', trained to be disciplined and used to enduring all kinds of hardship (heat, cold, hunger) despise the 'crowd of citizens', considering them inferior. In reality, however, no one with a 'sound mind' could claim that, without them, the State would be less prosperous and stable: on the contrary, an *imperium* that has 'enough power to defend its own possessions, but not enough to seek those of others, and which for that reason tries in every way to avoid war and to preserve peace'[120] will always be more solid. As Spinoza puts it, echoing Grotius: '[w]ar ought to be waged only for the sake of peace so that when it's finished, the weapons may be set aside'.[121] Occupied cities should remain free from occupying forces, allowing the enemy to redeem them, or else be completely destroyed, and the inhabitants transferred and dispersed. Besides, peace will always be the aim of the majority of the Council for fear of losing their freedom and property, for the need to avoid huge expenses, and because otherwise 'their children and relations, occupied with private concerns, will be compelled to apply their zeal to arms and to go into military service'.[122] Aiming, once again, at the preservation of peace, it is advisable to abolish the private property of real estate. The fields, the land and, if possible, even the houses should be publicly owned and available to the monarch, who will lease them to the citizens in exchange for an annual fee, the only tax paid by the citizens, used to fund the works of fortification of the country, as well as the private needs of the king. Indeed, in the state of nature, nothing can be claimed as one's own less than the soil and all that adheres to it. And if no single person owns these material goods, the danger that comes from war will be the same for everyone. Everyone will thus focus mainly on trade, or lending money to each other, thus promoting projects that are 'entangled with one another' and which require the same means to be increased; in this way the will of the Supreme Council will converge on decisions in relation to common affairs and works of peace that are usually

---

[118] *TP* VII, 22; *CWS* II, 554–5.
[119] *TP* VI, 31; *CWS* II, 541.
[120] *TP* VII, 28; *CWS* II, 560.
[121] *TP* VI, 35; *CWS* II, 542.
[122] *TP* VII, 7; *CWS* II, 548.

unanimous, putting into practice the principle according to which 'everyone defends the cause of another just so far as he believes that in this way he makes his own situation more stable'.[123] Yet another way to safeguard the *pax* will be to forbid the king to marry a foreigner: the States are still in a condition of natural mutual hostility, and the society arising from such a marriage would often give rise to 'controversy and dissension'. Consider the case of Solomon, who married the daughter of the king of Egypt, and whose heir Rehoboam was then ruinously defeated by the pharaoh Sesac, as well as, in modern history, the example of the war of devolution between France and Spain.[124]

Finally, it will be necessary to establish another Council for the administration of justice, composed of only experts of the law, with the purpose of 'to decide lawsuits and punish criminals'. The goal to be achieved is the independence and fairness of the work of this body as a guarantee for the accused. All sentences, then, will have to be approved by the restricted Council in order to guarantee the respect of the procedures and the impartiality of the judgments. Verdicts will be only be issued in the presence of all the judges, and with a secret vote. These magistrates will also be numerous (to make it difficult for them to be corrupted by private individuals), elected when at least forty years of age, only one per family, and not for life, being instead offered a partial annual renewal of their role.[125] The assets of those condemned to the death penalty, and the emitted fines, will be used to retribute them and the members of the restricted Council. The condemned in a civil sentence will pay a share proportional to the entire sum being discussed, which will then be divided between the two bodies. In fact, it is inadvisable to pay the judges an annual salary, for that would make their work less efficient, encouraging long trials. Moreover, it is also advisable to forbid the king's confiscation of the property of a condemned individual, for this could engender slander and the fabrication of false accusations for the sole purpose of stripping the richest citizens of their possessions.[126]

Now, if we focus on the characteristics of such a political-institutional structure from the perspective of the king (the figure that should represent its central pivot, the 'sovereign', considering the monarchic nature of the form in question), we seem to reach paradoxical results. Firstly, the king is chosen by the *multitudo*, and he cannot change the fundamental structures

---

[123] *TP* VII, 8; *CWS* II, 548. See also *TP* VI, 12 (*CWS* II, 535) and VII, 19 (*CWS* II, 553).
[124] *TP* VI, 36; *CWS* II, 542.
[125] *TP* VI, 26–8 (*CWS* II, 540–1) and VII, 21 (*CWS* II, 554).
[126] *TP* VI, 29; *CWS* II, 541.

of the State and the norms that establish and regulate their functioning: the division into clans, the Supreme Council, the restricted Council, the College of judges, and the civic army. Secondly, the king appoints the councillors, but only by choosing among the candidates proposed by noble families (constrained by an age limit and their civil condition). Thirdly, the king has the last word, but only among those decisions already vetted and taken by the Council. Fourthly, he is 'powerful', but this power derives from his army, so that he prefers peace to war, unlike the monarchic *imperium* in which the sovereign 'can best show his virtue' in the case of war (while 'the chief feature of a Democratic state is that its excellence is valued much more highly in peace than in war').[127] Finally, and most importantly, he is not allowed to appoint a successor; the monarch may abdicate, but not 'unless the multitude, or its strongest part, acquiesces': the *multitudo* is also responsible for deciding how political power will be transmitted in such a way that the first election would also be 'eternal', preferably opting, for simplicity's sake, for power to be transmitted to the male first born. Otherwise, the *civitas* also die along with its king (it would be as if that particular kind of *civitas*, crystallised around the figure and the role of the king, would dissolve) and the supreme power would then return to the constitutive power of *multitudo*, the only social group able to emanate new laws to abolish the old ones, the only party with the power to take decisions in a 'state of exception'.[128]

'The King's power is determined only by the power of the multitude, and is preserved by the multitude's support': when applied to a monarchy, the *multitudo-imperium* circularity – and the implicit assumption that the deficit of reason from which the necessity of power (*potestas*) derives must be supplemented both with repression and (above all) with the re-orientation of human passions towards positive opportunities for the civil order – produces a government that is both established and supervised by the *multitudo*. This would be a sort of *monarchy with popular sovereignty*, where the power of the king is determined, regulated, and limited by that of the 'armed people', so that 'the King's sword, or right, is really the will of the multitude itself or of its stronger part'.[129] Before this outline takes on the contours of precise historical figures and of actual, established institutions, Spinoza clearly sees (to the point of elevating it to a lucid yet paradoxical political programme) that a constitutional monarchy actually represents the end of all kings.

---

[127] *TP* VII, 5; *CWS* II, 547.
[128] *TP* VI, 37–8 (*CWS* II, 542–3) and VII, 25 (*CWS* II, 556–7).
[129] *TP* VII, 25; *CWS* II, 557.

The Aristocracy

Organised in the complex structure of Councils outlined in the *TP*, Spinoza considers the aristocratic *imperium* to be a stronger, more compact form of power (*potestas*) than the monarchical one:

> a King absolutely requires counsellors. But a Council doesn't require anything of the kind. Second, Kings are mortal, but Councils are everlasting. [. . .] Third, a King's rule is often precarious, either because he's a child, or sick, or aged, or for other causes of this kind. But the power of a Council always remains one and the same.[130]

The greater political solidity of the aristocracy depends, first of all, on a sort of *democratisation* of the order of the fathers, on the wider and equal fruition, within them, of freedom and equality, compulsion and consent, reasons and passions.[131] Keeping the *multitudo* away from power is the other fundamental, structural goal of this kind of power (*potestas*):

> [i]t's evident, then, that the condition of this state will be best if it's so organised that it comes nearest to being absolute, that is, so that the multitude is as little to be feared as possible, and maintains no freedom except what must necessarily be granted it from the constitution of the state itself, which is therefore a right, not so much of the multitude itself, as of the whole state, which only the best claim and preserve as theirs.[132]

This objective can be achieved, on the one hand, by keeping the inevitable threshold of fear to a minimum level, since 'the multitude is terrifying to its rulers so it maintains some freedom for itself. If it does not claim that freedom for itself by an explicit law, it still claims it tacitly and maintains it.'[133] But, on the other hand, the maximum power of the aristocracy derives from the most accurate selection/co-optation of those who can be admitted to the administration of the *res publica*, and from the promotion of the rights of the patricians only on the basis of value and of merit. The most rigid exclusion of the *multitudo* from the *imperium* thus ends up being realised through the most effective circulation from the *multitudo* to the elite, allowed by the

---

[130] *TP* VIII, 3; CWS II, 566.
[131] *TP* VIII, 11–12 (CWS II, 569–70) and 19–20 (CWS II, 572–3).
[132] *TP* VIII, 5; CWS II, 567.
[133] *TP* VIII, 4; CWS II, 567.

imperium itself: patricians 'selected from the multitude'.[134] This is a solution that makes this political form almost eternal, as long as its structure is not corrupted; something that, however, rarely happens whether due to private feelings and immediate personal interests – in essence, due to politically irrational criteria (kinship, friendship, clientele), which weaken the quality and the 'superiority' of the patrician order,[135] a corruption that very often takes place.

An aristocratic *imperium* is not held by one person but by some, the patricians to whom also belongs the right to elect, choosing among the multitude, their own peers. Compared to a democracy, the essential difference consists in the fact that here the right to govern depends precisely on this 'choice', while in the democratic *imperium* it is determined by a prerogative of citizenship, either innate or 'a right acquired by fortune'.[136] Even if, paradoxically, the entire *multitudo* was accepted in the order of 'the best (*optimates*)' by means of the Patricians' appointment, and not by their own right, we would still be in the context of an aristocratic power. When all the patricians belong to the same city – the capital of the State, which also takes its name, as in the case of Rome, or Genoa, or Venice – the *imperium* is centralised. When, on the other hand, they live in different cities, and are linked together by shared powers and interests, then the aristocratic form is federal: the 'Republic of the Hollanders' is precisely such a federation, which takes its name from a province, and in which the subjects enjoy a greater freedom.[137]

In order for a unitary aristocracy to be stable, a minimum number of *optimates* is necessary, which will be proportional to the overall size of the city. For a medium-sized republic it would be sufficient for the 'supreme power of the state' to be in the hands of one hundred patricians. However, having the power to elect new 'colleagues' to replace those who died, they would always favour their own children, their closest relatives, or their friends, so that the management of power would end up in the hands of those who are related to the nobles by pure chance – a lucky birth. And since out of a hundred men who obtain public offices, only three can be found who are 'powerful and influential because of their skill and judgment', the government would thus end up in the hands of very few, who – eventually seized by the inevitable 'human desire' – would easily pave the way to monarchy. In order to have

---

[134] *TP* X, 10; *CWS* II, 600–1.
[135] *TP* XI, 2; *CWS* II, 602.
[136] *TP* VIII, 1 and 2; *CWS* II, 564–6.
[137] *TP* VIII, 3 and IX, 2; *CWS* II, 566 and 589.

a hundred patricians worthy of their duty, it will therefore be necessary to choose among at least five thousand. And to avoid that their power (*potentia*) might be overwhelmed by that of the *multitudo*, it will also be necessary to maintain a strict proportional relationship between the two orders: which can reasonably be one optimate to every fifty plebeians.[138]

Following a logic of articulation and of balancing of powers, Spinoza outlines, for this first form of aristocratic republic, a complicated mechanism of councils, which includes the Supreme Council, holder of the sovereignty (of the '*summa potestas*'), the Council of Syndics (an institutional guarantee body), the Senate (functioning halfway between legislative and executive power), and the Consuls, responsible for daily governance.

It is essential for the aristocratic republic to rest solely on the will and on the power (*potentia*) of the Supreme Council, organised and composed in such a way as to be completely free, in both its activity and its decisions, from any fear of *multitudo*. All citizens of at least thirty years of age will be eligible to this body on the basis, as we have seen, of the patricians' choice, with the exception of those who have been guilty of crimes, or someone who performs a servile job, or those who have married a foreigner. The inheritance of the patriciate is also prohibited (something already established by the Venetian model, after the 'lockdown' of the *Maggior Consiglio*). This is because, in the long run, the noble families could become extinct, and because such an exclusion would appear ignominious for all the others. It would then be absurd, and impossible, to prevent them from choosing their children and relatives: what matters is that such an eventuality is not explicitly sanctioned by the law.[139] Convened on set dates and in a certain place in the city, this first Council holds the *supremum jus*, having the task of making and repealing laws and of appointing new patricians and public officials. For this reason it is very dangerous to put a *princeps* as head of the Council for life – like the Doge of the Venetians – or even for a fixed term, as among the Genoese: the many precautions and limitations with which both cities have defined the role of these figures prove their precarious status, which can easily open avenues towards a monarchical order.[140] Since, finally, the 'supreme power of the state' is in the hands of the Council as a whole as an organism and not of any single one of its members, it is necessary to ensure that all the patricians are united, so as to form a single body guided by a single mind. And since the norms appear ineffective, and are

---

[138] *TP* VIII, 1–2 (*CWS* II, 564–6), and 11 and 13 (*CWS* II, 593).
[139] *TP* VIII, 7 (*CWS* II, 567) and 14 (*CWS* II, 571).
[140] *TP* VIII, 18; *CWS* II, 572.

easily violated, when their custodians are also possible transgressors, it will be necessary to find a *medium* through which all the 'rights provided by the state' are respected, without compromising the guiding principle of aiming for 'as much equality among the patricians as possible'.[141] This need will be answered by the Council of Syndics, subject to the Supreme Council, also composed of patricians. This Council has the task of monitoring and ensuring that the procedures and the rights pertaining to the structures of the republic and its officials are always safeguarded. With a proportion of one to fifty compared to the *optimates* (the same ratio, that is, that must be maintained between the patricians and the *plebs*), and elected for life (to prevent them from finding themselves in other official positions, those submitted to their control), the members of the Council of Syndics must be at least sixty years old and have already been senators, in order 'to prevent their becoming too proud'.[142] In order for them to perform their duties properly, they will have a part of the army at their disposal and, like all those who hold public offices, will not receive a fixed salary, but a remuneration proportionate to their commitment and the quality of their work. They will certainly be paid, because they take care of the public good, while the *multitudo* attends to private occupations. But since, as we have seen, 'no one defends another's cause except insofar as he believes that he thereby makes his own situation more stable', it will be necessary to dispose of things in such a way that everyone might 'consult their own interests most when they look out most diligently for the common good'.[143] Therefore, each year the syndics will receive: a small-value token from each householder (so that they will always keep the exact number of patricians under control), a large sum from the newly elected nobles, the fines paid by those who are absent at board meetings, or by the officials subjected to trial and convicted, as well as the fees paid to receive the 'badge' that is destined for those who, having reached the age of thirty and who are not explicitly excluded by law from the government, will arrange to have their name registered in a special, public register.[144] The Syndics must also summon the Supreme Council, propose the topics to be discussed therein, and occupy its 'first place', although without the right to vote. The task of convening their College will be the responsibility of the president who, along with ten or more other members (elected by the Supreme Council for six months and without the possibility of confirmation

[141] *TP* VIII, 19; *CWS* II, 572.
[142] *TP* VIII, 21–23; *CWS* II, 332–3.
[143] *TP* VIII, 24; *CWS* II, 573.
[144] *TP* VIII, 25; *CWS* II, 573–5.

before three or four years), will permanently preside over it, in order to listen to 'complaints and secret accusations' moved against public officials.[145]

'The second Council to be subordinated to the Supreme Council we'll call the Senate': this body will have the responsibility of managing 'public business', of promulgating the 'laws of the state', of providing for the fortification of the cities, of giving 'instructions to the armed forces', of imposing taxes, of dealing with foreign ambassadors (as well as establishing whether to send their own), and finally of deciding 'about war and peace' (requiring, in this case, ratification by the Supreme Council).[146] As for the number of its members, it is necessary to ensure that all the patricians can have an equal chance of being part of it, and that the role will always be accessible to experienced and capable men, wise and virtuous. Therefore, there will be four hundred senators (preserving, in any case, a ratio of one to twelve with respect to all the patricians) and they must be at least fifty years of age. They will hold office for one year, with the possibility of being re-elected after an interval of two years. Their compensation will be such that peace will always be more advantageous to them than war: they will therefore receive the earnings of a tax corresponding to the hundredth or fiftieth part of the value of exported or imported goods. Even so, in fact, the tributary system of the aristocratic *imperium* will be less exorbitant than that of the monarchic one, for the courts of kings are always more expensive. And that which, when power (*potestas*) is held by a single individual, goes only to the monarch or to a few, is here distributed to the many. Moreover, kings and their functionaries do not submit to taxes themselves while, in an aristocratic order, the patricians have to contribute, and considerably so, especially considering that they are generally chosen among the richest and wealthiest men:

> [w]hen the burdens of the state are imposed to safeguard peace and freedom, even if they're great, they're still endured, and borne because of the advantage peace brings. What nation ever had to pay so many and such heavy duties as the Dutch? But not only has this nation not been drained dry, on the contrary, their wealth has made them so powerful that everyone has envied their good fortune.[147]

The state secrets of kings crush their subjects: 'the virtue of Kings is worth more in war than in peace, and those who wish to rule alone must strive

---

[145] *TP* VIII, 26 and 28; *CWS* II, 575–6.
[146] *TP* VIII, 29; *CWS* II, 576.
[147] *TP* VIII, 31; *CWS* II, 579.

to their utmost to have poor subjects'.[148] In the Senate there will be some syndics – chosen by the Supreme Council and without the right to vote – who will be given the task of monitoring compliance with the procedures and rules, as well as summoning the sovereign body when the other has to communicate guidelines or problems.[149] Finally, in order to provide adequately for peace, it will be necessary to allocate a number of nobles also to the cities in the peripheries of the State, and to elect each year, among these, some senators and a syndic, elected for life.[150]

The entire Senate will also meet on predetermined dates, and during the time between one assembly and the next a part of its members will be chosen to take its place, executing the Senate's decrees, summoning it in case of need on the basis of a specific agenda, and examining letters and documents sent to the Supreme Council.[151] These, called Consuls, will either be jointly elected by the other two assemblies, or randomly chosen. There will be at least thirty of them – a numerous group – in order to avoid their possible corruption: they could, in fact, deceive the Senate, presenting matters of little relevance for discussion while silencing the most important ones. The Consuls will propose the question to be examined as well as its possible solution; should their opinion be unanimous, the senators will vote without further discussion. If instead there are diverging opinions, those that have obtained the largest approval will be put to the vote, in sequence (on the basis of complex and meticulous procedures).[152]

As for the '*forum*', the number, the remuneration, and the appointments of the judges will follow the logic already envisaged for the monarchical form of governance. Both the magistrates elected by the Supreme Council and those appointed in each city will be *optimates*. Supervised by the syndics, they will never be able to resort to torture in order to extort confessions from the accused, and '[t]his will be a sufficient precaution against their being unfair to plebeians and favoring the Patricians too much out of fear'. The plebeians, among other things, will be granted the possibility of making a direct appeal to the syndics, who, were they not successful in avoiding 'being hated by many Patricians', will on the other hand

---

[148] Ibid.
[149] *TP* VIII, 33; *CWS* II, 579–80.
[150] *TP* VIII, 42; *CWS* II, 584.
[151] *TP* VIII, 34; *CWS* II, 580.
[152] *TP* VIII, 35–6; *CWS* II, 580–1.

always be in favor with the plebeians, whose applause they'll be anxious to win, as much as they can. To that end they'll take any opportunity they're given to reverse judgments which violate the laws of the court, to examine any judge, and to impose penalties on those who are unfair. Nothing wins the hearts of the multitude more than this.[153]

Regarding the military, it will be particularly important to fortify both the capital and the frontier cities. Since in a republic there is no universal equality, it is not necessary for the army to be only composed of citizens. Instead, it is fundamental for the *optimates* to acquire a good knowledge of the techniques and the strategies of war. To exclude the people from the army and from the functions of command would in any case be 'sheer stupidity'. Moreover, in this way the money remains within the country; whoever is holding arms 'for their altars and homes' always does so 'with singular courage', and soldiers who can hope for glory and honours will fight with great and particular boldness. Conversely, it is wrong and contrary to the supreme *jus* of the patricians to forbid them to command, in case of need, foreign troops. Finally, the general 'of the whole armed forces' is elected among the *optimates* only in time of war, with a one-year appointment without any possibility of extension. Indeed it often happens that the patricians become submitted to their generals – as evidenced by the history of late-republican Rome – and when this happens the degeneration of the State is even worse than in the case of a monarchy, because it implies not only a change of the power held by individuals, but a complete reversal of the form of the *imperium* itself.[154]

The inequality which, in an aristocratic system, separates the *optimates* from the *multitudo*, makes the division of inhabitants into clans irrelevant, something that is instead common in the monarchical kinds of government. And since all non-patricians are in the *civitas* as 'foreigners', if all real estate was to remain public, the people would abandon the country during periods of adversity, being able easily to bring with them everything they own. Houses and land should therefore be sold, not rented, to private individuals, provided that part of their annual income is taxed, 'as is done in Holland'.[155] Moreover, the Treasury Officials and the secretaries and the officials of every council can be of plebeian origin: one should only try to prevent, in this case, the continuity of their practice and of their technical-administrative

---

[153] *TP* VIII, 41; CWS II, 584–5.
[154] *TP* VIII, 8–9; CWS II, 568–9.
[155] *TP* VIII, 10; CWS II, 569.

experience from overlapping with the political decision-making bodies: '[t]his has been disastrous for Holland' (in the 'Republican' Holland of De Witt).[156]

As for institutional religion, it would be appropriate for all patricians to share a single creed, preferably the Catholic faith, rich in civil implications, as outlined in the *TTP*, avoiding at all costs divisions and conflicts between the various denominations. Even if everyone is guaranteed freedom of speech, it will nevertheless be appropriate not to allow large gatherings. Large and sumptuous, official temples are the appropriate place for all essential acts of worship (baptisms, weddings, and laying on of hands), rituals that are reserved for the *optimates* (thus again manifesting their different status, along with the special garments they will always have to wear). On the other hand, other denominations will be granted the possibility of having smaller temples, built far from each other, and funded by private capital.[157]

Spinoza goes on:

[u]p to this point we've considered only the Aristocratic state which takes its name from one city, which is the capital of the whole state. Now it's time to treat aristocracies which have several cities. I think these are preferable to the previous kind.[158]

On the basis of this second typology, the cities will be 'combined with one another and united', so as to form 'one state', but in such a way that each city might get 'greater right in the state than the others do just to the extent that its power is greater'. Indeed 'to seek equality among unequals is to seek something absurd' and if all individuals are equal with respect to their *civitas* (since the power of the single has no significance with respect to that of the political order), the strength of each city which corresponds to its size constitutes instead 'a great part of the power of the state itself'. It follows, then, that even the right of each city must be directly proportional to its *magnitudo*.[159] The fundamental structures of confederate power will be the Senate and the court. The first, having the purpose of dealing 'with the common business of the state', will have the same characteristics and follow the same procedures as that of the centralised public office, the only difference being that it will also hold the necessary authority to settle the disputes

---

[156] *TP* VIII, 44; *CWS* II, 585–6.
[157] *TP* VIII, 46–7; *CWS* II, 587–8.
[158] *TP* IX, 1; *CWS* II, 588–9.
[159] *TP* IX, 4; *CWS* II, 589–90.

that may arise between cities. The patricians of each city will elect senators with a ratio of one to twelve with respect to their global number, so that in each order of the Senate they will be able to rely on a greater or smaller number of 'representatives' according to their size and power. All cities will also send some syndics, with the right to participate in Senate meetings but without the right to vote, and with the task of monitoring compliance with fundamental laws and regulations. For the court, the *optimates* will choose a number of 'supreme judges' proportional to their total number, once again with the aim of safeguarding the principle that 'the more powerful a city, the greater is its right, both in the Senate and in the court'.[160] The seat of the Senate and of the court will not be a city with political rights (because otherwise it would effectively become the capital, thus re-proposing a centralised form of the aristocratic *imperium*). Rather it will be a village or a city with no 'right to vote' (like The Hague in the case of the United Provinces).[161] All *civitates* will have to maintain ample autonomous powers. The Supreme Council, the general assembly of the patricians of each city, will retain the power (*potestas*) to ratify the decisions of the Senate (in institutional matters, in the choice of generals and ambassadors, in declarations of war, and peace treaties), together with the authority to carry out all the acts that are deemed useful for the maintenance and development of the city: to build fortifications, enlarge the walls, impose duties and taxes (even those meant to support federal expenses), make and repeal particular laws, and to appoint officials. Appointed by their respective patricians, the Consuls will form for this purpose (like the Senate) the executive power of each city. Even local judges will be elected by the *optimates* of the various cities, it being understood that it will always be possible to appeal against their decisions to the 'supreme judgment of the state', unless 'the person's guilt is proven unambiguously' or when a debtor confesses his or her insolvency.[162] Lastly, a city that is not 'its own master' and is part of a region or a province of the republic, and whose inhabitants share a common language and nationality, will be merged with the nearest autonomous ones. Conversely, those that were conquered 'by the right of war' will become allied or 'else Colonies should be sent there, which will enjoy the right of Citizenship', or 'should be completely destroyed'.[163]

This particular variant of the aristocratic form of governance, as it has been said, appears to Spinoza as better and preferable to the centralised one.

---

[160] See *TP* IX, 5–6 and 10; *CWS* II, 590–1 and 592.
[161] *TP* IX, 9; *CWS* II, 592.
[162] *TP* IX, 5–6, 8, 11 and 12; *CWS* II, 590–3.
[163] *TP* IX, 13; *CWS* II, 593.

Following the impulses of human desire, the patricians of each city will in fact strive to preserve and increase their right/power, seeking to win the favour of the multitude, to exercise the *imperium* through aid rather than fear, and also to increase of their own number, the only factor able to give them more power within the federation. This form, moreover, will be less subject to the danger of sudden acts of violence, since its supreme organ convenes (and takes its decisions) in different cities at different times. And then, with this power, the citizens will have less to fear and will always enjoy greater freedom, both because it will not be enough to subdue one city to demolish the State since more cities can take advantage of the same political rights, and because where a single *civitas* reigns 'the good of the others is considered only insofar as it serves the interests of the ruling city'.[164] Nor does the fact that each city prioritises its own interest, and that tensions and conflicts may arise because of this, represent an obstacle: the theme (already present in the *TTP*, in relation to democracy) of the positivity of disputes, and of discord as safer guarantee of 'rationality' in public deliberations, is here explicitly extended as a model for the government of the *optimates*:

> [s]ome will remind us of the saying 'while the Romans deliberate, Saguntum is lost.' On the other hand, when the few decide everything, simply on the basis of their own affects, freedom and the common good are lost. For human wits are too sluggish to penetrate everything right away. But by asking advice, listening, and arguing, they're sharpened. When people try all means, in the end they find ways to the things they want which everyone approves, and no one had ever thought.[165]

The equality between the *optimates* and the cities does not exclude the positive function of disagreements, the propulsive nature of competitions and comparisons that take place, according to Machiavellian motto, within the 'orders'. That of Spinoza is a theoretical and scientific stance that never loses sight of current events and of historical-political reality. It was not the discussions and the disagreements that undermined Holland's republican structure, but rather the institutional uncertainties characteristic of that very structure:

> [b]ut if someone retorts that this state of the Hollanders has not lasted long without a Count, or a Representative who could act in his place,

---

[164] *TP* IX, 15; *CWS* II, 595.
[165] *TP* IX, 14; *CWS* II, 594.

I would reply: the Hollanders thought that to maintain their freedom it was enough to renounce their Count and cut the head off the body of the state. They didn't think about reforming it, but left all its members as they'd been set up before, so that Holland remained a county without a Count, or a body without a head, and the state itself remained without a name.

This confusion of roles and institutions is accompanied in the concrete reality of the United Provinces by the even more serious and dangerous limit, that of an extremely narrow political representation:

> [s]o it's not at all strange that most subjects didn't know who possessed the supreme power of the state. Even if this hadn't been so, those who really had the authority were far too few to be able to govern the multitude and overcome powerful opponents. The result was that their opponents were often able to plot against them with impunity and eventually to overthrow them. The sudden overthrow of the Republic did not result from the fact that it wasted time in useless deliberations, but from the defective constitution of the state and the small number of its regents.[166]

The two variants of the aristocratic *imperium* (mostly the second one) stand out for their compact nature, their solidity and stability. They appear, in essence, to be the political forms that are most impervious to *change*, the only true source of their possible decline: '[n]ow that we've explained and shown the foundations of each kind of Aristocratic state, it remains to ask whether they can, from some inherent defect, be dissolved or changed into another form'.[167] In this regard the 'most acute Florentine' teaches that the *imperium*, not unlike the human body, tends to become corrupt because 'something is added daily which eventually requires treatment'. In order to avoid an uncontrolled growth of the vices, to such an extent that they could not be eliminated without also liquidating the aspects of power, a periodic *reduction* of power (*potestas*) towards its own principle is therefore necessary (following the Machiavellian lesson). A readjustment that could take place 'by chance or by the judgment and wisdom either of the laws or of a man of outstanding excellence'. The first remedy often offered for this predicament, that of appointing a supreme dictator, threatens to steer towards Scylla those who want to avoid Charybdis: if held by a single individual, such power will

---

[166] *TP* IX, 14; *CWS* II, 595.
[167] *TP* X, 1; *CWS* II, 596.

be very similar to that of a monarch, and 'the state can't be changed for a time into a Monarchy without great danger to the Republic, however short the time is'.[168] The case of the institutional control assigned to the syndics is different. For this does not pertain to a person but to a college, subject to the Supreme Council, excluded from any other public office, without a real influence on the army, made up of members too numerous to be able to divide the *imperium* among themselves, and in any case having already reached an advanced age, when the security of the present is preferred to the dangers of novelties and change.[169] And yet even such a governing body, while avoiding that the form of *dominion* might be modified, will still be unable to prevent the penetration of vices that laws cannot prohibit and which might weaken – in times of peace and during everyday life – the republican spirit and attachment to *civitas*:

> [i]n peace, when fear has been set aside, men gradually change from being savage and warlike to being political or civilised, and from being civilised, they become soft and lazy. One tries to surpass another, not in excellence, but in arrogance and extravagant living.[170]

Nor are 'sumptuary laws' able to prevent these inconveniences, since all those rules that can be transgressed without harming others 'are objects of derision. Far from reining in men's desires and lusts, they make them stronger. We always strive to have what is prohibited, and desire what we're denied.'[171] Those vices, then, should not be explicitly prohibited, but indirectly defused, building power on foundations such as that, even if the majority of citizens do not live 'wisely', they will at least be guided by passions that are useful for the *civitas*. For example, instead of thrift and parsimony, avarice could be encouraged, by establishing that insolvent debtors will lose their status of *optimates*, and above all by creating structures of power so wide, articulated, and dynamic as to allow most of the rich to access governmental and public offices. Spinoza explains that

> [t]here's no doubt that if this affect of greed, which is universal and constant, is fostered by an eagerness to be esteemed, most people will put

---

[168] *TP* X, 1; *CWS* II, 596–7. For Machiavelli see *Dis*, III, 1.
[169] *TP* X, 2; *CWS* II, 598.
[170] *TP* X, 4; *CWS* II, 598.
[171] *TP* X, 5; *CWS* II, 599.

their greatest zeal into increasing their possessions without disgrace. That way they achieve honors and avoid the greatest shame.[172]

It is necessary to make sure that the subjects perform their duty spontaneously, rather than being forced by the law. The *imperium* that aims to govern through fear 'will lack vices rather than possess virtue'.[173] According to Spinoza:

> Men must be so led that they seem to themselves not to be led, but to live according to their own mentality and from their free decision, so that they're restrained only by love of freedom, the desire to increase their possessions, and the hope of achieving honors.[174]

Civic virtue will therefore be a worthy reward for civic virtue itself. On the other hand, where 'triumphs and portraits' are flaunted – where distinguished men enjoy special honours and privileges – 'equality has been set aside, the common freedom necessarily perishes'.[175]

Now, when an eternal *imperium* is given, its fundamental rights will remain intact, since they are continuously supported both 'by reason and by men's common affects', and the two forms of the aristocracy – since 'we've shown that the fundamental laws of each Aristocratic state agree both with reason and with the common affect of men' – will tend to remain immutable: 'we can maintain that if any state is everlasting, this one must be everlasting, or that it can't be destroyed by any inherent defect, but only by some inevitable fate'.[176] The aristocratic form of government will be resilient enough to withstand even the most unpredictable of external dangers. It is true that there is no affect 'which isn't sometimes overcome by a stronger, contrary affect'; for example, we often see the fear of death prevailing, and overcoming every other passion. And it is also true – once again Spinoza has in mind the painful Dutch experience of its conflict with France – that in times of great difficulty 'everyone is seized by panic' and, blindly and dangerously, 'all heads turn toward a Man who is famous for his victories', freeing him from all laws, rules, and limits of power. But it is also true that, in a well-ordered republic, terror can only arise due to some justified reason, nor can

---

[172] *TP* X, 6; *CWS* II, 599.
[173] *TP* X, 8; *CWS* II, 599.
[174] *TP* X, 8; *CWS* II, 600.
[175] Ibid.
[176] *TP* X, 9; *CWS* II, 600.

it happen that only 'one man or another has such an outstanding reputation for excellence', since it is easier, and necessary, for many to compete with each other, and for everyone to enjoy the favour of many. The aristocratic *imperium*, being composed by institutes aimed at continually transforming reasons and passions into vital energetic substance, would therefore represent the culmination of the experiences of the political order. Indeed:

> I can assert unconditionally, then, that both a state which one city alone controls, and especially a state which several cities control, is everlasting, or can't be dissolved or changed into another form by any internal cause.[177]

The first lines of the last chapter of the *TP* (the unfinished chapter on democracy) are meant to better explain and to circumscribe the meaning of these claims:

> I come, finally, to the third, and completely absolute state, which we call Democratic. We've said that the difference between this state and an Aristocratic one consists chiefly in this: that in an Aristocratic state it depends only on the will and free Choice of the supreme Council that this or that person is made a Patrician. So no one has a hereditary right to vote or stand for political offices, and no one can demand this right for himself by law, as happens in the state we're now discussing.[178]

If a law establishes the criteria on the basis of which one can have the *jus* of being part of the Supreme Council, then such an *imperium* must be considered to be democratic and no longer aristocratic, even in the borderline case in which the citizens thus identified are found to be fewer than those of the previous form of government. And although a power of this type – where those destined to government are not the 'best', but rather those who more or less by chance have the necessary characteristics (birth-right, age, economic condition) to access power (*potestas*) – may seem, at first sight, inferior to the aristocratic one, the results will not appear substantially different, as soon as we consider 'actual life, or the common condition of men': indeed 'the men who seem best to the Patricians will always be the rich, or their own close relatives, or their friends'. Of course, if the patricians were able to choose their colleagues free from any passion and guided solely by

[177] *TP* X, 10; *CWS* II, 601.
[178] *TP* XI, 1; *CWS* II, 601.

the concern of public health, then '[t]here would be no state to compare with an Aristocracy. But experience has shown abundantly that things don't work that way'.[179] The aristocratic *imperium* is built on the basis of an original caesura, one which, contradicting the heart of the political order (its relationship – both of opposition and of dependency – with the multitude) does not make it truly 'absolute' (absolute in Spinozan terms). Although stable and long-lasting, it will be neither immutable nor eternal. The crucial point, at once the strength and the *hybris* of aristocratic power, is precisely the separation between the two orders of the patricians and the *plebs*, the *optimates* and the *multitudo*. As we have seen, the preservation of such a caesura is a vital node of this form of power, the other being the greatest possible equality among the *optimates*. Different to the monarchical order (Spinoza's monarchy), the aristocratic *imperium* never returns to the *plebs*, nor is the *plebs* ever consulted about its workings: it is the will of the Council of the *optimates* – and not the 'vigilance of the multitude' – that is an absolute rule. This form of government will therefore be more optimal the closer it comes to absolute power, that is, when the multitude will instil the least amount of fear in the patricians, who will have to exclude it from any freedom that has not been explicitly delineated by the constitution of the *imperium*, so that their power (*potestas*) will be inversely proportional to the rights that the *plebs* are able to seize for themselves. A sufficiently large aristocratic council will certainly be able to make decisions inspired by reason more than by greed, and therefore there will be no danger of the *multitudo* falling into a condition of cruel slavery. However, it is always 'terrifying to its rulers':[180] excluded from power, the *multitudo* remains power's most serious threat. Well beyond contingency, beyond the 'reasonableness' of the resolutions that the *imperium* will be able to take, or the effectiveness of its selection/co-optation choices which – even when unaffected, as it generally happens, by personal and passional criteria – would still be unable to resolve the substance of that exclusion, the obstacle of the power (*potentia*) of the *multitudo* and its constant, unavoidable subversive danger remains a reality. Near the absolute – firm in the functionality of its institutions, meant to withstand the impact of reasons and passions, and indeed to use them to guarantee its own persistence – the rule of aristocratic *imperium* will however never be absolute due to its very constitution, such as to achieve the most complete overlap, the most complete circulation of *potestas* and of *potentia*, of the *multitudo* and of the *potestas*: '[f]or if there's

[179] *TP* XI, 2; *CWS* II, 602.
[180] *TP* VIII, 4; *CWS* II, 567.

any absolute rule, it is the rule which occurs when the whole multitude rules'.[181]

Absolutum, sive democratia

Grounded on the newly acquired centrality of the *multitudo* – and freed from the ideological-rationalist structures of the *TTP* – the *TP* (as much of it as Spinoza managed to write) aims towards the logical-ontological primacy of democracy. In the monarchical *imperium* there is civic equality, there are large shares of substantial and popular power, and the identity of armed militia and citizenship. In the order of the *optimates*, there is a widespread political freedom among those who govern, and a positive role for conflict between orders and within laws that are defended by both reason and by the common passions of men. The other forms of the *imperium* are strengthened by broadening the *social basis* of their power and through the introduction of the demands of the *societas universalis* into the circuit of power (*potestas*). And if the inevitable partiality and 'non-completeness' of such an input will always represent their constitutive limit, these forms will still play a positive and propulsive function: the more effective, the more they manage to approximate the 'integral' circulation of *imperium* and *multitudo*, its only truly fluid and constituent propulsive force, both extremely powerful and utterly fragile.[182] Of course, we will never know which explicit direction the last part of the *TP* could have taken. And yet, taking into account the general theoretical assumptions and the analytical framework relating to the first two 'species' of government, it is perhaps possible to hypothesise that Spinoza's attention to democracy would have focused on the determination of the structures, the institutions, and the most functional and organisational criteria for promoting and simultaneously channelling the 'absolute' of this form of government, such as to reach its maximum power while regulating, as far as possible, its continuous mobility (its unstable mutability) within the *certainty* of an organism, the positive of a procedure. Moreover, the whole second part of the *TP* (dedicated to the analysis of the various kinds of political order), tends to show how the *static* nature of passions, the annihilation of drives and the compression of interests, magnify fear, which in turn hinders the effective functioning of the *imperium*. Only a *dynamic* of forces feeds the 'reason' of power (*potestas*). The relative nature of the *imperium* remains active and productive only as long as there is some possibility

---

[181] *TP* VIII, 3; CWS II, 566.
[182] *TP* VI, 3–4; CWS II, 517–28.

of mutual determination between the sovereign (the single subject of power) and the *multitudo* (the seething multiplicity of powers). The very existence, the political persistence of the *multitudo*, including that of its role in the monarchy and (in some way) in the aristocracy, is fundamental for that movement which, starting from the prevailing passion of men, leads to the *ratio* of power (*potestas*), to the crystallisation of in-principle mobility into a fundamental norm (*Grundnorm*), the reification of its original 'interactivity' into the materiality of an order, the positivity of a constitution (*Verfassung*). The immediate and isolated physicality of the sovereign – the Machiavellian 'personal' virtue of the prince – is no longer enough; 'art' is also needed, as well as an 'apparatus' able to create and nurture that decisive convergence which recognises each person as a legitimate public actor of his own utility, and the *imperium* as the only possible universal, a relationship of force – a part determined by the parts, because implicating the *vis* of coercion – guiding the coexistence and the progression of forces. The greater stability of the State is found in its 'constitution' while still preserving the subordination and the consequentiality of the 'rule' to the continuous relocation of passions, to the unstoppable reciprocation of powers (*potentiae*). There is no transcendental with respect to force: neither the Hobbesian-Hegelian one of the 'decision', nor the liberal, Lockean-Kantian one of a *proprietary* reason, of a *meta-relational* constitutionalism produced by the intrinsic and self-legitimating claims of a new substantial knowledge.

Due to the way in which it is presented – as oriented towards the totality of human interactions, towards *conservatio* – the pre-eminence of democracy does not imply, in any case, its being the 'end', the 'objective' or the 'fulfilment' of a unitary and unchangeable path in the experiences of the *imperium*. Spinoza never gives in to any finalistic temptation, not even in this case. Open to the inexhaustible intersections of the 'modes', the metaphysics of the cause does not leave any real space to *anakyklosis*, the possibility of normalising, or reducing, conservation and political change to a 'norm' or a constant rule, neither the imperturbable naturalistic (classic-Polybian) necessity of life cycles, nor a teleological logic of the gradual transformation – through decay or progression – of the forms of the *imperium*. It is not by chance, then, that both of Spinoza's political works reserve only a few and incidental considerations to this problem. In the *TTP*, as we have already seen, it seems to Spinoza that the political history of the Jews, following their liberation from slavery in Egypt, started from a sort of theological democracy (by virtue of which the people, under the leadership of Moses, are persuaded to give up their right to God, in order to really remain free), and ends with a declining and quarrelsome ecclesiastical monarchy, after 'the

High Priests took for themselves the right to rule'.[183] In the *TP* the question is explicitly addressed only once, where the probability of a similar principle of the *imperia* is theorised, starting from a kind of primordial 'nomos of the earth' which, collectivised within an original occupying *multitudo*, would then remain strictly precluded to foreigners (to 'pilgrims'), thus creating the conditions for the separation of rights and the division of forces which ultimately turns primitive democracy into an aristocratic form:

> [b]ut in the meantime, the multitude is increased by the influx of foreigners, who gradually take on the customs of the native people, until at length they're distinguished only by the fact that they don't have the right to acquire honors. While the number of the immigrants grows daily, the number of citizens is for many reasons diminished. [. . .] So gradually the rule is reduced to a few, and finally, because of factions, to one.[184]

As we can see, this is a disruptive, degenerative process. But it is also little more than an aside (of probable Machiavellian origin),[185] part of the analysis of the aristocratic government and meant as an example among many unknown and possible scenarios 'which destroy states'.[186] A different trend would seem to be derived, implicitly, from the overall structure of the *TP*, which examines first the monarchy, then the aristocracy, and finally democracy: considering the two previous ideas, such a succession could lead to the suggestion of a recurrent path, proceeding from theological freedom to the split forms of the *potestas*, up to a 'mature' democratic power, built on the free, conscious, and plural aggregation of a *multitudo*. But it would only be a suggestion. In reality, there is no necessary step that regulates the relationships between the various forms of *potestas*. Indeed, under certain conditions the constitutive duplicity of the *conatus* makes it possible to appreciate, as we have seen, how the stability of the 'transfer', of the passage of the *imperium* to one or to the few as a more immediate and safe refuge is easier to reach, as compared to the risky precariousness of an uncertain and wavering democratic form.

This, moreover, was the specific 'transition' which was favoured by Spinoza in his analysis of monarchy and aristocracy. Not because, from here, the transformations of the *imperium* could be reduced to a rigid typology, or

---

[183] *TTP* XVII, 112; *CWS* II, 322.
[184] *TP* VIII, 12; *CWS* II, 570.
[185] See *Dis.*, I, 6.
[186] See *TP* VIII, 12; *CWS* II, 570.

a single, invariable principle, but rather because it represents a 'scientific choice', focusing on contexts that gave 'experience *or* praxis' to theory, the chance of power (*potentia*) to 'doctrine', an option that, while mindful of 'principles', still allowed firm connections to the empirical reality of the contemporary world. Focused on the prospect of a rationalisation of power which, although aimed at widening the basis of consensus and participation, would still remain a minority prerogative of society, the *TTP* had avoided having to fully deal with the *plebs*, the *vulgus*, which was reduced to a passive and negative object of a closed, aggressive, and intolerant political-religious hegemony. Just as it imputes the republican defeat of the narrowness of the *dominion* – to the 'small number of regents' – Spinoza's *TP* also presents itself as a sort of self-critical revision of his previous work, which could have only partially and inadequately overcome such a narrow approach. Having defeated the democratic/republican perspective, and undermined the idea of a high-density ideological compromise between the rationalising vectors of knowledge and the most open and libertarian religious denominations, now the task becomes that of preventing, as far as possible, that a new concentration of the *imperium* – tendentially 'monarchic' – might produce the dogmatic annihilation and the authoritarian compression of the *multitudo*. Even from the uncertain defensive trenches of folding, reflux, and concealment, the imperative remains to continue to aim at the principle and the essence of political order.

The Patience of the Excluded

Even when read in this context, the first four paragraphs of Chapter XI of the *TP*, which should have introduced the discussion of the free Republic, appear rough and impervious; and not only because this is clearly a sketchy and approximate draft, even more so than the pages that immediately precede it. They are indeed the very last pages, a sort of *décalage*, of progressive incompleteness, easily ascertainable, proceeding from the first chapters onwards. But, most pertinently, they can be considered as the 'last words' due to their content, which are far from flowing in a smooth and linear way towards the general 'principles' of the treatise. Indeed, it does not seem easy to reconcile, or even to bring together, the hasty exclusion of majority sectors of the multitude – the servants and the women – from the active government of a democracy (this is the most relevant and significant theme of this final part), with the overall theoretical framework, the broader philosophical-political structure of the *TP*. For the latter presents democracy and the *multitudo* – in the first five chapters, and in occasional mentions in the following ones – as fully congruent, and indeed mutually convertible without residue. When it comes to the last chapter, the four concluding paragraphs of the *TP* – i.e., when we move from the general pronouncements about the democratic *imperium* to the construction of its positive form and to the outline of its own particular type – the logic of general inclusion, the horizon of a more or less universal admission, quickly deviates towards a rigid and 'limiting' solution: surprisingly, a problematically 'exclusive' one.

In the first paragraph, the distinction between democracy and aristocracy still seems to look at the former's greater breadth as compared to the latter:

> [f]or [in a Democracy] everyone whose parents were citizens, or who was born on the country's soil, or who has deserved well of the Republic, or who has the right to be a citizen for any other reasons on account of which the Law commands that someone be granted the right of a citizen – all such people, I say, rightly demand for themselves the right to vote in the supreme Council and to stand for political offices. They can be denied this only on account of a crime or disgrace.[187]

It is not by coercion that an individual actively participates in citizenship (the *ius civis*) but fundamentally by virtue of his or her nature or descent; one is a *cives* because their 'parents were citizens'. This is a very general criterion, which would seem to extend political rights beyond all those borders imposed by other forms of government, both the monarchical and the aristocratic. And yet, already from the second paragraph the apparent breadth of this universal inclusion is sharply narrowed and foreclosed. Introducing some examples of active citizenship (the right to vote and the right to manage the business of the State), Spinoza refers to cases that immediately seem to suggest that governance should be limited to some classes of citizens: only the elders who have reached a certain age; or only first-born adults; or to those who pay a certain cash contribution to the republic. Compared to his previous position – establishing a criterion of access to power mainly based on 'nature' (and, apparently, implicitly 'broad') – here a 'legal' and juridical dimension is imposed, deliberately calibrated on the reduction and the restriction of that access. A decisive element to distinguish democracy from aristocracy is that the right to rule is not acquired by election but granted by law, even when the law – and this is the point – assigns the right of *imperium* to a smaller number of citizens than of the *optimates* alone. States of this kind, however, 'ought to be called Democratic. For their citizens, who

---

[187] *TP* XI, 1; *CWS* II, 602.

are destined to govern the Republic, are not chosen by the supreme Council as the best, but are destined for this status by law.'[188] The natural *datum*, the broad criterion of birth, thus appears to be quickly and abruptly regulated, conditioned, scaled down.

The third paragraph confirms and proposes once again this position, moving from pure exemplification to a 'project', to the beginning of a sociopolitical construction. Among the many possible different kinds of democracy, Spinoza looks at one in particular, rather 'narrow' with respect to the area of government: that form in which the right to vote and access to offices is forbidden not only to, as is obvious, foreigners, criminals, and underage children (and perhaps 'madmen', as is mentioned in Chapter VI[189]), but also to servants and the women, because they are not independent, they are not *sui iuris*, since they are submitted to (*in potestate*) their masters and husbands – with a difference of no small importance, between these two 'categories', which should be immediately highlighted.

The 'servile' condition, as Alexandre Matheron has shown, in one of the few relevant studies on the subject,[190] must be understood in a very broad sense, such as to extend to wage-workers, and to all literally 'dependent' activities. Not to morally 'unworthy' professions (as per the traditional Aristotelian classification), nor to poverty as such, but rather to subjection, to personal submission, which certainly draws its first origin from poverty, but which, however, does not present itself as an automatic consequence of it. The servile condition is a situation of economic dependence which implies individual submission. In sum, this is both a personal and social condition, and for this very reason, as can be deduced, beyond its literal presentation, is neither static nor immutable. Pending the emergence, during the Industrial Revolution, of conditions for economic subordination that no longer excluded civil-political autonomy, in the terms posed by Spinoza it is already possible to conquer political autonomy, even if only through the achievement of economic autonomy. In Spinozan terms, the possibility is (implicitly) accepted that the worker might change career, that one could become, for example, a merchant, even if only of wine or beer.[191] Conversely, the personal, and therefore political, subjection of the women

[188] *TP* XI, 2; *CWS* II, 602.
[189] *TP* VI, 11; *CWS* II, 535.
[190] Matheron 1977.
[191] See Matheron 1977, 185. My translation, where he corrects 'the little mistake, caused by carelessness, that generations of translators have piously passed on to each other', regarding *TP* VIII, 14, thus giving *Oenopolae* and *Cerevisiarii* that right of citizenship, as self-employed workers, that Spinoza actually recognises.

appears to be firm and unchangeable, because it is obtained not by custom but from 'nature'. It is presented (again, in the sixth chapter) as the consequence of a sort of 'impairment', a case of organic 'minority', a bit like that of the 'mute'.[192] This is the topic of the fourth paragraph: the exclusion of women – on which, as we know, the TP comes to an abrupt end.

Spinoza affirms that it is 'experience' that attests to an inferiority of power (*potentia*) (and therefore of right) of females, as compared to males. A lack of intelligence and of strength of character, factors in which the *humana potentia* mainly consists:

> [w]herever we find men and women [living together], they have never ruled together. What we see is that there the men rule and the women are ruled, and that in this way both sexes live in harmony. On the other hand, the Amazons, who according to tradition once ruled, did not allow men to remain on their soil, but raised only the females, and killed the males they bore. If women were by nature equal to men, both in strength of character and in native intelligence – in which the greatest human power, and consequently right, consists – surely among so many and such diverse nations we would find some where each sex ruled equally, and others where men were ruled by women, and so educated that they could do less with their native intelligence.[193]

In this regard, critics have often insisted on Spinoza's all-too-rapid sublimation – the hasty transformation – of the raw, partial (and not even linear) data of experience into 'nature' and 'principles'.[194] The claim, for example, that men and women never governed together, neglects the existence of great queens, especially the greatest of them all – Elizabeth I of England. Furthermore, the discussion of the Amazons appears somewhat specious: the same argument to which Hobbes had resorted to demonstrate

---

[192] *TP* VI, 11; *CWS* II, 535.

[193] *TP* XI, 4; *CWS* II, 603.

[194] 'Here Spinoza himself seems to fall into the error of which, at the beginning of the book, he accused the "philosophers": that of confusing the things as they are with what one would like them to be' (Droetto 1958: 368n. My translation). 'From the weakness of the opposite sex, which seemed evident to him, he drew the conclusion of the juridical incapacity of the female sex, a logical conclusion by virtue of the identity of law and power (*potentia*). I cannot, however, refrain from observing that if, according to him, contingency is only a necessity that is ignored, then necessity – even when provided with evidence – is sometimes only a contingency that is forgotten' (Breton 1979: 196. My translation).

the absurdity of the principled exclusion of women from government.[195] The fact that the Amazons killed men, or used them exclusively for reproduction, does not exclude, as Spinoza would claim (and indeed implies), an iron-clad and most ferocious capacity of women to dominate men. But it may also be that, in this case, the objective was simply to demonstrate the purely mythical and legendary character of such an example. And finally, as argued at the end of the paragraph and of the book as a whole, the fact that women must consider themselves the cause of jealousies and emotional conflicts between men[196] cannot be considered a demonstration. If anything, it is a reasoning about the *consequences* of a possible demonstration: it is the (presumed) inferiority of *mulieres* which would make them a politically negative presence, a mere object of disturbance and confusion.

In an insightful essay, Antonio Negri examines the reader's perplexity (the reader's 'restlessness' as he puts it) when approaching these pages and facing 'the great tension' between 'the incompleteness of the text' and the two 'very strong concepts' that traverse it: democracy as a 'completely absolute state', and the strict legalism – the positivistic construction – through which the conditions for democratic participation are rigidly fixed and foreclosed to many.[197] There is a sort of constitutive tension between nature and custom from which Negri discerns, on at least two occasions, the emergence of the ontological primacy of one element over the other. In the third paragraph, where Spinoza argues for the possibility of conceiving different kinds of democratic *imperium* (a claim that in itself reduces and relativises the impact and scope of the strong legalism that both precedes and follows it),[198] and in the fourth one, in which the condition of political subordination of women is not deduced by custom but, precisely, by nature: on the basis, that is, of a 'natural process, unbound, foundational and not founded', with respect to which the institution is presented as a merely 'extrinsic' element.[199] And it could also be said that it is the very alternative between 'by

---

[195] *Lev.*, XX.

[196] 'Furthermore, if we consider human affects, namely, that for the most part men love women only from an affect of lust, and that they judge their native intelligence and wisdom greater the more beautiful they are, and furthermore, that men find it intolerable that the women they love should favor others in some way, etc., we'll have no difficulty seeing that men and women can't rule equally without great harm to the peace. But enough of these matters'; *TP* XI, 4; *CWS* II, 604.

[197] Negri 1992: 313–42.

[198] *TP* XI, 3: 'From what we said it's evident that we can conceive different kinds of Democratic state. I don't plan to discuss each one [. . .]'; *CWS* II, 602–3.

[199] Negri 1992: 333.

nature' and 'by custom' that ultimately presents itself, in Spinozan terms, as unthinkable and unfounded. Spinoza is not Hobbes. For Spinoza no human 'artifice' can ever be posited *against nature*, outside (above or beyond) that 'nature' of which every *fabrica*, every human convention and construction, always and inevitably is an 'expression': a mode, a *modification* of nature/substance, and for this very reason invariably involved in its own, unceasing productive mobility. Even when the problem is posed in these terms it remains to be understood, and as far as possible to be clarified, why in the face of democracy as a completely absolute state, Spinoza chooses and works on, among the many admissible varieties, a particularly 'restricted' form of democratic government. This explains why, proceeding to quash the women (a good half of the people that make up the *multitudo*), he overturns the meaning of the nature-institution relationship, by quickly and roughly erasing the complexity, multiplicity, and mobility of 'nature' in favour of simplicity, singularity, and the fixity of its 'extrinsic figure'. Such is the external, superficial stillness of a particular bond, as a consequence of which someone (always the same person) *commands*, and someone else (again, always the same person) *obeys*.

Matheron has drawn metaphorically dramatic conclusions from this kind of 'reversal', such as to involve both the philosopher's theory and his biography. The fact that the *institutum* is configured as a direct and immediate expression of *nature* is a consequence of Spinoza's identification of right with power (*potentia*). Starting from this identity, the alternative between being or not being *sui iuris* bends the Roman juridical tradition, from which Spinoza draws for his own distinction, towards the flat recognition of effective powers, of the subalternities in act. The hypothesis of the perpetual subjection of women and servants (as long as they remain so), then, appears to be not only a prejudice, but the coherent consequence of that identity, which offers ontological foundation and substance to *all* existing power relationships. Matheron concludes that 'perhaps, in the final analysis, there was a reason to stop and something to die for!'[200] The last pages of the *TP* thus become the symbolic representation of the philosopher's end, induced by what has become a terrified gaze cast upon the consequences of his own philosophy. Before accepting 'desperate' conclusions such as these, however, it is possible to frame the problem somewhat differently.

Perhaps the 'political science' approach of the *TP* originates precisely from the new theoretical paradigm that regulates the relationships between *multitudo* and *imperium*. The selection and the construction of variants of

---

[200] Matheron 1977: 200. My translation.

political power pertains, as we have seen, to the triple constitutive movement that sees a) the *multitudo* establishing the *imperium*; b) the *imperium* as an essential condition (*una veluti mente*) for the unfolding of the *multitudo*; and c), nevertheless, the continuous exceeding and overflowing of the movements of the one on the 'fixations' and the stabilisations of the other. And so, as long as political power must be thought of starting from the multitude's relative weakness (from its greater or lesser 'impotence'), as long as the *imperium* must be framed with respect to the multitude through separation (the space between the king or of the *optimi*), the problem of the political scientist and of the 'Good Republican', which still animates and directs the political scientist, will be that of defining positive institutions aimed at opening communication channels with the *multitudo*. These will be institutions aimed at recognising, and in some way putting into practice, the constitutive role that the multitude always maintains with respect to *all* forms of political order. In the case of a monarchy, this can take the paradoxical shape of that very strange kind of 'king by popular sovereignty', a figure which Spinoza outlines in the two central chapters of the *TP*, the sixth and the seventh. In the case of the aristocracy, it can lead to the no less paradoxical mechanism in virtue of which the most rigid exclusion of the *multitudo* from the *imperium* ends up taking place through a careful selection, among the ranks of the *optimi*, of some selected from the *multitudo*: this is realised when choosing government personnel through a most effective circulation *from the multitude to the elite*.

When, on the other hand, we move to the democratic kind of government, the perspective of the analysis and of the political *fabrica* shifts decidedly towards the *imperium*. The accent here goes on the essential function played by political power in the expression of the *multitudo*. In this case, what is problematised is no longer a break or a gap, but rather the immediate connection, the continuous, direct pouring of the disordered and chaotic elements of the *multitudo* into the *imperium*. The problem is now the stability and the duration of this *species*: at once the most powerful, because the only completely absolute one and the one less prone to rebellions, it is permanently threatened by its own plural power (*potentia*), and structurally undermined by the multiple intensity of its own strength.[201] It becomes most urgent to emphasise their differences precisely where the line that joins but also distinguishes the *multitude* (the substratum of every form of the *imperium*) from its positive democratic variant, risks being blurred. Of course, nothing would rule out, in principle, a more 'inclusive' and 'comprehensive'

---

[201] *TP* VI, 4; *CWS* II, 533.

design, such as to involve rather than exclude the active participation to kinds of popular government. But this structural tension, which is central and decisive for the other forms of government, slides into the background with respect to the urgent stabilising needs typical of democracy. So, the simplest way becomes that of resorting to existing relations of force (the exclusion of the 'servants'), and that of the transfiguration in 'nature' of the 'institution' and of prejudice, the exclusion, that is, of women. However, such an outcome would not be enough to silence the principle in the face of the *datum*, to decree the definitive dissolution of philosophy into the existent, ignoring the incompleteness of the argumentative structure just sketched which aims at that outcome.

The continual need to traverse the substantial concretisations of the *summa potestas* neither eliminates nor erases the constituent primacy of the multitude. It does not annihilate its uncontainable overabundance with respect to power. The *imperium* is born out of the *power* (*potentia*) of the *multitudo* and it codifies it by fixing it into a *ius*, a positive law. But by the very fact of structuring itself within a political power, the multitude continually surpasses and exceeds such power. The natural plurality, ductility, and versatility of *potentia* endures and threatens the artificial singularity, fixity, and rigidity of *potestas*, even while the former feeds the latter. There is no *natural* 'dialectic': Spinoza's 'nature' does not allow any dialectical process, purpose, or teleology. If anything, there is a constitutive tension that structurally keeps *multitudo* and *imperium* balanced between power (*potentia*) and crisis, between strength and dissolution. It applies to the more 'contracted' form of political power, where the role of the *multitudo* appears restricted to a mere disposition to be acted upon (*aptitudo patientis*) (for example, as it applies to the masses subjected to a tyrant, as explained in the *TTP*). But this also applies to 'established' democracy, in which gaps of 'endurance' as well as residues of 'patience' or of subversive resistance can still be found: it applies to women and to servants (and maybe even to the mute and the mad) as compared to men and slave owners. And it also applies to the political scientist, who excludes them. As the only Spinozist form of tolerance, the patience of the excluded goes beyond the planning strategies of the *TP*, and beyond its 'science', there where the physical, individual death of the philosopher does not suffice to contain or break the grandiose and vital projections of his philosophy.

Bibliography

Works by Spinoza

Abbreviations for Spinoza's works

    PP   Descartes' Principles of Philosophy Parts I and II
   CM   Metaphysical Thoughts
    KV   Short Treatise on God, Man, and His Well-Being
  TdIE   Treatise on Emendation of the Intellect
  Ethics   Ethics
   TTP   Tractatus theologico-politicus
    TP   Tractatus politicus
    Ep.   Letters

Abbreviations for the internal structure of PP and Ethics

     A.   Article
   App.   Appendix
    Ax.   Axiom
   Cor.   Corollary
   DA #   [Arabic numeral] (Definitions of the Affects from part three)
   Def.   Definition
  Dem.   Demonstration
   Lem.   Lemma
   Post.   Postulate
  Praef.   Preface
  Schol.   Scholium

Editions

Original texts

Spinoza Opera, im Auftrag der Heidelberger Akademie der Wissenschaften, hrsg. von C. Gebhardt. Heidelberg 1924, rist. 1972, 4 vols (a fifth volume was published in 1987, including Gebhardt's commentary to the TTP and the TP, as well as an Appendix by C. Altwicker).

Korte Verhandeling van God, de Mensch en deszlvs Welstand. Breve Trattato su Dio, l'uomo e il suo Bene, with an introduction, Italian translation, and commentary by F. Mignini. L'Aquila: Japadre, 1986.

Tractatus de intellectus emendatione, ed. B. Rousset. Paris: Vrin, 1992 (cited by an R followed by the Arabic numeral indicating the page number).

Opera posthuma, complete photographic reproduction, ed. P. Totaro, with an introduction by F. Mignini. Macerata: Quodlibet, 2008.

English translation

The Collected Works of Spinoza, ed. E. Curley. Princeton: Princeton University Press, 1985, 2016. Abbreviated as CWS I and CWS II.

Other Abbreviations

Aristotle	Met	= Metaphysics, trans. by W. D. Ross. Oxford: Oxford University Press, 1924.
	Phys.	= Physics, trans. and ed. Jonathan Barnes, in The Complete Works of Aristotle. Volume 1. Princeton: Princeton University Press, 1984.
	NE	= Nicomachean Ethics, trans. C. D. C. Reeve. Indianapolis: Hackett, 2014.
	DA	= De Anima, trans. Hugh Lawson-Tancred. London: Penguin, 1987.
	Pol	= The Politics, trans. C. D. C. Reeve. Indianapolis: Hackett, 1998.
Augustine	DO	= De ordine. South Bend: St. Augustine's Press, 2007.
Bacon, F.	Ess	= Essays, in The Works of Francis Bacon, ed. J. Spedding, R. L. Ellis, and D. D. Heath, vol. VI (1861). Reprint Stuttgart: Bad Cannstatt, 1963.
Besold, C.	De arc.	= De arcanis rerumpublicarum, in appendix to Clapmayer, De arc. (corresponding to Chap. V, di Politicorum libri duo, 1618).

Cicero, M. T. Tusc = *Tuscolan Disputationes*, trans. J. E. King. Loeb Classical Library, Cambridge, MA: Harvard University Press, 1927.

De Off = *De officiis*, trans. Walter Miller. Loeb Classical Library, Cambridge, MA: Harvard University Press, 1913.

Clapmayer, A. *De arc.* = *De arcanis rerumpublicarum libri sex, iterato illustrati a Jh. Arn. Corvino*. Amsterdam, 1644.

Descartes, R. *Disc* = *A Discourse on the Method*, trans. Ian MacLean. Oxford: Oxford University Press, 2006.

Med = *Meditations on First Philosophy*, trans. John Cottingham. Cambridge: Cambridge University Press, 1996.

Ouvr = *Oeuvres et lettres*, ed. A. Bridoux. Paris: Gallimard, 1958.

Pass = *The Passions of the Soul*, trans. Stephen H. Voss. Indianapolis: Hackett, 1989.

Princ = *Principles of Philosophy*, in *The Philosophical Writings of Descartes*, trans. John Cottingham. Cambridge: Cambridge University Press, 1985.

Reg = *Regulae ad directionem ingenii*, in *The Philosophical Writings of Descartes*, trans. John Cottingham. Cambridge: Cambridge University Press, 1985.

Resp = *Replies to the Objections*, in *Meditations, Objections, and Replies*. Indianapolis: Hackett, 2006.

have also referred to Descartes' *Opera philosophica*, editio ultima, Francofurti ad Moenum, MDCXCII.

Galilei, G. GCL = *A madama Cristina di Lorena, granduchessa madre di Toscana*, in *Opere*, ed. F. Brunetti. Torino, 1964, vol. I, 551–93.

Hegel, G. W. F. VG = *Vorlesungen über die Geschichte der Philosophie* (1833–1836), in *Werke*. Berlin, 1844, vol. XV.

Hobbes, T. EW = *The English Works*, ed. G. Molesworth, XI vols (1829–1845). Reprint. London, 1966.

De cive = *Philosophical Rudiments concerning Government and Society*, in *EW* II.

De corp = *De corpore*, in *EW* I.

Elements = *The Elements of Law Natural and Politic*, ed. F. Tönnies, London 1969.

Lev = *Leviathan*, in *EW* III.

Leibniz, G. W. CDE = *Considérations sur la doctrine d'un esprit universel* (1702), in *Die philosophische Schriften von G.W. Leibniz*, ed. C. I. Gerhardt, 7 vols. Berlin 1875–1890, reprinted in Hildesheim 1965, vol. VI, 1965.

RIS = *Réfutation inédite de Spinoza*, ed. A. Foucher de Careil. Paris, 1854.

Locke, J. T2 = *The second Treatise of Government*, ed. Thomas P. Peardon, New York: The Liberal Arts Press, 1952.

Machiavelli, N. Dis. = *Discourses on Livy*, in *Discourses*. London: Penguin, 1984.

Princ. = *The Prince*. Oxford: Oxford University Press, 2005.

FH = *Florentine Histories*. Princeton: Princeton University Press, 1990.

Plato Phaed. = *Phaedo*, in *Complete Works*, ed. John M. Cooper. Indianapolis: Hackett, 1997.

Rep. = *The Republic*, in *Complete Works*, ed. John M. Cooper. Indianapolis: Hackett, 1997.

Plotinus Enn = *Enneads*, trans. Lloyd P. Gerson. Oxford: Oxford University Press, 2018.

Schopenhauer, A. SG = *Skizze einer Geschichte der Lehre vom Idealen und Realen*, in *Parerga und Paralipomena, Sämtliche Werke*, cit., Bd. 6. Berlin: Globus Verlag, 1902.

WW = *Die Welt als Wille und Vorstellung, Ergänzungen*, in *Sämtliche Werke*, Hrsg. A. Hübscher. Wiesbaden 1972, Bd. 3; trans. E. F. J. Payne. New York: Dover, 1969.

Suárez, F. DM = *Metaphysicarum disputationum, tomi duo*.

Thomas Aquinas CG = *Commentary on the Gospel of John*.

SG = *Summa de veritate fidei catholicae contra Gentiles*.

ST = *Summa Theologiae*.

Secondary Literature

Adelphe, L. (1914) 'La formation et la diffusion de la politique de Spinoza', *Revue de Synthèse historique*, XXVIII: 253–80.

Althusser, Louis (1978) *Essays in Self-Criticism*. London: Verso.

Appuhn, C. (ed.) (1928) *Spinoza: Traité politique – Lettres*. Paris: Flammarion.

Armour, L. (1992) *Being and Idea: Developments of Some Themes in Spinoza and Hegel*. Hildesheim–Zürich–New York: Lubrecht & Cramer.

Aurélio Pires, D. (2019) 'Introdução' to B. de Espinosa, *Tratado Teológico-Politico*, ed. D. Aurélio Pires. Lisbon: Impresa Nacional–Casa da Moeda.

Baensch, O. (1927) 'Ewigkeit und Dauer bei Spinoza', *Kant-Studien*, XXXII (*Spinoza-Festheft*): 44–84.

Balibar, E. (1985) '*Spinoza, l'anti–Orwell. La crainte des masses*', *Temps Modernes*, 470: 353–98.

Balibar, E. (1990) *Spinoza et la politique*. Paris: Presses universitaires de France.

Balibar, E. (2020) *Spinoza: The Transindividual*. Edinburgh: Edinburgh University Press.

Balibar, E. and Morfino, V. (eds) (2014), *Il transindivuale. Soggetti, relazioni, mutazioni*. Milan: Eterotopie.

Balibar, E., Seidel, H., and Walther, M. (eds) (1994), *Freiheit und Notwendigkeit: Ethische und politische Aspekte bei Spinoza und in der Geschichte des (Anti-)Spinozismus*. Würzburg: Königshausen & Neumann.

Banfi, A. (1969) *Spinoza e il suo tempo. Lezioni e scritti*, ed. L. Sichirollo. Florence: Vallecchi.

Baron Salo, W. (1973) [1937] *A Social and Religious History of the Jews*. New York: Columbia University Press.

Battelli, G. (1904) *Le dottrine politiche dell'Hobbes e dello Spinoza*. Florence: Tip. di S. Landi.

Bayle, P. (1965) [1697] *Historical and Critical Dictionary*. Indianapolis: Bobbs-Merrill.

Beckkötter, O. (1920) *Hobbes und Spinoza*. Munchen.

Belaief, G. (1971) *Spinoza's Philosophy of Law*. The Hague.

Bernard, W. (1977) 'Psychotherapeutic Principles in Spinoza's "Ethics"', in *Speculum Spinozanum 1677–1977*, 63–80.

Bertrand, M. (1983) *Spinoza et l'imaginaire*. Paris: Presses universitaires de France.

Bertrand, M. (1984) 'Spinoza: le project éthique et l'imaginaire', *Bullettin de l'Association des Amis de Spinoza*, XIV: 1–12.

Bettini, A. (2005) *Il Cristo di Spinoza*. Milan: Mimesis.

Bloch, O. (ed.) (1993) *Spinoza au XX^a siècle: Actes des journées d'études*. Paris: Presses universitaires de France.

Bloom, H. I. (1937) *The Economic Activities of the Jews of Amsterdam in the Seventeenth and Eighteenth Century*. Williamsport: Kennikat Press.

Bobbio, N. (1979) 'Il modello giusnaturalistico', in N. Bobbio and M. Bovero (eds), *Società e Stato nella filosofia politica moderna*. Milan: Il Saggiatore, 15–109.

Bodei, R. (1991) *Geometria delle passioni. Paura, speranza, felicità: filosofia e uso politico*. Milan: Feltrinelli.

Bonicalzi, F. (1999) *L'impensato della politica*. Naples: Guida.
Bonifas, H. (1904) *Les Ideés bibliques de Spinoza*. Mazamet.
Bordoli, R. (1989) 'Spinoza politico nella critica francese contemporanea', *Critica Marxista*, XXVII(6): 115–51.
Bordoli, R. (1997) *Ragione e scrittura tra Descartes e Spinoza: saggio sulla 'Philosophia S. Scripturae Interpres' di Lodewijk Meyer e sulla sua recezione*. Milan: Franco Angeli.
Boss, G. (1985) 'La conception de la philosophie chez Hobbes et Spinoza', *Archive de Philosophie*, 48: 311–26.
Bostrenghi, A. (ed.) (1992) *Hobbes e Spinoza. Scienza e Politica*. Atti del Convegno Internazionale (Urbino, 14–17 ottobre 1988). Naples.
Bostrenghi, A. (2003) 'Baruch Spinoza e la cosa a noi simile', *Il cannocchiale. Rivista di studi filosofici*, 2: 3–12.
Bove, L. (1996) *La stratégie du conatus. Affirmation et résistance chez Spinoza*. Paris: Vrin.
Breton, S. (1979) *Spinoza. Teologia e politica*. Assisi: Cittadella Editrice.
Brochard, V. 1974 [1926] *De l'eternité des âmes dans la philosophie de Spinoza*. Paris: Librairie Félix Alcan.
Brugère, F. and Moreau, P.-F. (eds) (1999) *Spinoza et les affect*. Paris: Presses universitaires de France.
Brunschvicg, L. (1904) 'Descartes et Spinoza', *Révue de la Métaphysique et Morale*, XII.
Brunschvicg, L. (1927) *Le progrès de la conscience dans la philosophie occidentale*. Paris: Presses universitaires de France.
Brunschvicg, L. (1971) [1894] *Spinoza et ses contemporains*. Paris: Presses universitaires de France.
Bunge, M. (1959) *Causality: The Place of the Causal Principle in Modern Science*. Cambridge, MA: Harvard University Press.
Burbage, F. and Chouchan, N. (1993) *Freud et Spinoza. La question de la transformation et le devenir actif du sujet*, in *Spinoza au XX^a siècle: Actes des journées d'études*, 527–48.
Burman, F. (1704) *Der Spinosisten hoogste goed vergeleken met den Hemel op aerde van F. van Leenhof*. Enkhuizen.
Caporali, R. (1993) 'Spinoza: l'anomalia e il moderno', *Filosofia Politica*, VII(3): 531–6.
Caporali, R. (2012) *La pazienza degli esclusi. Studi su Spinoza*. Milan: Mimesis.
Caporali, R. (2014) *Il netto e il sospetto. A proposito di Machiavelli*. Cesena: Il Ponte Vecchio.
Caporali, R. (2016) 'Il moderno incompiuto (sullo Spinoza di Strauss)',

Preface to L. Strauss, *Il testamento di Spinoza*, ed. R. Caporali. Milan: Mimesis, 7–32.

Carnois, B. (1980) 'Le désir selon les Stoiciens et selon Spinoza', *Dialogue*, XIX: 255–77.

Carp, J. H. (1921) 'Naturrecht und Pflichtbegriff nach Spinoza', *Chronicon spinozanum* I: 81–90.

Cascione, G. (1999) *Libertà e paura. Echi e discrimina hobbesiani nel pensiero di Spinoza*. Milan: Ennerre.

Cassirer, E. (1922) *Das Erkenntnisproblem in der Philosophie und Wissenschaft der Neueren Ziet. Erster Band*. Berlin: Verlag Bruno Cassirer.

Cassirer, E. (1961) [1946] *The Myth of the State*. New Haven: Yale University Press.

Castrucci, E. (1981) *Ordine convenzionale e pensiero decisionista*. Florence: Giuffrè.

Cavarero, A. (1987) 'La teoria contrattualistica nei "Trattati sul governo" di Locke', in G. Duso (ed.) *Il contratto sociale nella filosofia politica moderna*. Bologna: Il Mulino, 149–90.

Cerroni, U. (1998) 'La politica moderna', in P. De Nardis (ed.) *Le Nuove frontiere della sociologia*. Rome: Carocci, 109–58.

Chaui, M. (1980) 'Direito natural e direito civil em Hobbes e Espinosa', *Revista latinoamericana de filosofia*, 6: 57–71.

Chaui, M. (2005) *Spinoza e la politica*, Milan: Ghibli.

Chaui, M. (2007) *Societé et politique: les conflits au sein de la multitudo*, in Caporali R., Morfino V. and Visentin, S. (eds) *Spinoza: individuo e moltitudine*. Cesena: Il Ponte Vecchio, 129–44.

Ciccarelli, R. (2003) *Potenza e beatitudine. Il diritto nel pensiero di Baruch Spinoza*. Rome: Carocci.

Colerus, J. (1994) [1705] *Korte, dog waarachtige Levens-Beschryving van Benedictus de Spinosa, Uit Autentique Stukken en mondeling getuigenis van nog levende Personen, opgestelt*. Amsterdam.

Corsi, M. (1978) *Politica e saggezza in Spinoza*. Naples: Guida.

Couchoud, P. L. (1902) *B. de Spinoza*. Paris.

Cremaschi, S. (1979) *L'automa spirituale. La teoria della mente e delle passioni in Spinoza*. Milan: Vita e Pensiero.

Crippa, R. (1965) *Studi sulla coscienza etica e religiosa del Seicento, Le passioni in Spinoza*. Milan.

Cristofolini, P. (1985) *Spinoza e la gioia*, in Giancotti, E., ed. *Spinoza nel 350° anniversario della nascita*, 197–204.

Cristofolini, P. (1987) *La scienza intuitiva di Spinoza*. Pisa: Edizioni ETS.

Cristofolini, P. (1993) *Spinoza per tutti*. Milan: Feltrinelli.

Cristofolini, P. (1999) 'Per leggere il "Trattato politico"', Preface to B. Spinoza, *Trattato politico*, ed. P. Cristofolini. Pisa: Edizioni ETS.
Cristofolini, P. (2002) *Spinoza edonista*. Pisa. Edizioni ETS.
Cristofolini, P. (2007) *Popolo e moltitudine nel lessico politico di Spinoza*, in R. Caporali, V. Morfino, and S. Visentin (eds) *Spinoza: individuo e moltitudine*. Cesena: Il Ponte Vecchio, 145–59.
Cristofolini, P. (ed.) (1985) *Studi sul Seicento e sull'immaginazione*. Pisa: Scuola Normale Superiore.
Curley, E. M. (1991) 'The State of Nature and its Law in Spinoza and in Hobbes', *Philosophical Topics* 19: 97–117.
De Angelis, E. (1964) *Il metodo geometrico nella filosofia del Seicento*. Pisa: Universita Degli Studi Di Pisa
De Lachelière, R. (1963) *Étude sur la théorie democratique. Spinoza, Rousseau, Hegel, Marx*. Paris: Payot.
De Vries, T. (1970) *Spinoza in Selbstzeugnissen und Bilddokumenten*. Hamburg: Rowohlt Taschenbuch.
Del Lucchese, F. (2003) 'Democrazia, multitudo e terzo genere di conoscenza', in F. Del Lucchese and V. Morfino (eds), *Sulla scienza intuitiva di Spinoza. Ontologia, politica, estetica*. Milan: Ghibli, 95–127.
Del Lucchese, F. (2004) *Tumulti e indignatio. Conflitto, diritto e moltitudine in Machiavelli e Spinoza*. Milan: Ghibli.
Del Vecchio, G. (1922) *Il concetto della natura e il principio del diritto*. Bologna: Kessinger.
Delbos, V. (1893) *Le problème moral dans la philosophie de Spinoza et dans l'histoire du spinozisme*. Paris.
Deleuze, G. (1990) *Expressionism in Philosophy: Spinoza*. New York: Zone Books.
Deleuze, G. (1988) *Spinoza: Practical Philosophy*. San Francisco: City Lights Books.
Den Uyl, D. J. and Warner, S. D. (1987) 'Liberalism and Hobbes and Spinoza', *Studia Spinozana* 3: 261–318.
Derathé, R. (1950) *Rousseau et la science politique de son temps*. Paris: Vrin.
Deugd, C. V. (1968) *The Significance of Spinoza's First Kind of Knowledge*. Assen: Humanities Press.
Di Vona, P. (1969) *Studi sull'ontologia di Spinoza*. Florence: La Nuova Italia.
Di Vona, P. (1990) *Aspetti di Hobbes in Spinoza*. Naples: Loffredo.
Di Vona, P. (1995) *La conoscenza 'sub specie aeternitatis' nell'opera di Spinoza*. Naples: Loffredo.
Droetto, A. (1958) 'Introduzione e note'. Introduction and notes to the Italian edition of the *TP*.

Droetto, A. and Giancotti, E. (1972) 'Note'. Notes commenting the Italian edition of the *TTP*.
Duff, R. A. (2012) [1903] *Spinoza's Political and Ethical Philosophy*. London: Hardpress.
Dunin-Borkowski, S. V. (1933–1936) *Spinoza*. Münster, Aschendorff (4 vols).
Dunn, J. (1959) *The Political Thought of John Locke: An Historical Account of the Argument of the Two Treatises of Government*. Cambridge: Cambridge University Press.
Duso, G. (1988) *La rappresentanza. Un Problema di Filosofia Politica*. Milan: Franco Angeli.
Dyroff, A. (1918) 'Zur Entstehungsgeschichte der Lehre Spinozas vom Amor Dei intellectualis', *Archiv für Geschichte der Philosophie*, 1–28.
Eckstein, W. (1944) 'Rousseau and Spinoza', *Journal of the History of Ideas* V: 259–91.
Eckstein, W. (1971) [1933] 'Zur Lehre vom Staatsvertrag bei Spinoza', in N. Altwicker (ed.), *Texte zur Geschichte des Spinozisums*. Darmstadt: Wissenschaftliche Buchgesellschaft.
Erdmann, E. (1848) 'Die Grundbegriffe des Spinozismus', in *Vermichte Aufsätze*. Leipzig: Verlag Von Fr. Chr. Wilh. Vogel.
Esposito, R. (1984) *Ordine e conflitto. Machiavelli e la letteratura politica del Rinascimento italiano*. Naples: Liguori.
Fassò, G. (1964) *La legge della ragione*. Bologna: Giuffrè.
Fassò, G. (1983) 'Giusnaturalismo', entry in N. Bobbio, N. Matteucci, and G. Pasquino (eds), *Dizionario di Politica*. Torino: UTET, 469–74.
Faucci, D. (1954) '"Amor Dei intellectualis" e "charitas erga proximum" in Spinoza', *Giornale Critico della Filosofia Italiana* 4: 461–80.
Feuer, L. S. (1958) *Spinoza and the Rise of Liberalism*. Boston: Beacon Press.
Filippi, I. (1985) *Materia e scienza in B. Spinoza*. Palermo: Flaccovio Dario.
Finelli, R., Manzi-Manzi, S., Moreau, P-F. and Toto, F. (eds) (2015) *Corporis humani fabrica. Percorsi nell'opera di Spinoza. Il cannocchiale*, XL, 2/3.
Fischer, K. (1865) *Baruch Spinozas Leben und Charakter. Ein Vortrag*. Heidelberg: Carl Winter.
Fischer, K. (1909) 'Spinozas Leben, Werke und Lehere', in C. Gebhardt (ed.) *Geschichte der neueren Philosophie*, vol. II. Heidelberg: Carl Winter.
Francès, M. (1937) *Spinoza dans les pays néerlandais de la seconde moitié du XVIIe siècle*. Paris: Librairie Félix Alcan.
Francès, M. (1951) 'Les réminiscences spinozistes dans le Contrat Social de Rousseau', *Revue philosophique*, 141(1): 61–84.

Francès, M. (1954) 'Introduzione a B. Spinoza *Traité de l'autorité politique*', in R. Callois, M. Francès e R. Misrahi (eds) *Ouvres Complètes*. Paris: Gallimard.
Francès, M. (1958) 'La liberté politique selon Spinoza', *Revue philosophique* 148: 317–37.
Freudenthal, J. (1887) *Spinoza und die Scholastik*, in Zeller, E. (ed.) *Philosophische Aufsätze: Eduard Zeller zu seinem fünfzigjährigen Doctor-Jubiläum gewidmet*. Leipzig: Fues Verlag, 85–138.
Freudenthal, J. (1899) *Lebensgeschichte Spinoza's in Quellenschriften, Urkunden und Nichtamtlichen Nachrichten*. Leipzig: Fues Verlag.
Friedman, J. I. (1978) 'Spinoza's Denial of Free Will in Man and God', in J. Wetlesen (ed.) *Spinoza's Philosophy of Man*, 51–84.
Fütscher, L. (1933) *Akt und Potenz*. Innsbruck: F. Rauch.
Galli, C. (1988) *Modernità. Categorie e profili critici*. Bologna: Il Mulino
Galli, C. (1996a) 'Ordine e contingenza. Linee di lettura del "Leviatano"', in *Percorsi della libertà. Scritti in onore di Nicola Matteucci*. Bologna: Il Mulino, 81–106.
Galli, C. (1996b) *Genealogia della politica. Carl Schmitt e la crisi del pensiero politico modern*. Bologna: Il Mulino.
Gallicet Calvetti, C. (1972) *Spinoza lettore di Machiavelli*. Milan: Vita e Pensiero.
Gallicet Calvetti, C. (1981) 'In margine a Spinoza lettore del "De cive" di Hobbes', *Rivista di filosofia neo-scolastica* LXXIII: 52–84, 235–63.
Garulli, E. (1982) 'Forme del "soggetto collettivo" in Spinoza (Per un dibattito storiografico)', *Hermeneutica* 2: 106ff.
Gebhardt, C. (1908) *Spinoza als Politiker*. Heidelberg.
Gebhardt, C. (1923) *Juan de Prado*, Chronicum Spinozanum III: 269–91.
Gebhardt, C. (ed.) (1922) *Die Schriften des Uriel Da Costa*. Amsterdam: M. Hertzberger.
Geismann, G. (1989) 'Spinoza jenseits von Hobbes und Rousseau', *Zeitschrift für philosophische Forschung* 43(3): 405–31.
Gentile, G. (2019) [1963] *Commentary to Spinoza's Ethics*, trans. G. Durante, annotated G. Gentile. Milan: Bompiani
Geyl, P. (1951a) *The Revolts of the Netherlands 1559–1609*. London: Ernest Benn.
Geyl, P. (1951b) *The Netherlands in the Seventeenth Century. Part One, 1609–1648*. London: Ernest Benn.
Geyl, P. (1964) *The Netherlands in the Seventeenth Century. Part Two, 1648–1715*. London: Ernest Benn.
Giancotti, E. (1970) *Lexicon Spinozanum*. La Haye: M. Nijhoff.

Giancotti, E. (1972) 'Introduzione', in Spinoza, *Trattato teologico-politico*. Milan: Einaudi.
Giancotti, E. (1985a) *Baruch Spinoza*. Rome: Editori Riuniti.
Giancotti, E. (1985b) 'Il Dio di Spinoza', in *Spinoza nel 350° anniversario della nascita*, 35–50.
Giancotti, E. (1988) 'Introduzione', in Spinoza, *Etica*. Rome: Editori Riuniti.
Giancotti, E. (1990) 'Sui concetti di potenza e potere in Spinoza', *Filosofia Politica* 1: 103–18.
Giancotti, E. (1995) *Studi su Hobbes e Spinoza*, ed. D. Bostrenghi and C. Santinelli. Naples: Bibliopolis.
Giancotti, E. (ed.) (1985) *Spinoza nel 350° anniversario della nascita*. Atti del Congresso Internazionale (Urbino 4–8 ottobre 1982). Naples: Bibliopolis.
Gierke, O. von (1880) *Johannes Althusius und die Entwicklung der naturrechtlichen Staattheorien*. M. & H. Marcus.
Gilson, E. (1949) *Introduction a L'etude De Saint Augustin*. Paris: Vrin.
Glicksman Grene, Marjorie (ed.) (1979) *Spinoza: A Collection of Critical Essays*. Notre Dame: Notre Dame University Press.
Gonella, G. (1934) 'Il diritto come potenza secondo Spinoza', in *Spinoza nel terzo centenario della sua nascita*. Milan: Sacro Cuore, 149–80.
Graeser, A. (1991) 'Stoische Philosophie bei Spinoza', *Revue internationale de philosophie* CLXXVIII(3): 336–46.
Guéret, M., Robinet, A., and Tombeur P. (1977) *Ethica, concordances, index, listes de fréquences, tables comparatives*. Louvain-la-Neuve: Publications du CETEDOC.
Gueroult, M. (1953) *Descartes selon l'ordre des raisons, Tome I*. Paris: Aubier.
Gueroult, M. (1968) *Spinoza, I, Dieu (Ethique, I)*. Paris: Aubier.
Gueroult, M. (1974) *Spinoza, II, L'âme (Ethique, II)*. Paris: Aubier.
Haddad-Chamakh, F. (1980) *Philosophie systématique et sistème de philosophie politique chez Spinoza*. Tunis: University of Tunis.
Haddad-Chamakh, F. (1985) *L'imagination chez Spinoza. De l'imbecillitas imaginationis à l'imaginandi potentia*, in P. Cristofolini (ed.) *Studi sul Seicento e sull'immaginazione*, 75–94.
Hadot, P. (1976) 'Causa sui', in J. Ritter (ed.) *Historisches Wörterbuch der Philosophie*. Basel (first ed. 1971). Berlin: Schwabe Verlag.
Hallet, H. F. (1930) *'Aeternitas': A Spinozistic Study*. Oxford: The Clarendon Press.
Hallet, H. F. (1957) *Benedict De Spinoza*. London: Bloomsbury.
Hampshire, S. (1951) *Spinoza*. London: Penguin.
Hazard, P. (2005) [1935] *La Crise de la conscience européenne 1680–1715*. Paris: Livre de Poche.

Heerich, T. (2000) *Transformation des Politikkonzepts von Hobbes to Spinoza: da Problem der Souveränität*. Würzburg: K&N.
Hessing, Siegfried (ed.) (1977) *Speculum Spinozanum 1677–1977*. London: Routledge.
Hubbeling, H. G. (1964) *Spinoza's Methodology*. Assen: Van Gorcum–Prakke & Prakke
Hubbeling, H. G. (1978) [1966] *Spinoza*. Freiburg/München: Karl Alber Verlag.
Huizinga, J. (1968) *Dutch Civilisation in the Seventeenth Century*. New York: F. Ungar Pub. C.
Iodice, A. (1901) *Le teorie di Hobbes e Spinoza studiate nella società moderna*. Naples: Tip. A e S. Festa.
Jacob, P. (1974) 'La politique avec la physique à l'âge classique. Principe d'inertie et conatus: Descartes, Hobbes et Spinoza', *Dialectique* 6: 99–121.
Jaquet, C. (2001) *Le Corps*. Paris: Presses universitaires de France.
Jaquet, C. (2018) *Affects, Actions and Passions in Spinoza: The Unity of Body and Mind*. Edinburgh: Edinburgh University Press.
Jaspers, K. (1974) *Spinoza*. Boston: Mariner Books
Jelles, J. (1677) 'Praefatio' to B. Spinoza, *Opera posthuma*.
Kather, R. (1994) 'Der Begriff der Causa sui bei Spinoza und Whitehead', in *Philosophische Jahrbuch* 1: 55–75.
Kolakowski, L. (1969) *Chrétien sans Eglise. La conscience religieuse et le lien confessionel au XVII siècle*. Paris: Gallimard.
Kortholt, S. (1701) 'Praefatio' to C. Kortholt *De Tribus Impostoribus*. Hamburg.
Kouznetsov, B. (1967) 'Spinoza et Einstein', in *Revue de Synthèse* LXXXVII: 31–52.
Koyré, A. (1957) *From the Closed World to the Infinite Universe*. Baltimore: Johns Hopkins University Press.
Kreische, J. (2000) *Konstruktivistische Politiktheorie bei Hobbes und Spinoza*. Baden-Baden: Nomos Verlagsges.
Lazzeri, C. (1999) *Droit, pouvoir et liberté: Spinoza critique de Hobbes*. Paris: Presses universitaires de France.
Lécrivain, A. (1977) 'Spinoza et la phisique cartésienne', *Cahiers Spinoza* I(1): 235–65.
Liesenfeld, C. (1994) 'Einsteins spinozistische Ethik', in E. Balibar, H. Seidel and M. Walther (eds) *Freiheit und Notwendigkeit*, 219–24.
Lods, A. (1982) [1950] *Histoire de la littérature hébraïque et juive*. Paris/Geneve: Slatkine.

Lucas, J.-M. (1927) [1719] *The Oldest Biography of Spinoza*, ed. A. Wolff, Bristol: Thoemmes.
Macherey, P. (1979) *Hegel ou Spinoza*. Paris: La Decouverte.
Macherey, P. (1992) *Avec Spinoza. Études sur la doctrine et l'histoire du Spinozism*. Paris: Presses universitaires de France.
Macherey, P. (1994) *Introduction à l'Éthique de Spinoza. La cinquième partie. Le voies de la liberation*. Paris: Presses universitaires de France.
Macherey, P. (1995) *Introduction à l'Éthique de Spinoza. La troisième partie. La vie affective*. Paris: Presses universitaires de France.
Macherey, P. (1997a) *Introduction à l'Éthique de Spinoza. La deuxième partie. La réalité mentale*. Paris: Presses universitaires de France.
Macherey, P. (1997b) *Introduction à l'Éthique de Spinoza. La quatrième partie. La condition humaine*. Paris: Presses universitaires de France.
Macherey, P. (1998) *Introduction à l'Éthique de Spinoza. La première partie. La nature des choses*. Paris: Presses universitaires de France.
Macpherson, C. B. (1962). *The Political Theory of Possessive Individualism: Hobbes to Locke*. Oxford: Oxford University Press.
Mansveld, R. van (1674) *Adversus anonymum Theologo-politicum Liber singularis*. Amsterdam: Abrahamum Wolfgang.
Matheron, A. (1969) *Individu et communauté chez Spinoza*. Paris: Minuit.
Matheron, A. (1971) *Le Christ et la salut des ignorants chez Spinoza*. Paris: Aubier.
Matheron, A. (1972) 'Remarques sur l'immortalité de l'âme chez Spinoza', *Les Études philosophiques*, July–September: 369–78.
Matheron, A. (1977) 'Femmes et serviteurs dans la démocratie spinoziste', *Revue Philosophique de la France et de l'Etranger* 102: 181–200.
Matheron, A. (1985) 'Le droit du plus fort: Hobbes contre Spinoza', *Revue philosophique de la France e de l'Étranger* 110: 115–33.
Matteucci, N. (1970) 'Niccolò Machiavelli politologo', *Rassegna italiana di sociologia* 2: 169–206.
Matteucci, N. (1989) 'Riflessioni su Thomas Hobbes', *Filosofia Politica* III: 417–21.
Mcshea, R. J. (1968) *The Political Philosophy of Spinoza*. New York: Columbia University Press.
Meinecke, F. (1957) [1924] *Die Idee der Staatsräson in der neueren Geschichte*. Munich: R. Oldenbourg Verlag.
Meininger, J. V. and van Suchtelen, G. (1980) *Liever met wercken, als met woorden: de levensreis van doctor Franciscus van den Enden, leermester van Spinoza, complotteur tegen Lodewijk de Veertiende*. Amsterdam: Heureka.
Meinsma, K. O. (1983) *Spinoza et son cercle*. Paris: Vrin.

Menzel, A. (1898) 'Wandlungen in die Staatslehre Spinozas', in *Festschrift für J. Unger zum 70. Geburtstag*. Stuttgart: Scientia Verlag.
Menzel, A. (1904) *Homo sui juris. Eine Studie zur Staatslehre Spinozas*. Vienna.
Meozzi, A. (1915) *Le dottrine politiche e religiose di B. Spinoza. Confronto con Hobbes*. Pisa: Vallerini.
Messeri, M. (1990) *L'epistemologia di Spinoza. Saggio sui corpi e le menti*. Milan: Il Saggiatore.
Mignini, F. (1981a) *Ars imaginandi. Apparenza e rappresentazione in Spinoza*. Naples: Edizioni scientifiche italiane.
Mignini, F. (1981b) 'Il sigillo di Spinoza', *La Cultura* XIX: 351–89.
Mignini, F. (1983) *Spinoza*. Rome/Bari: Laterza.
Mignini, F. (1986) 'Introduction' and 'Commentary' to B. Spinoza, KV, L'Aquila, 7–118 and 371–800.
Mignini, F. (1989) 'Somiglianza e riconoscimento', in G. Galli (ed.), *Interpretazione e riconoscimento. Riconoscere un testo, riconoscersi in un testo*. Genova: Marietti
Mignini, F. (1995a) *L'Etica di Spinoza. Introduzione alla lettura*. Rome: La Nuova Italia.
Mignini, F. (1995b) 'La dottrina Spinozana della religione', *Studia spinozana* 11: 53–80.
Misrahi, R. (1977) *Le système et la joie dans la philosophie de Spinoza*, in *Giornale Critico della Filosofia Italiana* LVI (3–4): 458–77.
Moreau, P. F. (1988) 'La méthode d'interprétation de l'Ecriture sainte: détermination et limites', in R. Bouveresse (ed.), *Spinoza, Science et religion*. Paris: Vrin, 108–14.
Moreau, P. F. (1991) 'Le principes de la lecture de l'Ecriture sainte au temps de Spinoza et dans le système spinoziste', *Travaux et documents du GRS*, Pups, no. 4.
Moreau, P. F. (2021) [1994] *Experience and Eternity in Spinoza*. Edinburgh: Edinburgh University Press.
Moreau, P. F. and Bouveresse, R. (1979) *Spinoza. Traité politique*. Paris: Editions République.
Morfino, V. (1994) *Spinoza contra Leibniz. Documenti di uno scontro intellettuale (1676–1678)*. Milan: Unicopli.
Morfino, V. (1997) *Substantia sive organismus: immagine e funzione teorica di Spinoza negli scritti jenesi di Hegel*. Milan: Guerini e associati.
Morfino, V. (2002) *Il tempo e l'occasione. L'incontro Spinoza-Machiavelli*. Milan: LED Edizioni Universitarie.
Morfino, V. (2005) *Il tempo della moltitudine. Materialismo e politica prima e dopo Spinoza*. Rome: Manifestolibri.

Mousnier, R. (1989) *Monarchies et royautés de la préhistoire à nos jours*. Paris: Perrin.
Mugnier-Pollet, L. (1976) *La philosophie politique de Spinoza*. Paris: Vrin.
Musaeus, J. (1674) *Tractatus Theologico-Politicus* [. . .] *ad veritatis lancem examinatus*. Jenae.
Nadler S. (2001) *Spinoza's Heresy*. Oxford: Oxford University Press.
Nadler, S. (2011) *A Book Forged in Hell*. Princeton: Princeton University Press.
Negri A. (1981) *L'anomalia selvaggia. Saggio su potere e potenza in B. Spinoza*. Milan: Feltrinelli.
Negri A. (1992) *Spinoza sovversivo. Variazioni (in)attuali*. Rome: Pellicani.
Negri A. (1998) *Spinoza*. Rome: DeriveApprodi.
Neri, D. (1992) 'La teoria delle definizioni in Hobbes e Spinoza', in Bostrenghi (ed.) *Hobbes e Spinoza. Scienza e Politica*, 71–112.
Neu, J. (1978) *Emotion, Thought and Therapy: A Study of Hume and Spinoza and the Relationship of Philosophical Theories of the Emotions to Psychological Theories of Therapy*. Berkeley: University of California Press.
Osier, J. P. (1987) 'L'hermenéutique de Hobbes et Spinoza', *Studia Spinozana* III: 319–49.
Pacchiani, C. (1979) *Spinoza. Tra teologia e politica*. Padova: Francisci.
Passerin d'Entrèves, A. (1954) *La dottrina del diritto naturale*. Milan: Edizioni di Comunità.
Paty, M. (1986) 'Einstein and Spinoza', in M. Grene and D. Nails (eds) *Spinoza and the Sciences*. Boston: Springer, 267–302.
Pezzillo L. (1991) 'Introduction' to B. Spinoza *TP*, vii–xxix.
Piovani, P. (1961) *Giusnaturalismo ed etica moderna*. Bari: Liguori.
Pocock, J. G. A. (1975) *The Machiavellian Moment: Florentine Political Thought and the Atlantic Republican Tradition*. Princeton: Princeton University Press.
Pollock, F. (1880) *Spinoza, his Life and Philosophy*. London: Kegan Paul.
Pollock, F. (1921) 'Spinoza's Political Doctrine with Special Regard to His Relation to English Publicists', *Chronicum spinozanum* I: 45–57.
Preposiet, J. (1967) *Spinoza et la liberté des hommes*. Paris: Gallimard.
Procacci, G. (1995) *Machiavelli nella cultura europea dell'età moderna*. Rome/Bari: Laterza.
Proetti, O. (1985) 'Adulescens luxu perditus. Classici latini nell'opera di Spinoza', *Rivista di Filosofia neo-scolastica* LXXVII(2): 210–57.
Ravà, A. (1958) 'Un contributo agli studi Spinozani: Spinoza e Machiavelli', in A. Ravà (ed.) *Studi su Spinoza e Fichte*. Rome: Pubblicazioni dell'Istituto di Filosofia del Diritto dell'Università di Rome, 91–113.

Rensi, G. (1993) [1929] *Spinoza*, ed. A. Montano. Milan: Guerini e Associati.
Revah, I. S. (1959) *Spinoza et Juan de Prado*. Paris: Den Haag.
Revah, I. S. (1962) 'La religion d'Uriel Da Costa, marrane de Porto, d'après des documents inédits', *Revue de l'histoire des religions* 161: 45–76.
Rice, L. C. (1969–1970) 'The Continuity of "Mens" in Spinoza', *The New Scholasticism* XLIII: 75–103.
Richter, G. T. (1913) *Spinoza philosophische Terminologie*. Leipzig.
Ritter, G. (1948) *Die Dämonie der Macht*. Berlin: De Gruyter.
Rivaud, A. (1909) *Les notions d'essence et d'existence chez Spinoza*. Paris: FB&C Ltd.
Robinson, R. (1928) *Kommentar zu Spinoza Ethik*, vol. I, *Einleitung, Kommentar zum ersten und zweiten Teil der Ethik*. Leipzig: F. Meiner.
Röd, W. (1985) *Die Grenzen von Spinoza Rationalismus*, in E. Giancotti (ed.) *Spinoza nel 350° anniversario della nascita*, 89–111.
Rodis-Lewis, G. (1986) 'Questions sur la Cinquième Partie de l'"Ethique"', in *Revue Philosophique* II: 207–21.
Rossi, L. (1993) 'Prolegomeni al TIE di Spinoza', in *Occasioni. Saggi di varia filosofia*. Bologna: CLUEB, 30–62.
Roth, C. (1932) *History of the Marranos*. Philadelphia: Sepher-Hermon Press.
Rovere, M. (2017), *Le clan Spinoza*. Paris: Flammarion.
Rowen, H. H. (1978) *John de Witt, Grand Pensionary of Holland, 1625–1672*. Princeton: Princeton University Press.
Saccaro Battisti, G. (1977a) 'Sistemi politici del passato e del futuro nell'opera di Spinoza', *Giornale critico della Filosofia Italiana* 48: 1–44.
Saccaro Battisti, G. (1977b) 'Democracy in Spinoza's Unfinished "Tractatus Politicus"', *Journal of the History of Ideas*, 38: 623–34.
Saccaro Battisti, G. (1984) 'Spinoza, l'utopia e le masse: un'analisi dei concetti di "plebs", "multitude" "populus" e "vulgus"', *Rivista di storia della filosofia*, 1 and 3, 61–90 and 453–74.
Salazar, L. (2002) 'El problema de la obligacion politica en Hobbes y Spinoza', *Dianoia* 47: 67–88.
Santos Campos, A. (2010) *Jus sive potentia. Dereito Natural e Individuação em Spinoza*. Lisbon: Centro de Filosofia da Universidade de Lisboa.
Sasso, G. (1966) *Studi su Machiavelli*. Naples: Morano.
Sasso, G. (1980) *N. Machiavelli*. Bologna: Il Mulino.
Schäfer, A. (1989) *Spinoza. Philosoph des europäischen Bürgentums*. Berlin: Spliz Verlag.
Schmitt, C. (1986) *Scritti su Thomas Hobbes*, ed. C. Galli. Florence: Giuffrè.
Schnur, R. (1962) *Individualismus und Absolutismus. Zur politischen Theorie vor Thomas Hobbes (1600–1640)*. Berlin: Duncker & Humblot.

Schumann, K. (1987) 'Methodenfragen bei Spinoza und Hobbes: Zum Problem des Einflusses', *Studia Spinozana* 3, 47–86.

Scribano, E. (1988) *Da Descartes a Spinoza. Percorsi della teologia razionale nel Seicento*. Milan: Franco Angeli.

Scribano, E. (1990) 'Introduction' to B. Spinoza, *PP* and *CM*. Rome/Bari: Laterza.

Semerari, F. (1992) *Potenza come diritto. Hobbes Locke Pascal*. Bari: Dedalo.

Semerari, G. (1970) *La teoria Spinozana dell'immaginazione*, in *Studi in onore di Antonio Corsano*. Bari: Piero Lacalta, 435–41.

Sibilla, G. (2015) *Modernidad, critica de la religión y escritura: cómo leer el Spinoza de Leo Strauss*, in M. J. Solé (ed.), *Spinoza en debate*. Buenos Aires, Miños y Dávila

Signorile, C. (1970) *Politica e ragione. Spinoza e il primato della politica*. Padova: Marsilio.

Simson, O. v. (1988) *The Gothic Cathedral*. Princeton: Princeton University Press.

Siwek, P. (1930) *L'âme et le corps d'après Spinoza (la psychologie spinoziste)*. Paris: Librairie Felix Alcan.

Siwek, P. (1947) 'Le libre arbitre d'après Spinoza', *Revue philosophique de Louvain* XLV: 339–54.

Skalweit, S. (1982) *Der Beginn der Neuezeit: Epochengrenze und Epochenbegriff*. Darmstadt: Wissenschaftliche Buchgesellschaft

Solari, G. (1927) 'La dottrina del contratto sociale in Spinoza', *Rivista di Filosofia* 18(3): 317–53.

Solari, G. (1930) 'La politica religiosa di Spinoza e la sua dottrina del 'ius sacrum'', *Rivista di Filosofia* 21(4): 306–44.

Spizelius, T. (1680) *Infelix Literatus*. Rotterdam.

Sportelli, S. (1995) *Potenza e desiderio nella filosofia di Spinoza*. Naples: Edizioni Scientifiche Italiane.

Steinberg, D. B. (1981) 'Spinoza's Theory of the Eternity of the Mind', *Canadian Journal of Philosophy* XI: 35–68.

Strauss, L. (1947) 'How to Study Spinoza's "Theological-Political Treatise"', *Proceedings of the American Academy for Jewish Research* 17: 69–131

Strauss, L. (1953) *Natural Right and History*. Chicago: University of Chicago Press.

Strauss, L. (1965) *Spinoza's Critique of Religion*. New York: Schocken Books.

Strauss, L. (1988) *What is Political Philosophy? And Other Studies*. Chicago: University of Chicago Press.

Tatián, D. (2014) *Spinoza. Filosofia terrena*. Buenos Aires: COLIHUE.

Taylor, A. E. (1938) 'The Ethical Doctrine of Hobbes', *Philosophy* 13(52): 406–24.
Tenenti, A. (1978) 'La religione di Machiavelli', in *Credenze, ideologie, libertinismi tra Medioevo ed età moderna*. Bologna: Il Mulino.
Terpstra, M. (1994) 'What Does Spinoza Mean by "potentia multitudinis"'?, in E. Balibar, H. Seidel, and M. Walther (eds) *Freiheit und Notwendigkeit*, 85–98.
Terrenal, Q. C. (1976) *Causa Sui and the Object of Intuition in Spinoza*. Cebu City: University of San Carlos.
Tönnies, F. (1971) *Thomas Hobbes Leben und Lehre* (1925/3). Stuttgart-Bad: Cannstadt.
Torres, S. (2007) 'Machiavelli y Spinoza: entre seguritas y libertas', *Conatus. Filosofia de Spinoza* 1(1): 87–103.
Tosel, A. (1984) *Spinoza ou le crepuscule de la servitude*. Paris: Aubier.
Totaro, G. and Canone, E. (1991) 'Il "Tractatus de intellectus emendation" di Spinoza. Index locorum', *Lexicon Philosophicum* V: 21–127.
Totaro, G. and Veneziani, M. (1993) 'Indici e concordanze del *Tractatus theologico-politicus* di Spinoza', in *Lexicon Philosophicum* VI: 51–204.
van Blyenberg, W. (1674) *De waarheid van den Christelyken Godsdienst en de authoriteyt der H. Schrifte*. Leiden.
van der Linde, A. (1961) [1871] *Benedictus Spinoza, Bibliographie*. Nieuwkoop: B. de Graaf.
van Gelderen, M. (1990) 'The Machiavellian Moment and the Dutch Revolt: The Rise of Neostoicism and Dutch Republicanism', in G. Bock, Q. Skinner, and M. Viroli (eds) *Machiavelli and Republicanism*. Cambridge: Cambridge University Press, 205–23.
Vasoli, C. (1970) *La filosofia medievale*. Milan: Feltrinelli.
Vaughan, C. E. (1925) *Studies in the History of Political Philosophy Before and After Rousseau*, vol. I (*From Hobbes to Hume*). Manchester: University of Manchester Press.
Vaz Dias, A. M. and Van der Tak, W. G. (1932) *Spinoza Mercator & Autodidacticus*. Amsterdam: Den Haag.
Vernière, P. (1954) *Spinoza et la pensée française avant la Révolution*. Paris: Presses universitaires de France.
Vincieri, P. (1984) *Natura umana e dominio. Machiavelli, Hobbes, Spinoza*. Ravenna: Longo.
Vinciguerra, L. (2001) *Spinoza et le signe. La genèse de l'imagination*. Paris: Vrin.
Vinciguerra, L. (2015) *Spinoza*. Rome: Carocci
Visentin, S. (2001) *La libertà necessaria*. Pisa.

Visentin, S. (2004) '*Acutissimus aut prudentissimus?* Intorno alla presenza di Machiavelli nel trattato politico di Spinoza', *Ethica & Politica* 1.
Visentin, S. (2017) 'Aliter Hobbesius. Spinoza e il suo "altro"', in V. Brodsky, G. Farga, G. G. Urquijo, and A. Viñas (eds), *Spinoza. Decimo segundo coloquio*. Córdoba: Altamira, 8–18.
Voegelin, E. (1996) *Die politischen Religionen*. München: Vilhelm Fink.
Voss, H. S. (1981) 'How Spinoza Enumerated the Affects', in *Archiv für Geschichte der Philosophie* 63: 167–79.
Walther, M. (1985) 'Die Transformation des Naturrechts in der Rechtsphilosophie', *Studia Spinozana* I: 73–104.
Walther, M. (1992) 'Biblische Hermeneutik und/oder theologische Politik bei Spinoza und Hobbes', in A. Bostrenghi *Hobbes e Spinoza. Scienza e Politica*, 623–69.
Warrender, H. (1957) *The Political Philosophy of Hobbes: His Theory of Obligation*. Oxford: The Clarendon Press.
Wernham, A. G. (1978) 'Le contrat social chez Spinoza, in Spinoza 1636–1677', *Revue de Synthèse* 89–91.
Wetlesen, Jon (ed.) (1978) *Spinoza's Philosophy of Man*. Notway: Univetsitsfotlaget.
Wilson, C. (1968) *La République hollandaise des Provinces-Unies*. Paris: Hachette.
Wolf, A. (1927) *The Oldest Biography of Spinoza. Edited and translated with an introduction and annotations by A. Wolf*. London: Allen & Unwin.
Wolfson, H. A. (1934) *The Philosophy of Spinoza: Unfolding the Latent Processes of his Reasoning*, 2 vols. Cambridge, MA: Harvard University Press.
Worm, K. (1904) 'Spinozas Naturrecht', *Archiv für Geschichte der Philosophie* 17(4): 500ss.
Wynecken, G. A. (1898) *Amor Dei Intellectualis, eine religionsphilosophische Studie*. Greifswald.
Yakira, E. (1994) *La causalité de Galilée à Kant*. Paris: Presses universitaires de France.
Yovel, Y. (1985) 'Psychology of the Multitude', *Studia Spinozana* I: 305–33.
Yovel, Y. (1989) *Spinoza and Other Heretics*. Princeton: Princeton University Press.
Zac, S. (1963) *L'idée de vie dans la philosophie de Spinoza*. Paris: Presses universitaires de France.
Zac, S. (1965) *Spinoza et l'interpretation de l'Ecriture*. Paris: Presses universitaires de France.
Zac, S. (1968) Introduction and notes to B. Spinoza, *Traité politique*. Paris: Vrin.

Zac, S. (1977) 'Vie, conatus, vertu: rapports de ces notions dans la philosophie de Spinoza', *Archives de Philosophie* XL: 51–84.
Zac, S. (1979) *Philosophie, théologie, politique dans l'œvre de Spinoza*. Paris: Vrin.
Zaltieri, C. and Marcucci, N. (eds) (2019) *Spinoza e la storia*. Mantova: Negretto.
Zaltieri, C. (2013) *Il divenire della Bildung in Nietzsche e Spinoza*. Milan: Mimesis.
Zanetti, G. (1993) *La nozione di giustiza in Aristotele*. Bologna: Il Mulino.
Zeppi, S. (1976) *Studi su Machiavelli pensatore*. Milan: Cesivet.
Zourabichvili, F. (1992) 'Spinoza, le "vulgus" et la psycologie sociale', *Studia Spinozana*, VIII: 151–69.

Index

Adam (the first man), 81, 82, 148
Adelphe, L., 143n
Alfakhar, J., 103, 103n
Alfieri, V., 165n
Althusser, L., 46n
Appuhn, C., 172n, 173n
Aristotle, 5, 24, 24n, 25, 32n, 51, 51n, 55, 59n, 86n, 87, 87n, 125
Armour, L., 45n
Arnauld, A., 22, 23, 26
Augustine, 5, 51, 51n, 55, 55n
Aurélio Pires. D., 101n

Baensch, O., 71n
Balibar, E., 18n, 74n, 80n, 127n, 138n, 143n, 153n
Banfi, A., 14n
Baron, S.W., 8n
Bayle, P., 6, 6n, 7n, 8n, 12, 12n, 14n, 15n
Bertrand, M., 106n
Besold, C., 175n
Bettini, A., 116n
Blijenbergh, W., 4n, 38n, 39n, 47n, 156n, 157n
Bloom, H.I., 7n
Bobbio, N., 89n
Boccalini, T., 165n
Bodei, R., 61n, 134n, 155n
Bonicalzi, F., 161n
Bonifas, H., 100n
Boss, G., 91n
Bostrenghi, D., 91n, 162n
Bouveresse, R., 153n

Bouwmeester, J., 3n
Bove, L., 56n, 99n, 153n
Boxel, U., 38n, 44n, 154n
Breton, S., 47n, 80n, 100n, 103n, 116n, 201n
Brochard, V., 71n
Brugère, F., 69n
Brunschvicg, L., 22, 22n, 28
Bunge, M., 46n
Burbage, F., 62n
Burgh, A., 38n, 157n
Burman, P., 4n

Calvin, J., 29
Campanella, T., 155n
Canone, E., 153n
Caporali, R., 29n, 120n, 164n
Carnois, B., 55n
Carp, J.-H., 138n
Cascione, G., 91n
Cassirer, E., 28n, 52n
Castrucci, E., 88n
Caterus, J., 23
Cavarero, A., 83n
Cerroni, U., 86n
Chaui, D., 91n, 153n
Chouchan, N., 62n
Ciccarelli, R., 153n
Cicero, M.T., 51n, 55n, 63n, 66n
Clapmayer, A., 175n
Colerus, J., 4n, 6, 6n, 7n, 12n, 14n, 15n
Condé (Prince), 14, 15n
Corsi, M., 143n

Couchoud, P., 96n
Cremaschi, S., 62n
Crippa, R., 30n, 63n
Cristofolini, P., 13n, 14n, 159n, 162n, 165n, 167n
Curley, E.M., 91n

D'Holbach, P.-H. D., 17
Da Costa, U., 8, 8n
Daniel (Book of), 113
Dante Alighieri, 55n, 140
David (King of the Jews), 81
De Angelis, E., 21n
De Lachelière, R., 134n
De Vries, S.J., 6n
De Witt, C., 3, 11, 11n, 20, 141
De Witt, J., 3, 4, 9, 10n, 11, 11n, 20, 141, 176
Del Lucchese, F., 91n, 133n, 153n, 165n
Del Vecchio, G., 138n
Deleuze, G., 6, 6n, 25, 25n, 28n, 30n, 43, 73n
Den Uyl, D.J., 91n
Derathé, R., 134n
Descartes, R., 21, 22, 23–29, 30, 33, 33n, 36n, 37n, 42, 46, 47, 54, 55, 57n, 59n, 63n, 66, 66n, 67n
Deugd, C., 106n
Di Vona, P., 23, 23n, 25, 25n, 29n, 71n, 91n
Droetto, A., 9n, 11n, 13n, 78n, 98n, 143n, 172n, 173n, 201n
Duff, R.A., 17n
Dunin-Borkowski, S., 6n, 10n, 22n, 30n
Dunn, J., 81n
Duns Scotus, 28, 55n
Duso, G., 90n

Eckstein, W., 134n, 138n
Elizabeth I, Queen of England, 201
Enden, F., 15, 15n
Erdmann, E., 43n
Esposito, R., 133n
Euclid, 102
Ezra, 113

Fabritius, L., 11n, 13, 13n, 14n
Fassò, G., 78n
Feuer, L.S., 138n
Filippi, I., 56n
Fischer, K., 43n, 79n, 138n
Foscolo, U., 165n
Francès, M., 11n, 134n, 143n, 173n
Freud, S., 62n
Freudenthal, J., 6n, 22n, 30n, 31n
Fütscher, L., 41n

Galilei, G., 21, 47, 56n, 112n
Galli, C., 88n, 90n
Gallicet Calvetti, C., 91n, 165n
Garulli, E., 153n
Gebhardt, C., 8n, 11n, 33, 33n, 173n
Geismann, G., 78n, 79n, 134n
Gelderen, M., 165n
Gentile, G., 22n
Gentili, A., 165n
Geyl, P., 9n
Giancotti, E., 14n, 22n, 30n, 36n, 39n, 44n, 91n, 96n, 98n, 138n, 143n
Gierke, O., 17n, 138n
Gilson, É., 51n
Grotius, U., 78n, 177
Guéret, M., 153n
Gueroult, M., 28n, 30n, 33n, 36n, 37n, 42, 42n, 43n, 106n

Haddad-Chamakh, F., 106n
Hadot, P., 22n
Hallet, H.F., 30n, 71n
Hampshire, S., 5n, 30n
Hazard, P., 88n
Heereboord, A., 37n
Heerich, T., 91n
Hegel, G.W.F., 17, 22, 22n, 43n, 46n, 164
Hobbes, T., 3, 20, 21, 37n, 47n, 52, 53, 56, 56n, 62n, 63n, 66, 66n, 78, 80n, 82n, 83, 84, 85, 86, 87, 88, 88n, 89n, 90, 90n, 93, 99, 111, 122, 126n, 127, 129, 134, 135, 146, 149, 164, 175, 201, 203
Hubbeling, H.G., 21, n, 30n, 51n, 52n
Hudde, J., 33n, 58n, 158n
Huizinga, J., 9n

Jacob, P., 56n
Jaquet, C., 59n
Jaspers, K., 11n
Jelles, J., 5, 5n, 7, 142n, 146, 146n
Jesus Christ, 114, 115, 116, 116n
John (the evangelist), 115
Joshua, 111, 113

Kant, I., 53, 164
Kather, R., 44n
Kolakowski, L., 10n
Kortholt, C., 5n
Koyré, A., 21n, 88n
Kreische, J., 91n

La Mettrie, J.O., 17
Laberium, D., 155n
Lazzeri, C., 91n
Leibniz, G.W., 11n, 35n,
Linde, A., 4n
Locke, J., 52, 53, 81, 81n, 82n, 83n, 85, 87, 164
Lods, A., 100n
Louis XIV, king of France, 3, 5, 6, 15
Lucas, J.-M., 6n, 7n, 11n, 12n, 13n, 15n
Ludwig, K. (prince-elector of the Palatinate), 13

Macherey, P., 45n, 46n, 48n
Machiavelli, N., 5, 110, 111n, 133n, 144, 147, 158, 158n, 159n, 161n, 165, 165n, 189, 191n
Macpherson, C.B., 85n
Mcshea, R.J., 143n
Maimonides, M., 103, 103n
Mallarmé, S., 47n
Mansweld, R., 4n
Marcucci, N., 101n
Martelli, M., 133n
Marx, K., 142
Masaniello, 4
Matheron, A., 18n, 78n, 91n, 116n, 138n, 143n, 153n, 200, 200n, 203, 203n
Matteucci, N., 86n, 133n
Matthew (the evangelist), 116
Meinecke, F., 17n, 143n, 175n
Meininger, J.V., 15n

Meinsma, K.O., 6n
Menzel, A., 17n, 143n
Messeri, M., 56n
Meyer, L., 2, 20, 44n, 51n, 61n, 96, 158n
Mignini, F., 15n, 30n, 51n, 105n, 106n, 120n
Montesquieu, C. de Secondat, 17
Moreau, P.-F., 35n, 48, 48n, 69n, 100n, 127n, 173n
Morfino, V., 35n, 46n, 74n, 153n
Moses, 109, 110, 111, 113, 114, 116, 136, 165n, 196
Mugnier-Pollet, I., 18n, 143n, 148n
Musaeus, J., 4n

Nadler, S., 6n, 8n, 11n
Negri, A., 9n, 18n, 21n, 30n, 134n, 138n, 143n, 153n, 164n, 202, 202n
Neri, D., 30n
Nietzsche, F., 6
Noah, 81

Oldenburg, H., 2n, 4, 11n, 20n, 38n, 44n, 51n, 62n, 72n, 95, 95n, 114, 114n, 115, 115n
Osier, J.P., 111n

Pacchiani, C., 158n
Passerin d'Entreves, A., 78n
Pezzillo, L., 143n, 172n
Philip II (King of Spain and Portugal), 7
Piovani, P., 78n
Plato, 5, 47n, 133, 142
Plotinus, 43n
Pocock, J.G.A., 165n
Pollock, F., 17n, 43n, 138n
Prado, J., 8, 8n
Preposiet, J., 18n, 92n, 138n
Procacci, G., 165n
Proietti, O., 176n

Ravà, A., 165n
Rehoboam (son of Solomon), 178
Rensi, G., 55n
Revah, I.S., 8n
Rice, L.C., 71n

Ritter, G., 89n
Rivaud, A., 22n
Robinet, A., 153n
Robinson, R., 43n
Rodis-Lewis, G., 71n
Roth, C., 7n
Rousseau, J.-J., 17, 52, 53, 134, 134n, 165n
Rovere, M., 11n
Rowen, H.H., 10n

Saccaro Battisti, G., 153n, 154n
Salazar, L., 91n
Samuel (Book of), 113
Santos Campos, A., 153n
Sasso, G., 133n
Saul (King of the Jews), 111
Schäfer, A., 140n
Schmitt, C., 88n
Schnur, R., 88n
Schopenhauer, A., 47
Schuller, H., 37n, 63n
Schumann, K., 91n
Scribano, E., 33n
Semerari, F., 106n
Semerari, G., 82n
Seneca, L.A., 69n
Sesac (pharaoh), 178
Signorile, C., 8n, 15n
Simson, O., 52n
Skalweit, S., 88n
Solari, G., 17, 17n, 18, 18n, 93n, 126n, 138n, 143n
Solomon, 178
Spizelius, T., 4n
Sportelli, S., 43n, 55n
Steinberg, D.B., 71n
Strauss, L., 17, 17n, 18, 86n, 120n
Suárez, F., 24, 24n, 25
Suchtelen, G., 15n

Tak, W.G., 12n
Tatián, D., 165n
Taylor, A.E., 86n
Telesius, B., 55n
Tenenti, A., 111n
Terpstra, M., 164n
Terrenal, Q.C., 45n

Thomas Aquinas, 24, 24n, 51n, 55n, 59n
Tombeur, P., 153n
Tönnies, F., 63n, 85n, 88n
Torres, S., 165n
Tosel, A., 18n, 92n, 120n, 138n, 140n, 153n
Totaro, P., 153n
Tschirnhaus, E.W., 158n

Ulysses, 171

Vanini, G.C., 15n
Vasoli, C., 52n
Vaughan, C.F., 17n, 52n, 138n
Vaz Dias, A.M., 12n
Veneziani, M., 153n
Vernière, P., 17n, 118n, 134n
Vico, G.B., 21
Vincieri, P., 39n, 133n
Vinciguerra, L., 69n, 106n
Visentin, S., 91n, 153n, 165n
Voltaire, 17
Vries, T., 6n

Wagner, A., 142
Walther, M., 78n, 111n
Warner, S.D., 91n
Warrender, H., 86n
Wernham, A.G., 143n
William II of Orange, 174
William III of Orange, 174, 176
Wilson, C., 9n
Wolf, A., 6n
Wolfson, H.A., 22n, 30n, 43, 55n
Worm, K., 138n

Xenophon, 155n

Yakira, E., 46n
Yovel, Y., 8n, 153n

Zac, S., 30n, 54n, 56n, 93n, 101n, 115n, 116n, 172n
Zaltieri, C., 101n
Zanetti, G., 87n
Zeppi, S., 133n
Zourabichvili, F., 153n

EU representative:
Easy Access System Europe
Mustamäe tee 50, 10621 Tallinn, Estonia
Gpsr.requests@easproject.com

www.ingramcontent.com/pod-product-compliance
Lightning Source LLC
Chambersburg PA
CBHW070349240426
43671CB00013BA/2448